Famous Men of the Second World War

by Clark Highsmith

Famous Men of the Second World War
by Clark Highsmith

ISBN 061553029X
EAN-13 978-0615530291

November 2011 updated edition correcting minor errors.
Published in United States by Alacrity Press, 2011
www.alacritypress.com

ALACRITY
PRESS

Photo Credits

Front Cover - U.S. National Archives
Back Cover - U.S. Farm Service Administration,
   Photos from left are of an M3 tank, the cruiser USS Quincy, and a Boeing B-17 Flying Fortress.
Interior photos as noted on image.

TABLE OF CONTENTS

Visit the Famous Men of the Second World War Website at:

www.famousmenww2.com

About the author

Clark Highsmith lives in Midlothian, Texas along with his wife and son. He enjoys hiking, reading, wargaming, teaching Sunday School and spending time with his family. This is Clark's second book.

PREFACE

More than 100 years ago, educator and writer John Haaren wrote a series of history books for children. Using an approach in which history was taught through the biographies of those who lived it, Haaren wrote, "There is something in life that makes its own personal appeal to life. The living man — be he soldier, sailor, statesman or hero — forms a fixed and abiding center around which the pupil can gather the prominent events of the country to which the man belongs."

I realized Haaren was on to something while reading his *"Famous Men of Rome"* and *"Famous Men of Greece"* to my 9-year-old son. After reading both books, he begged me to buy *"Famous Men of the Middle Ages."* A child motivated and hungering to learn medieval history? Haaren understood the correct approach to history. Needless to say, I owe the format and inspiration for this book to him.

I made it a point to keep the book kid-friendly. I avoided colorful quotations and graphic photos. I do not want to glorify war or gloss over the evil that was committed, but I believe parents should be allowed to choose when to discuss the darker issues of life. That said, I do suggest that parents preview Raoul Wallenberg's chapter on the Holocaust to decide if a child is emotionally mature enough for the content.

Shortly after beginning this project I began to feel overwhelmed by the magnitude of what I was trying to encapsulate. The Second World War was the most complex event in history. I struggled with which Famous men to include. Many worthy men were left out — there simply is not enough room. I attempted to include men through whom the story of the war could best be told. I chose not to write a chapter about Adolph Hitler, as he is mentioned throughout the book and his story is widely published elsewhere.

One specific goal I have for this book is to raise awareness among Americans concerning the struggle on the Eastern Front between Germany and Russia. The Eastern Front is typically only mentioned in passing in many American history books. It is my belief that the Second World War was won and lost on the Eastern Front — invading Russia was Hitler's greatest mistake and it ultimately led to Germany's defeat. The suffering and sacrifice of the people of the Soviet Union, during the war is a story that deserves telling. Almost one-seventh of the population of the Soviet Union perished during the war, while American deaths, though great, accounted for less than one-third of a percent.

I thank my wife for her patience and forbearance while I researched and wrote. I thank Charlotte Marsch for copyediting. I would also like to thank the Midlothian High School Library in Midlothian, Texas, the Sims Library in Waxahachie, Texas and the Titusville Public Library in Titusville, Florida for stocking their shelves with many wonderful resources.

Most importantly, I thank God for his providence even in such an awful tragedy as the Second World War. Researching this book I continually saw how in the midst of suffering he was at work. Proverbs 16:9 is true: "The heart of a man plans his way, but the Lord establishes his steps."

I dedicate this book to my son Benjamin. I love you and look forward to sharing this book with you.

Clark Highsmith

Neville Chamberlain

Prime Minister of Great Britain
Born: March 18, 1869
Died: December 9, 1940

On November 11, 1918 at 11 a.m. an armistice took effect ending the First World War. Germany reeled from the sting of defeat as guns in Europe fell silent, but little had been settled by the four-year conflict. While the causes of the Second World War, still debated today, are complex and many, the roots can be traced to the end of the First World War.

The end of the First World War came as a shock to the German people, who had been told they were winning. They believed that politics, not military shortcomings led to defeat. The Treaty of Versailles that officially ended the war placed harsh terms on Germany. Per terms of the treaty, the German government accepted sole responsibility for the war, gave up its colonies, severely restricted the size of its army and surrendered territory to France and Poland. In addition, the Allies imposed war damages that would require decades to pay down. The treaty led to instability, resentment and the rise of Adolph Hitler and the Nazi party.

Other nations faced problems of their own. In Russia, a bloody civil war began after Communists seized power in 1917. The people of Europe feared that Communism might engulf their nations. Germany's ally, Austria-Hungary, was carved into several smaller nations, trapping many Germans under foreign rule. The United States, hoping to sit out any future European wars, looked to the idealistic but weak League of Nations to keep the peace. Great Britain and France, nearly bankrupt and broken by the war, desired to keep Germany weak lest another war break out.

RISE OF FASCISM

Germany established a new government, known as the Weimar Republic, in 1919. Unable to prevent the collapse of the economy, by 1923 German currency was worthless and the economy in shambles. During this troubled time Adolph Hitler joined the German Workers Party — later to become the Nazi Party. Hitler's strong personality and radical ideas appealed to the resentful and restless populace. He soon won a large following.

Hitler was named chancellor of Germany in early 1933. The Nazis won a majority in the March elections. By outlawing all other political parties, Hitler and the Nazis gained firm control of Germany. In 1934 Hitler was elevated to *Führer* (leader). Hitler renounced the terms of the Treaty of Versailles and began to rebuild the German war machine.

Neville Chamberlain (left) and Adolf Hitler exit a building after a September 1938 meeting that eventually resulted in the Munich Agreement.

Like Germany, Italy faced a severe economic situation after the war. Prices had increased 500% from 1914. Strikes by angry workers were common as many small political parties vied for control of the government. In 1919 Benito Mussolini formed the Fascist Party. In 1922 Mussolini's Fascist Party took control of Italy's government. Over the next two decades he would seek to establish a new Roman Empire.

Japan, bristling at what it saw as unfair treatment by western powers, sought to unite all of East Asia under the *Greater East Asia Co-Prosperity Sphere.* As Japan extended its control over Asian countries in the 1930's and early '40's it became clear that the Japanese idea of prosperity was self-centered.

APPEASEMENT

In this time of turmoil, Arthur Neville Chamberlain of Great Britain became a key player in world events. Chamberlain first entered Parliament at the age of 49 in 1918. In the 1920's he served in a number of positions, including the prestigious position of Chancellor of the Exchequer, handling economic and financial matters for the Empire. Even as he helped balance the national budget by cutting military spending, Chamberlain could discern from world events that it would be prudent for Great Britain to rearm. He preferred air power, as he believed the English Channel would provide inadequate protection from air attacks.

In 1937 Chamberlain became Prime Minister. The world had recognized the resurgence of Germany and anxiously pondered the implications. Chamberlain believed Germany could be a partner in stabilizing Europe. He went so far as to suggest returning some of the colonies Germany gave up as a condition of the Treaty of Versailles. He opened up direct talks with Italy shortly after its invasion of Ethiopia that had drawn worldwide criticism.

Many Germans, including Hitler, believed that Austria should be part of Germany. While Chamberlain was open to the idea, the Austrian government did not agree. In March 1938, threatened by use of force, Austria was coerced into joining Germany. Chamberlain denounced the method used, but nothing more. While most Austrian people initially welcomed

German propaganda book Mein Weg nach Scapa Flow/Naval History & Heritage Command

The German submarine U-47 (right) sank the British Battleship Royal Oak (left) during a daring raid inside Scapa Flow in the early days of the war. Behind the U-47 is the German battleship Scharnhorst.

Polish cavalry cross the Weichsel River in September 1939. Like many other nations, Poland had a cavalry at the beginning of the war. It is a myth that Polish cavalry brandishing spears charged German tanks.

Anschluss, the unification of Germanic people groups, they soon realized they were under an oppressive occupation.

Hitler next targeted the Sudetenland region of Czechoslovakia in which 3 million ethnic Germans lived. These ethnic Germans desired to be part of Germany. Czechoslovakia fielded a formidable army made up of 44 divisions. It had defense agreements with both France and the Soviet Union, but both were hesitant to intervene. Chamberlain flew to Germany to serve as an intermediary between Hitler and the Czechs. The result of the meetings was the 1938 *Munich Pact.* Bullied, Czechoslovakia gave the Sudetenland to Germany. Hitler promised he had no other territorial ambitions.

Chamberlain, clutching a paper signed by himself and Hitler, received a hero's welcome upon his return to Great Britain. He believed the Munich Pact "symbolic of the desire of our two people never to go to war again." French politician Léon Blum summed it up well when he said, "I felt relieved and ashamed." Hitler had no intention of keeping his promise. In March 1939, Hitler demanded that what remained of Czechoslovakia be made German "protectorates." Emil Hácha, the Czech leader, signed away independence rather than face a military assault. Czechoslovakia ceased to exist while France and Great Britain failed to intervene.

Chamberlain initiated talks with Britain's allies in early 1939, encouraging them to form alliances to protect one another. Great Britain and France signed pacts with Greece, Romania (later to reluctantly join the Axis), Poland and Turkey guaranteeing military assistance if attacked by Germany.

INVASION OF POLAND

Hitler turned his attention to preparing *Case White*, an attack on Poland. On August 23rd, 1939 a German-Russian nonaggression pact was announced in which the Germans and Soviets promised not to attack one another. Secretly they also agreed to carve up Poland and much of eastern and central Europe. Assured that Russia would not interfere and emboldened by his previous successes in Austria and Czechoslovakia, Hitler was certain that no one would help Poland.

The Second World War officially began on September 1, 1939 as 55 German divisions poured into Poland. The Polish borders were long and the land flat. Instead of taking advantage of natural barriers such as rivers, Polish soldiers were spread out all along the frontier. The German *Luftwaffe* (air force) concentrated its attacks on communications, supply depots and columns of troops heading for the front. The Polish army, numbering about 1 million men, lacked adequate amounts of armor. German infantry pinned down the Polish infantry while their 15 motorized and armored divisions moved quickly behind to cut off and surround the Poles in what proved to be the first *Blitzkrieg* (Lightning war)of the conflict. The Poles were steadily pushed back.

Chamberlain, appalled by the German attack, issued an ultimatum demanding Germany to stop. The German attack continued, and on September 3, Great Britain and France declared war on Germany. At the outbreak of war Chamberlain said, "Everything I have worked for, everything I have hoped for, everything I have believed in during my public life, has crashed into ruins."

Polish Public Domain

The Grom ("Thunder") was one of three Polish destroyers to escape and continue the fight alongside the Western Allies. The Grom sank on May 4, 1940 after being struck by a bomb from a German plane. The other two Polish destroyers survived the war.

Realistically, Great Britain and France could do little to save Poland once the invasion had begun. The first British bombing raid on Germany took place September 4 when 10 Blenheim bombers attacked German naval ships and buildings at Wilhelmshaven. On September 7, France crossed the German frontier at three points. The offensive soon halted. Three Polish destroyers escaped to Great Britain where they were able to continue to fight. British troops began to deploy in France.

On September 17, Stalin sent Russian troops into the undefended eastern territories of Poland. On that same day, the first British military naval loss occurred when the German submarine *U-29* sank the aircraft carrier *Courageous* with the loss of 518 lives.

The citizens of Warsaw built 13 miles of interconnecting trenches and defenses, stalling the German offensive. The Germans began around-the-clock bombing of the city. Warsaw surrendered on September 27. The Polish Army fought bravely despite the hopelessness of the situation. Though the Polish government never officially surrendered, the last pocket of resistance gave up at Kock on October 6. In little more than a month Poland had been conquered.

TRIVIA

The opening salvo of the war was fired by the German pre-dreadnought battleship *Schleswig-Holstein* when she fired on a Polish base at Westerplatte early on the morning of September 1, 1939.

Hans Frank, the German placed in charge of Poland, said, "The Poles will be the slaves of the Greater German World Reich. The worst was yet to come for Polish Jews — only 10% of Poland's 3.3 million Jews would avoid extermination as part of Hitler's *"Final Solution."*

The war entered a time of relative quiet known as the *Phoney War*. It was six months later on April 9, 1940 that Germany made its next move, invading Denmark and Norway. A half-hearted attempt by the Western Allies to thwart the invasion failed.

Chamberlain resigned as prime minister on May 8, 1940. Winston Churchill became the new prime minister two days later, the same day Germany launched an invasion of the Low Countries. Chamberlain continued to serve his country for a short time before falling ill. He died of cancer on November 9, 1940 at the age of 71.

It is easier after the fact to judge how decisions concerning an event should have been handled. Though Chamberlain has often been criticized for giving too much to Germany and Italy through appeasement, he truly desired peace while working quietly to ready Great Britain for war. Chamberlain's ultimate failing might be that he never was viewed as a plausible and inspirational war leader.

REVIEW QUESTIONS

1. What was the name of the treaty that ended the First World War? The Treaty of Versailles

2. How old was Neville Chamberlain when he first entered Parliament? 49

3. What was the name of the failed German government formed after the First World War? Weimer Republic

4. The __Nazi__ Party derived its name from the Latin word fasces, a bundle of rods with an axe blade that was a symbol of power in ancient Rome.

5. Czechoslovakia was forced to give up part of its territory as a result of what 1938 agreement? Munich Pact

6. The Second World War officially began on September 1, 1939 when Germany attacked __Poland__.

7. What word meaning "lightning war" was used to describe Germany's quick offensives? Blitz Krieg

8. Approximately how many months did it take Germany to conquer Poland?
   a. 12
   b. 3
   c. 1
   d. 6

9. Which two countries signed a nonaggression pact shortly before the start of the Second World War? Germany/Russia

10. What was the period of time after surrender of Poland that saw little fighting called?
    a. The Phoney War
    b. Year of Peace
    c. The Quiet Time
    d. The False War

11. What aircraft carrier was the first British ship to be sunk during the war?
    a. Courageous
    b. Ark Royal
    c. Furious
    d. Illustrious

Carl Mannerheim

Marshal of Finland
Born: June 4, 1867
Died: January 27, 1951

Wikimedia Commons/Finnish public domain

One significant, though often overlooked, struggle of the Second World War took place in far northern Europe between the small country of Finland and the Soviet Union. Carl Gustaf Emil Mannerheim led Finland's determined struggle against an aggressor several times its size.

Finland was a grand duchy of the Russian empire when Gustaf Mannerheim was born in 1867. His family traced its lineage to a time when Finland was part of Sweden. As a young man, the future Marshal of Finland did not embrace his Finnish heritage. At age 16 he wrote, "I look forward happily to that moment when I can turn my back forever on Finland."

Mannerheim's military career almost ended as a youth after rebelliously going AWOL at a Finnish military academy. Being from a privileged family, he got a second chance at the prestigious Nicholas Cavalry School in Russia. He went on to serve the Russian czars for two decades. At the coronation of Nicholas II in 1895, Mannerheim was one of four officers given the honor of standing on the cathedral steps.

His command style avoided unnecessary risks that might waste the lives of his soldiers. He did not delegate responsibilities well and often took on work that his aides should have done.

During the First World War, Mannerheim was promoted to Lieutenant General and commanded the 6th Cavalry Corps against the Germans. He was the highest-ranking military commander in the First World War of any nation to later fight in the Second World War. In 1917, Communists took over Russia and killed the czar. Mannerheim, very opposed to Communism, fled for his life to his homeland of Finland.

Upon his arrival, Mannerheim found Finland on the brink of civil war. He led the *Whites* (capitalists) to victory over the *Reds* (Communists) in just three-and-a-half months. Between the wars, Mannerheim did much for Finland. He endowed a child-welfare society to care for orphans of soldiers killed on both sides of the civil war and secured a loan in order to buy wheat, which the grateful people used to bake "Mannerheim bread."

THE WINTER WAR

In the late 1930's, the Russians, led by Josef Stalin, looked to expand their influence over their weaker neighbors. The Russians, impressed by the success of the German *Blitzkrieg* of Poland, decided to take over Finland in a similar manner. Mannerheim knew war was likely. Despite shortages of transports, antiaircraft guns, heavy ammunition and many other items, Mannerheim did all he could to prepare Finland by inspiring the Finns to mobilize in the months before the war began.

The NKVD (Soviet police) secretly bombed one of their own villages near the Finnish bor-

The Mannerheim Line

Wikimedia Commons

The Mannerheim Line stretched across the Karelian Isthmus. In the background is a Finnish bunker known as the "Million Fortress."

Finnish Defense Forces

Tracers light up the sky near the Soviet-Finland border during the first month of the Winter War in 1939.

der, Mainila, and blamed the Finns, thus creating an excuse for the invasion. On November 30, 1939, Russia hurled 21 divisions, made up of more than 450,000 men at 150,000 Finns. The attack, launched in early winter instead of summer when the land would be boggy and muddy, is remembered as the *Winter War*. The winter of 1939-40 was especially cold; on January 16, 1940, the temperature dropped to -45° Fahrenheit on the Karelian Isthmus.

Russian leaders expected Finland to surrender within two weeks. Though much larger and better-equipped, the Red Army found conquering Finland difficult because of the many lakes, swamps, forests and lack of paved roads that greatly aided the defenders. In addition, the Russians, who would later use cold weather to their advantage against the Germans, were not prepared for the arctic conditions, wearing brownish overcoats and fielding tanks with summer camouflage.

Almost all the Finnish soldiers were excellent skiers. They would move quickly from place to place, removing their skis before entering combat. Russian soldiers who attempted to ski often failed to remove their skis before combat, with comical and often fatal results. Instead of attacking the Russians head-on, guerilla tactics

were used, including attacking field kitchens in order to deprive the Russians of warm food in the bitter cold.

The main Russian attack came across the Karelian Isthmus. During the summer of 1939, thousands of Finns had given up their summer vacations to help build a defensive line, known as the Mannerheim Line, across the Karelian Isthmus. The line was constructed mostly of trenches and log-covered dugouts. The Finns used an amount of concrete equal to only 4% of what the French had put into the Maginot Line. The true strength of the Mannerheim Line proved to be "stubborn defenders with a lot of *sisu* (guts)." Wave after wave of Russians was repelled. With few tanks of their own and little in the way of antitank weapons, brave Finnish

SA-kuva (Finnish Army Pictures)

A 76mm Finnish artillery piece stands guard near the city of Viipuri in 1940.

soldiers often jammed crowbars or logs in bogie wheels of Russian tanks. Molotov cocktails, bottles filled with rags and flammable liquid, were used for first time. Although outnumbered 4 to 1, the line held. The lack of progress infuriated Stalin.

The two Russian armies that crossed into Finland on the northern border experienced initial success but suffered critical losses in Finnish counterattacks. The Battle of Suomussalmi was one such great Finnish victory. The Finns initially fell back, allowing the Russian 163rd Division to enter Suomussalmi on December 7, 1939. While the Red Army dug in, the Finns waited for reinforcements. They then mounted a counterattack that encircled the entire Russian division.

Dividing the Russians into smaller groups known as *mottis*, the Finns were able to systematically reduce the enemy. Finnish soldiers ambushed the Russian 44th motorized division, sent in relief, pinning it along a forest road near Suomussalmi. The Russians dug in along a five-mile stretch of road. The Finns established camps, with warm food and shelter, near the Russians. The Russians, freezing and starving, were systematically reduced until they were no more. Not

SIMO HÄYHÄ

Perhaps the greatest Finnish soldier of the Second World War, Simo Häyhä was a man of modest stature. Only five feet tall, Häyhä was one of a number of skilled Finnish snipers. Häyhä's skills generated so much fear among Red Army troops that he came to be known as "The White Death."

A farmer and hunter, Häyhä developed his skills in shooting sports. Häyhä differed in his approach in that he preferred an iron sight rather than a telescopic sight on his rifle. A telescopic sight could easily fog up or reflect sunlight, revealing a sniper's position. Dressed in white camouflage, Häyhä recorded 505 confirmed sniper kills. An unofficial count raises the total to more than 800. He killed at least 200 more Russians with machine guns.

The war ended for Häyhä on March 6, 1940, when a Russian bullet destroyed half of his jaw. He was unconscious for a week, but survived. Mannerheim promoted him to second lieutenant. After the war, Häyhä became a dog breeder and continued to hunt. Häyhä passed away in 2002.

only did the Finns destroy two divisions during the battle, they recovered many tanks, field guns, trucks, horses and antitank guns for their own use.

For all their courage and valor, the Finns could only delay the Russians. In January 1940, the Russians brought in siege weapons under the command of General Semyon Timoshenko and began the systematic destruction of the Mannerheim line. Sheer exhaustion overcame the Finnish troops. By early March, the road to the Finnish capital, Helsinki, was open to the Russians. The Finns were forced to sign the Moscow Peace Treaty. In the treaty, Finland lost 11% of its land but retained its status as an independent nation. Stalin and the Soviet Union, though the victors, were humiliated.

FINLAND PARTNERS WITH THE AXIS POWERS

After the Winter War, Finland looked to Germany for food and support, though with misgivings. While they never signed a treaty to become part of the Axis, the Finns awkwardly embraced "co-belligerence with Germany," seeking to reclaim the land lost during the Winter War. On June 25, 1941, Finland declared war on Russia. German and Finnish troops crossed into Russia several days later.

Initially described as a defensive war, Mannerheim made the "Sword Scarab Declaration" on July 10, 1941, saying that Finland and East Karelia (a region of Russia which had ethnic and historical ties to Finland) must be free. Just 15 months after defeat in the Winter War, Finland moved to the offensive in what Finns called the *Continuation War*. Finnish forces stopped at the Svir River not far from Leningrad. By early December, the Finns had reclaimed all the land lost during the Winter War and captured East Karelia. Satisfied and not wishing to further anger the Russians, they dug in.

In December 1941, Britain declared war on Finland. The U.S. condemned the Finnish attacks but refrained from a declaration of war. A grateful nation promoted Mannerheim to "Marshal of Finland" in 1942. He is the only person to have ever held the title. When the tide of war turned in favor of the Russians after the German disaster at Stalingrad, Mannerheim and the Finns started to look for a way out of their uncomfortable alliance.

Finland angered the Germans by opening negotiations with the Soviet Union. The Russian terms were considered too harsh and were rejected. The Russians launched a ground offensive against Finnish positions on June 9, 1944. On just the second day, the Russians broke through and the Finnish soldiers were forced to retreat. As the situation became dire, Finland's president Risto Ryti asked for German help. Antitank weapons, assault guns and fighter bombers were sent along with a warning to the Finns not to sign any treaty with Russia. Mannerheim reluctantly supported the request, but did not sign, allowing him to later revoke it. The Finns managed to stop the Russian offensive near the lines, marking the end of the Winter War. The Russians turned their attention to central Europe, desiring to beat the Western Allies to Berlin.

Mannerheim was elected president of Finland in August 1944. Their military strength completely spent, the Finns were forced to sign another oppressive treaty with the Soviet Union. They remained an independent country but had to demobilize most of their army and give up additional land to the Russians. Mannerheim renounced all relations

SA-kuva (Finnish Army Pictures)

A Finnish light antiaircraft unit watches the skies for Soviet planes.

with Germany. Since many German soldiers had yet to retreat from Finland into Norway, a number of skirmishes was fought in northern Finland in what is known as the *Lapland War*. The Germans used scorched-earth tactics as they retreated, leaving behind many destroyed villages.

In 1946, at the age of 79, with World War II over and sensing his work was done, Mannerheim resigned from the presidency. In 1951, he died of a stomach attack at the age of 83. Mannerheim was given a state funeral and mourned by his nation. He is considered to be Finland's greatest statesman and military leader ever.

REVIEW QUESTIONS

1. What was the name of the 1939-40 conflict between Finland and the Soviet Union?
   a. The Lapland War
   b. The Murmansk War
   c. The Arctic War
   d. The Winter War

2. In what country did Gustaf Mannerheim receive his military education?
   Russia

3. Gustaf Mannerheim defeated which group in a three-and-a-half month civil war in Finland?
   a. Fascists
   b. Whites
   c. Reds
   d. Roundheads

4. During the summer of 1939, many Finns gave up their summer vacations in order to help construct what defensive fortification?
   Mannerheim Line

5. How many Finnish soldiers faced the 450,000 invading Russians in 1939?
   a. 150,000
   b. 100,000
   c. 400,000
   d. 800,000

6. What skill gave the Finnish soldiers superior mobility? *Skiing*

7. What crude weapon, made out of a bottle filled with rags and flammable liquid, was first used by the Finns?
   Molotov cocktails

8. The Finns succeeded in destroying two Russian divisions near what municipality?
   a. Helsinki
   b. Jyväskylä
   c. Suomussalmi
   d. Liinakhamari

9. Which Axis power did Finnish soldiers fight alongside in 1941? *Germany*

10. The June 1941 attack on Russia is known in Finland as:
    a. The Continuation War
    b. The Summer War
    c. The Germo-Finn Conflict
    d. Mannerheim's War

11. How did Mannerheim anger the Germans?
    By opening negotiations with the Soviet Union

12. Late-war skirmishes with retreating German soldiers are known as:
    a. Hitler's Debacle
    b. The Lapland War
    c. The German War
    d. Struggle on the Tundra

Heinz Guderian

German General and father of Blitzkrieg
Born: June 17, 1888
Died: May 14, 1954

Much of Germany's success in the early days of the war was due to its decided advantage in armor. More than any other person, Heinz Wilhelm Guderian worked to develop the equipment, organization and tactics that made German tanks effective.

Guderian, the son of a Prussian army officer, commanded a wireless station during the First World War before being named to serve on the general staff. When size limitations were placed on the German army after the war, Guderian was one of only 4,000 men allowed to serve as officers. For a time, Guderian was attached to the Swedish army, where he was first introduced to the tank. From this experience and from extensive reading, Guderian started to develop his theory of mobile warfare, better known as *Blitzkrieg* (lightning war).

During the early 1930's, Guderian set about creating a *panzer* (tank) force for Germany. He worked hard to convince his superiors of the merits of tank warfare. At first, unable to construct actual tanks because of treaty limitations, Guderian's men drew laughs from fellow soldiers as they ran around mock battlefields with tin cutouts and cars covered with cardboard. Germany's first tank, the *Panzer I* (intended to be a training tank), entered production in 1934 and saw service during the early part of the war.

Guderian believed that a panzer general should serve on the frontline, observing strongholds and locating weak spots that could be quickly crushed. In 1936, he was promoted to major general. In 1937, he published a book, *Achtung! Panzer*, detailing the tactics that would lead to German success in the early stages of the Second World War.

German tanks pause during the invasion of Poland in September 1939.

The soundness of Guderian's tactics were proven in the first Blitzkrieg campaign in Poland. Guderian led two panzer divisions in the short campaign. After Poland fell, Hitler next planned to attack France. He delayed the attack after plans for the invasion accidentally fell into Allied hands. During this time, General Erich von Manstein developed a cunning plan. Troops would be sent into the Low countries in

Panzer I

The Panzer I was the first German tank developed after the First World War. Intended for training only, it ultimately saw action in the Spanish Civil War, Poland, France, North Africa and Russia.

INVASION OF NORWAY

Group I: "Narvik" 2000 men, 10 destroyers and the battlecruisers *Scharnhorst* and *Gneisenau*

Group II: "Trondheim" 1700 men, four destroyers and the heavy cruiser *Admiral Hipper*

Group III: "Bergen" 1300 men, two destroyers and the light cruisers *Köln* and *Königsberg*

Group IV & V: "Kristiansand" and "Egersund," cruiser *Karlsruhe* and eight support ships

Group VI: "Oslo" 163rd Division spearhead, general staff, three destroyers and the cruisers *Blücher*, *Lützow* and *Emden*.

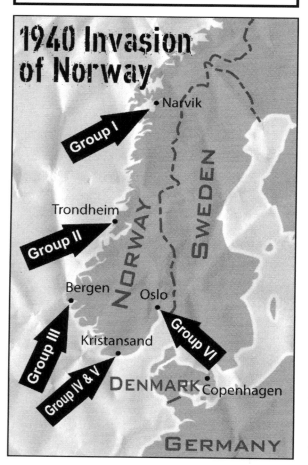

order to draw Allied troops to the north while an entire army group would drive through the Ardennes Forest and head for the sea, trapping the Allied troops. Guderian strongly supported the plan. Hitler loved the idea and approved it. While revised plans for France were being prepared, Hitler turned his attention toward Denmark and Norway.

ATTACK ON NORWAY

In early 1940, both Axis and Allies were confronted with the issue of the neutral country of Norway. The Allies wanted to stop shipments of iron ore that were passing through the country from Sweden to be used in the German war machine. Hitler wanted to protect the iron ore while also coveting the country as a potential U-boat base and buffer to protect Northern Germany. But which side would act first? When war did reach Norway, King Haakon VII, upon being told by an aide, "Majesty, we are at war!" asked "Against whom?"

German plans were put into action just as the Allies were preparing forces of their own. The Germans launched a daring attack known as *Operation Weserübung* in early April. The attack would bring both Denmark and Norway under German control.

On April 8, the British destroyer *Glowworm* skirmished with the German destroyers *Bernd von Arnim* and the *Hans Lüdemann*. The heavy cruiser *Admiral Hipper* soon arrived and attacked the *Glowworm*. Badly damaged by the cruiser's large guns, the *Glowworm* rammed *Hipper* before sinking. The Allies did not recognize that the German ships were part of an invasion, instead assuming they were sent to stop the planned Allied landings.

At 4:15 a.m. on April 9, 1940, German troops crossed into Denmark. At the same time, Danish King Christian X was handed an ultimatum. Meeting with his advisers while German bombers droned menacingly above Copenhagen, the

Danes reached the conclusion that they could not resist. Less than six hours after the invasion began, Denmark accepted what the Germans termed "protection of the Reich." Only several dozen soldiers died in the battle.

That same day, the Germans attempted six amphibious assaults intended to capture every major port along the coast of Norway. Three of the groups soon secured their objectives. At Narvik, three German destroyers used torpedoes to sink the outdated coastal defense ships *Eldsvold* and *Norge*. At Kristiansand the Germans were twice repulsed before securing the town.

The Germans encountered major problems attempting to land at the capital, Oslo. Forty-year-old torpedoes launched from the Oscarborg fortress sank the heavy cruiser *Blücher*. The *Lützow* withdrew, believing the *Blücher* had stumbled into a minefield. Off-loading troops 12 miles away from the intended destination delayed plans by 24 hours. The delay allowed the Norwegian King to board a train and escape to Hamar.

The Allies soon began landing British, French and Polish troops near the northern ports of Trondheim and Narvik. They fought valiantly for the next two months but never seriously threatened Germany's supremacy. Desperation engulfed France by early June. With Norway no longer a priority, the last troops were withdrawn from Narvik on June 8. On June 9, the Norwegians were told to cease all resistance.

King Haakon, along with a number of Norwegian naval, air and army forces, escaped to Great Britain and continued to serve with Allied forces. Despite five years of occupation, Norway never officially surrendered.

Though Germany had won, it came at a cost. Many soldiers who could have been used elsewhere were required to hold Norway for the remainder of the war. More importantly, the loss of three cruisers, 10 of its 20 destroyers and

six U-boats meant that the *Kriegsmarine* would never again be a major threat. Despite losing a carrier (the *Glorious*), two cruisers, seven destroyers, and one sub Great Britain could better absorb her losses.

The Battle of France

Hitler did not wait too long after the fall of Norway to launch *Fall Gelb* (Case Yellow) — the attack on the Low countries and France. The Germans once more anticipated a quick knockout of Allied forces.

The attack commenced on May 10, 1940 when 136 German divisions and 2500 planes faced off against half as many Allied troops. In

Heinz Guderian during the Battle of France. An Enigma code machine can be seen in the lower left-hand corner.

German troops roam the streets of Paris as conquerors.

the north, General Fedor von Bock led 30 divisions into the Netherlands and Belgium in the planned diversion to draw off Allied troops. The Allies took the bait and moved most of their troops north.

Four-thousand *Fallschirmjäger* troops parachuted into the Netherlands, capturing bridges and airfields. The Germans moved quickly. Only around Rotterdam was resistance fierce as the Dutch sealed off bridges so German tanks could not advance. On May 13, the Dutch government fled to Great Britain. Hitler, upset by lack of progress, ordered the city bombed into submission. Only a few buildings in the compact 642-acre city survived. The Dutch surrendered on May 15 at the cost of 2100 Dutch killed and 2700 wounded.

Glider troops captured the Belgian fort Eben Emael, a modern fortification with 1500 men expected to be able to hold out for weeks, in little more than a day. On May 17, German troops entered Brussels, the capital. The next day they entered Antwerp, a major seaport.

Guderian and General Erwin Rommel were among the corps commanders in *Army Group A.* As Allied forces moved north into Belgium, panzer divisions sped through Ardennes Forest. Success of the thrust through the Ardennes depended on exiting the forest before the French could block the advance. Only a few second-line forces were guarding the area. On May 12, Guderian's XIX Panzer Corps reached the Meuse River. The French defensive positions on the Meuse were quickly eliminated by *Luftwaffe* aircraft. Guderian crossed the river on an assault boat. French tanks counterattacked at Sedan on the 14th but were outmatched.

The German gains were so spectacular as to catch the German high command off guard. Guderian had to convince them to continue moving forward. On May 19, the French 4th armored division, led by Charles de Gaulle, counterattacked but was driven back. General Maxime Weygand took over as commander-in-chief of Allied forces. On May 20, Guderian's units moved into Amiens and Abbeville. The Germans had advanced farther along than at any time during the First World War. That night, units reached the sea, closing the net — 1 million Allied troops were trapped!

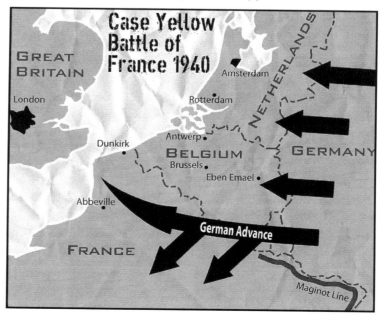

A triumphant Hitler visits Paris on June 23, 1940.

At this point, a curious thing happened. Hitler called a halt to operations. While many theories abound, the biggest reason is probably that he wished to capture Paris as soon as possible. During this time, the Allied troops were concentrated in the town of Dunkirk. A large-scale evacuation began in which more than 300,000 troops were evacuated to England. The surrender of Belgian forces on May 28 complicated the evacuation.

The Luftwaffe bombed Paris on June 3, and the invasion of France moved toward its inevitable conclusion. Only 65 Allied divisions stood against 143 German. Some Allied troops fought valiantly and many retreated, adding to the confusion of fleeing civilians on the French roads. The French lines broke in various places. Even the strongly fortified Maginot line broke.

The French government left Paris, and 46,000 French and British troops surrendered to Rommel at St. Valery-en-Caux.

Italian dictator Benito Mussolini, jealous of the German success and desiring a share of the glory, attacked France on June 10. The attack by the Italian army, unprepared for combat, was a disaster. The Italians were unable to dislodge the skeleton garrisons on the French border, and very little territory was captured. More than 600 soldiers died, and more than 2000 were wounded. Only 79 French soldiers died.

On June 13, Paris was declared an open city. Three-fourths of the city's population had already evacuated when German soldiers entered the next day. On June 17 Henri Petain replaced Paul Reynaud as leader of France. The next day, Petain asked the Germans for an armistice. France officially surrendered on June 21, signing the document of surrender at Compiégne. To humiliate the French, Hitler had the wall of a museum knocked down and a railway car, the same one in which the Germans had surrendered 22 years earlier, moved to the siding on which it sat in 1918.

The terms of the surrender were somewhat softened because Hitler did not want France to resume fighting. Part of France, known as *Vichy France*, remained unoccupied by German forces. More than 225,000 Jews from France and the Low countries would die as part of Hitler's *"Final Solution."*

General de Gaulle escaped to Britain, where he immediately began to organize the Free French forces. He made the first of many radio broadcasts urging his countrymen not to give up hope. "France has lost a battle. But France has not lost the war."

DISMISSAL BY HITLER

Guderian was on the front line again when the Germans launched *Operation Barbarossa* against Russia in the summer of 1941. Leading *Panzergruppe Guderian*, he captured Smolensk and set his sights on the Russian capital, Moscow. Protesting when his forces were redirected toward Kiev, he was relieved of command.

In 1943, he was brought back to oversee German armored strategy, tank design and production. Frustrated that Hitler planned so many different tank designs, Guderian argued for a greater number of proven medium tanks like the Panzer III's and IV's rather than larger designs. In 1944, he was named chief of staff. After a number of arguments about Hitler's handling of the war, Hitler dismissed Guderian in March 1945.

After the war, Guderian was arrested but not charged with war crimes. He assisted with the development of the West German army after the war. His son later became a commander in the *North Atlantic Treaty Organization* (NATO). Heinz Guderian passed away May 14, 1954.

REVIEW QUESTIONS

1. Heinz Guderian developed the theory of __Mobile__ warfare:
   - a. mobile
   - b. fortification
   - c. atomic
   - d. trench

2. Panzer is a German word for __tank__.

3. Guderian believed a panzer general should lead from the:
   - a. headquarters
   - b. back
   - c. front
   - d. center

4. What was the name of Guderian's book on armored tactics? __Achtung! Panzer__

5. Guderian led two divisions in what early war campaign?
   - a. North Africa
   - b. Poland
   - c. Russia
   - d. Denmark

6. One of the reasons Hitler attacked Norway was to protect delivery of iron ore from what country? __Sweden__

7. What small country surrendered within hours of invasion on April 9, 1940? __Denmark__

8. Which German cruiser was sunk during the attack on Oslo, Norway?
   - a. Graf Spree
   - b. Lützow
   - c. Bismarck
   - d. Blücher

9. Which Dutch city was leveled by German bombers? __Rotterdam__

10. The imposing Belgian fortress Eben Emael was captured by what kind of troops?
    - a. glider
    - b. infantry
    - c. airborne
    - d. naval

11. Which forest did panzer forces race through in order to trap Allied troops in northern France? __Ardennes Forest__

12. What country joined Germany in the invasion of France? __Italy__

13. What did Hitler do to humiliate the French when they signed the document of surrender? __the had a museum wall knocked down and railway car moved__

14. Which French leader escaped and organized the Free French forces that would continue to fight through the end of the war? __General de Gaulle__

15. What was the name of the part of France that remained unoccupied by German forces? __Vichy, France__

Karl Dönitz

Grand Marshall of the Kreigsmarine
Last leader of the Third Reich
Born: September 16, 1891
Died: December 24, 1980

Spreading war and death to all the world's oceans, submarines made the Second World War a truly global event. For Great Britain, an island nation, control of the seas was vital to survival. German admiral Karl Dönitz almost succeeded in isolating and vanquishing Great Britain by destroying its merchant ships with U-boats (short for *Unterseeboot* undersea boat.).

Dönitz was born in 1891 near Berlin. He joined the German Imperial Navy at the age of 18. In 1918, while in command of a U-boat, Dönitz was taken prisoner by the Allies. Between the wars, he wrote a number of studies on submarines even though Germany had none as a condition of the Treaty of Versailles.

When Hitler began to rebuild the German war machine in the 1930's into the *Wehrmacht*, the *Kriegsmarine* (navy) commanded lower priority than the *Heer* (army) and *Luftwaffe* (air force). Rebuilding the submarine fleet, Dönitz' efforts were further frustrated as he was forced to compete with the surface fleet for resources. At the outbreak of war, Germany had only 46 serviceable subs. Despite these disadvantages, Dönitz would oversee the construction of more than 1100 submarines that would sink more than 4600 merchant ships during the war. U-boats proved to be more effective than Germany's prized surface fleet.

BATTLE OF THE RIVER PLATE

On September 3, 1939, England declared war on Germany. That same day, *U-30* sank the British passenger ship *Athenia*, killing more than 100, including 28 Americans.

Two weeks later, another U-boat sank the aircraft carrier *Courageous*. Dönitz' U-boats were proving their value, but German Admiral Erich Raeder still gave priority to the surface fleet.

The first major naval battle of the Second World War took place far from Europe. As the German Navy was smaller than the British, the Germans preferred to avoid battle, focusing instead on destroying merchant ships. In the fall of 1939, the German pocket battleship *Graf Spee* moved into the South Atlantic and began capturing and sinking British ships. Unlike the unrestricted warfare engaged in by German submarines, Captain Hans Langsdorff saved all crew members before sinking a ship.

The British formed eight battle groups to hunt for the *Graf Spee*. On December 13, 1939, the heavy cruiser *Exeter* and light cruis-

The "pocket battleship" Graf Spee was a creative way around treaty limitations. German designers succeeded in placing battleship-caliber guns on a ship the size and weight of a cruiser.

ers *Ajax* and *Achilles* (a New Zealand cruiser) located the *Graf Spee*. *Exeter* retired from the battle after receiving heavy damage from *Graf Spee's* 11-inch guns but not before hitting *Graf Spee's* boiler room. The light cruisers peppered the German ship with their six-inch guns, causing significant damage.

The *Graf Spee* entered the neutral Uruguayan port of Montevideo in the River Plate estuary for repairs. The Uruguayan government demanded the ship leave within 72 hours. While not true, British intelligence convinced Langsdorff that a large task force blocked his escape. On December 17, the *Graf Spee* left the harbor at Montevideo. Langsdorff scuttled the ship in the estuary rather than subject his men to a losing battle. The ship settled into the muddy bottom of the shallow water while most of her superstructure remained above surface. Langsdorff afterward committed suicide.

HMS HOOD AND THE BISMARCK

The pride of the German Navy, the 35,000-ton battleship *Bismarck*, set sail in May 1941 to destroy Allied shipping in the Atlantic Ocean. With 11 convoys at sea or set to sail, the British Admiralty began an anxious search for the battleship.

The battlecruiser *Hood* and battleship *Prince of Wales* engaged the *Bismarck* in the North Atlantic between Greenland and Iceland. The third salvo from the *Bismarck* plunged into the deck of the *Hood*, striking the ship's ammunition magazine. A mighty explosion engulfed the ship, shattering her into pieces. Only three of the 1419 crew survived. The *Prince of Wales* disengaged after taking several hits, but not before damaging one of the *Bismarck's* fuel tanks, requiring her to head to France for repairs.

Sinking the *Bismarck* became the sole focus of the British Navy. After contact with the battleship was lost, it appeared that she

Armed with 15-inch guns, the Bismarck her sister ship, the Tirpitz, were the pride of the Kriegmarine. Though soon surpassed by other designs, the Bismarck was the largest warship (50,000 tons) at the time of her launching in February 1939.

Bismarck

might reach France safely. A *Consolidated PBY Catalina* flying boat located the *Bismarck*, and *Fairey Swordfish* biplanes from the carrier *Ark Royal* attacked the battleship. The canvas covering of the old-fashioned planes proved to their advantage as the *Bismarck's* antiair shells tore through but did not stop the attackers. Two torpedoes struck the ship. One did no damage, but the other doomed the *Bismarck* by hitting an engine room and jamming the rudders at an angle. As a result, the *Bismarck* was stuck sailing in a large circle.

British ships, led by the battleships *Rodney* and *King George V* converged on the stricken German ship. The *Bismarck* sustained hit after hit during the course of an hour-and-a-half. A torpedo from the cruiser *Dorsetshire* delivered the final blow. Only 110 of the *Bismarck's* 2000 crewmen survived.

In contrast to the brief journey of the *Bismarck*, nine old freighters converted into armed raiders succeeded in spreading fear and destruction around the globe. The ships were disguised to look like normal merchant ships, only revealing their true nature after it was too late for their prey to escape. In November 1941, a battle between the German raider *Kormoran* and the Australian cruiser *Sydney* resulted in the ships' mutual destruction. All 645 men onboard the *Sydney* perished.

The HMCS Quesnel was one of 267 Flower-class corvettes built to protect Allied convoys from German U-boats. In 1941, Canada aided the war effort by taking full responsibility for the western leg of of the Atlantic run.

THE BATTLE OF THE ATLANTIC

U-boat crews were held in high esteem by the German people. They were given the best rations and generous leave when not on duty. However, life onboard a U-boat was tough. Submariners spent three months at a time without showers, wearing the same clothes and living in very cramped quarters. The air stunk, and privacy was nonexistent. When under attack, submariners in submerged U-boats experienced periods of sheer terror, knowing they could be crushed at any moment. During the course of the war, 28,000 of Dönitz' 41,000 submariners perished.

After the Germans lost a large portion of their surface fleet during the invasion of Norway in early 1940, U-boats remained as the only significant naval threat. The early days of the war were known to German submariners as the "Happy Time." Great Britain, ill-prepared to counter the U-boat threat, agonized as ship after ship sank with little consequence. Dönitz organized his U-boats into "wolf packs," where multiple submarines would attack convoys at the same time. The top 10 German U-boat commanders alone sank a total of 318 ships.

Losing ships faster than they could be replaced, the British appealed to America for help. Though not yet in the war, President Roosevelt worked out a deal where the Americans gave the British 50 aging destroyers in exchange for British bases. The Americans also agreed to defend Greenland and Iceland in exchange for the right to build military bases.

In May 1941, the British destroyer *Bulldog* captured *U-100*, recovering an *Enigma* code machine that led to the "Ultra" program of deciphering German transmissions. By the fall of 1941, the Germans were able to keep 80 U-boats in service at one time. When Hitler began to move some of the U-boats into the Mediterranean, Dönitz became upset. Dönitz believed the key to the war was controlling the Atlantic. While they had some success, including the sinking of the *Ark Royal*, none of the 62 U-boats sent returned to the Atlantic.

The most successful year for U-boats was 1942. With the entry of the United States

Convoy WS-12 steams for Capetown, South Africa as a Vought SB2U Vindicator scout bomber launched from the carrier Ranger patrols for German submarines.

into the war, German subs prowled off the eastern coast of America. The Americans experienced heavy losses, as they were slow in learning to protect their ships. In the summer of 1942, the U-boats extended their reach into the Caribbean Sea and the Gulf of Mexico and even as far south as the coast of Brazil. The Battle of the Atlantic reached a climax in November 1942 with Allied losses at 860,000 tons (119 ships); U-boats accounting for more than 700,000 tons.

In January 1943, Dönitz replaced Raeder as the head of the German Navy. He lavished resources on his beloved U-boats. However, the fortune of war already was beginning to swing in favor of the Allies. That month as the number of operational German U-boats peaked at 212, Churchill and Roosevelt were meeting in Casablanca. The two leaders gave priority to waging war on the U-boats. In February 1943, new construction exceeded losses for the first time. By the spring of 1943, the Germans were losing one-and-a-half U-boats for each Allied ship sunk.

U-3008 was a late-war Type XXI submarine. The sub had a range of 13,000 nautical miles. Captured by the Allies, she was used as a test submarine in the U.S. Navy until she was scrapped in 1955.

U.S. Naval Historic Center

TRIVIA

Only two Liberty Ships are still operational today (2011): the *Jeremiah O'Brien* and *John W. Brown.*

THE ALLIES GAIN THE ADVANTAGE

Many factors contributed to the Allies winning the Battle of the Atlantic. A type of sonar known as ASDIC in use since the beginning of the war had proven useful but only could target U-boats underwater. The development of radar, especially the powerful microwave radar, located U-boats on the surface. The British Admiralty learned that larger convoys were less vulnerable, as U-boats could only sink a certain number of ships however large the convoy. Larger convoys meant fewer, allowing more escorts per convoy. The German wolf packs were dependent on radio contact with one another and headquarters. The development of the high-frequency direction-finder named "Huff Duff" allowed German subs to be located by their own radio transmissions. Two-hundred sixty-seven Flower-class corvettes built during the war ably protected convoys. Small escort carriers helped provide air cover. The Allies learned that airplanes, even if not armed, were effective in chasing away U-boats. After early, uncoordinated attempts failed to protect convoys, escort groups were kept together for the duration of the war in order to develop teamwork. American shipyards began to launch ships faster than the U-boats could sink them.

The U-boat would continue to be a threat for the duration of the war, but Dönitz wrote in his memoirs that he knew by May 1943 the Battle of the Atlantic would be lost. Improved Allied defensive measures and the ability to replace losses overwhelmed any damage the Germans could hope to generate.

Dwight Eisenhower said in 1944 of the merchant marines, "When final victory is ours there is no organization that will share its credit more deservedly than the American merchant marine." The same can be said of British and Canadian efforts.

LIBERTY SHIPS

U.S. National Archives

Liberty ships are lined up at a base in California in 1944.

Of all the Allied efforts, the single greatest contribution may have been a simple merchant vessel: the Liberty Ship. Based on the design of a British tramp steamer and known as "Ugly Ducklings," Liberty Ships were not pretty or fast. What they lacked in style they made up in sheer numbers. The ships were versatile, serving as both cargo ships and troop transports.

Shipbuilder Henry J. Kaiser devised a way to build much of each ship on land. The pre-fabricated components could then be quickly assembled in the shipyard. By the end of the war, the average time to build one was less than 40 days. As part of a publicity stunt, the *Robert E. Peary* was built in an astonishing four days and 15 hours.

The ships were inexpensive and said to pay for themselves in a single crossing of the Atlantic. Between October 1941 and the end of war, American shipyards produced more than 5000 merchant vessels, of which 2710 were Liberty Ships. The Germans sank 21.7 million tons of Allied ships during the war. The Americans built 19.4 million tons of Liberty ships alone.

On April 30, 1945, Dönitz learned that Hitler had committed suicide. Unexpectedly, Hitler had named Dönitz to be his successor. Realizing the war had been decided, Dönitz attempted to toss aside his Nazi image. His fleet's last action rescued thousands of refugees on the Baltic coast before they were overrun by the Soviets. On May 7, the German high command surrendered unconditionally. Dönitz was arrested on May 23.

Both his sons, one on a U-boat, were killed in action during the war. Accused of waging unrestricted warfare during his trial at Nuremberg, American commanders, including Chester Nimitz, came to Dönitz' defense citing that they, too, had waged unrestricted warfare in the Pacific Theater. While many other Nazi leaders were executed, Dönitz only served 10 years in prison.

Upon his release, Dönitz lived quietly in retirement. Karl Dönitz died in 1980 of a heart attack. He was buried without military honors because of his Nazi background. At his funeral, many men who served under him turned out to pay their respects to the man they called the "great lion."

REVIEW QUESTIONS

1. *What stealth weapons did the Germans use to attack Allied shipping?* V-boats

2. *How many serviceable submarines did Germany have at the beginning of the Second World War?*
   a. 110
   b. 46
   c. 1100
   d. 312

3. *What British passenger ship was sunk by a German submarine on the day Great Britain entered the war?* Athenia

4. Which ship did not take part in the Battle of the River Plate?
   a. HMNZS Achilles   b. HMS Exeter
   c. HMS Bulldog   d. Graf Spee

5. The Graf Spee was trapped in which South American port city? *Montevideo*

6. The British battlecruiser *Hood* was destroyed by the German battleship Bismarck.

7. What sealed the fate of the Bismarck?
   A torepedo hit the engine room

8. The Germans used nine old freighters to great effect to:
   a. destroy Allied shipping
   b. ram military vessels
   c. deliver secret payloads
   d. transport spies to America

9. Attacks by groups of submarines known as *U-boats* contributed to German success during the early part of the war.

10. The struggle between German U-boats and Allied convoys is known as the Battle of the *Atlantic*

11. What critical code machine did the Allies recover from a U-boat in May 1941?
   a. Oompa
   b. Distorter
   c. C1935
   d. Enigma

12. Which factor was NOT important in winning the Battle of the Atlantic?
   a. Flower-class corvettes
   b. B-29 bombers
   c. Microwave radar
   d. "Huff Duff"

13. The production of 2710 prefabricated *Liberty* ships was critical to replace losses caused by German U-boats.

Winston Churchill

Prime Minister of Great Britain
Knighted by Queen Elizabeth II
Born: November 30, 1874
Died: January 24, 1965

An artist, historian, prolific writer, British Army officer, accomplished statesman and an impassioned orator, few men have left as enduring a legacy as Winston Churchill. After having already served 40 years in British politics, his finest moment came during the dark early days of the Second World War. Churchill electrified Great Britain with his resolute determination to resist and eventually defeat Nazi tyranny.

Churchill was born November 30, 1874 at his family's home, Blenheim Palace. The son of Lord Randolph Churchill, who oversaw Great Britain's finances as Chancellor of the Exchequer, Churchill entered the Royal Military College at Sandhurst in 1893. He entered the British Army in 1895, serving in India and Africa. While in India, Churchill spent all his spare time reading in an effort to improve his education. He served as a war correspondent during the Cuban rebellion and the siege of Malakand in India.

He was in South Africa during the Boer War in 1899. The Boers were descendants of Dutch farmers who took up arms after the British built a railroad through their land. Taken prisoner by the Boers, Churchill managed to escape. The published account of his escape made him a hero to the British people. Experiencing several close brushes with death left Churchill feeling destined to accomplish much in life.

Churchill entered the House of Commons in 1901. His brilliant speeches attracted attention and fame. He wrote and lectured in England, America and Canada to earn an income, as Parliamentarians received no pay.

Churchill served in several key roles during the First World War. As First Lord of the Admiralty, Churchill worked hard to build up the British fleet. He resigned in the spring of 1915 after his plan to help supply Russia by seizing the Dardanelles Straits during the Gallipoli campaign turned into a disaster. For a short time, Churchill commanded a battalion of Royal Scots Fusiliers in France, where he earned the soldiers' respect for his coolness under fire. As Minister of Munitions, he helped develop the first tanks. The "landships" proved to be a decisive factor in the final battles of the First World War.

An 1895 photo of Winston Churchill wearing his military uniform as a member of the 4th Queen's Own Hussars.

Churchill struggled politically in the early 1920's, losing several elections. He was named Chancellor of the Exchequer in 1924, facing much criticism for the difficult financial times in England. A 1932 visit to Germany convinced Churchill that Adolph Hitler intended to rearm and fight. He pleaded for rearming to show Hitler that Great Britain would not back down.

After Prime Minister Neville Chamberlain agreed to the Munich Pact in 1938 Churchill said, "England has been offered a choice between war and shame. She has chosen shame, and will get war." A fierce critic of Neville's appeasement polices, Churchill said to him in a speech to the House of Commons, "You were given the choice between war and dishonor. You chose dishonor, and you will have war."

THE OUTBREAK OF WAR

The day on which Britain declared war on Germany, September 3, 1939, Churchill was again appointed First Lord of the Admiralty. During his time in the post, the first major naval battle of the war occurred when British ships battled and trapped the German pocket battleship *Graf Spee* in the Battle of the River Plate.

Chamberlain resigned as Prime Minister on May 10, 1940 just hours before Germany launched its *Blitzkrieg* attack on France and the Low Countries. Churchill became the new Prime Minister. He later said of that day, "I felt as if I were walking with Destiny, and that all my past life had been but preparation for this hour and for this trial."

DUNKIRK

As the Germans pushed into France they managed to trap a large number of French and British troops in a pocket near the coastal town of Dunkirk. Churchill strongly supported *Operation Dynamo*, an effort launched with the hope that 50,000 British troops could be evacuated by sea.

These British troops were taken prisoner by the Germans at Dunkirk in June 1940.

With only 41 destroyers were available, the Royal Navy sent out a call for personal ships, fireboats, paddle-wheels, fishing trawlers and any other seaworthy (and some dubious at that!) vessels. More than 800 ships from England, France, Belgium and Netherlands responded, and the evacuation began in earnest on May 26.

German dive bombers peppered troops gathered on the beaches. Limited support from the Royal Air Force and ship antiaircraft fire claimed more than 200 Luftwaffe planes. Oil tanks in Dunkirk were set on fire to provide a beacon for ships arriving from Great Britain. Troops formed a line two-thirds of a mile long on a jetty enclosing the harbor waiting to load. Others stood in lines extending far out into the surf. Smaller boats ferried soldiers out to waiting ships.

The situation became critical on May 28 when Belgian forces surrendered. Bernard Montgomery, long before success at El Ala-

THE DUNKIRK FLEET

It was a motley collection of ships that steamed, sailed or rowed to Dunkirk. Here are some of the more intriguing participants.

Tamzin - This 17-foot fishing boat is the smallest known to make the trip. Today it sits in the Imperial War Museum.

Endeavour - An America's Cup challenging yacht.

Fenella - This paddle-steamer was hit and sunk after loading 600 troops.

Count Dracula - This boat was once owned by a German admiral.

Mosquito - A Yangtze gun boat.

Sundowner - A 60-foot yacht piloted by C. H. Lightoller, the only surviving officer of the *Titanic*. Designed to carry only 20 people, the *Sundowner* succeeded in bringing back 130 men.

Shamrock - This tourist boat based at Folkestone shuttled soldiers from the beach to waiting ships. His life savings tied up in the boat, the captain lost everything when she sank near Dunkirk.

mein brought him fame, led his 3rd Division to plug the gap left by the Belgians. On May 29, in one of many heroic acts that characterized the operation, the *Oriole* beached herself at low tide to create a bridge to other ships. The high tide lifted the ship, now loaded with 700 soldiers and nurses from a field hospital. Forty-seven thousand British troops in all were evacuated that day.

By June 2, daylight evacuations became impossible. Forty thousand French troops willingly remained behind to delay the Germans. Two days later, the Germans entered Dunkirk. In a week, more than 200,000 British and 100,000 French, Dutch and Belgian troops had been evacuated to safety. Of the 861 participating ships, 231 were lost. British losses included the destroyers *Grafton*, *Grenade*, *Wakeful*, *Basilisk*, *Harvant* and *Keith*. The French Navy lost the *Bourrasque*, *Sirocco* and *Foudroyant*. Churchill referred to the great deliverance as a miracle.

BRITAIN FIGHTS ALONE

The fall of France jolted the British people with the reality that they stood alone against triumphant Germany. British leaders eyed Communist Russia with suspicion, and it would be 18 months before America entered the war. It was expected that Germany would follow up its lightning success with an invasion of England. Churchill encouraged the nation with a number of memorable speeches. He told his new government, "You ask what is our policy? I will say. It is to wage war, by sea, land and air, with all our might and with all the strength that God can give us; to wage war against a monstrous tyranny, never surpassed in the dark, lamentable catalogue of human crime. That is our policy."

Churchill supported the decision to attack French ships that did not scuttle or demobilize after the fall of France rather than allow the Germans to seize them. Most of the ships were neutralized without incident, but more than 1000 French sailors were killed at Mers-el-Kébir when they refused to surrender to the British. After the unfortunate incident, Churchill had to fight back tears while speaking to Parliament. He wrote later that the action showed Britain "feared nothing and would stop at nothing."

Churchill knew that the entry of the United States, with its great industrial capacity and military potential, would change everything. Churchill cultivated a friendship with U.S. President Franklin Roosevelt, whom he met for the first of their 10 wartime meetings at Placentia Bay, Newfoundland, in August 1941. Roosevelt refused to enter the war unless America was

Hawker Hurricane

Imperial War Museum / A 9534

Although the Spitfire left an enduring image as the champion of England during the Battle of Britain, the Hawker Hurricane accounted for more than half the German planes destroyed during the battle. The sturdy plane served in all the major theaters during the war.

Supermarine Spitfire

Imperial War Museum / CH 27

The agile Supermarine Spitfire proved to be the arch nemesis of Germany's Bf 109 during the Battle of Britain. The fighter remained in production throughout the war and continued to serve in a combat role into the 1950's.

attacked first. He did promise as much help as possible in the form of planes, tanks, destroyers and other weapons.

Compared to his chummy friendship with Roosevelt, Churchill's relationship with Josef Stalin was awkward at best. As fearful of Communism as Fascism, Churchill initially greeted the German invasion of Russia with approval. He secretly hoped that the two evil leaders, Stalin and Hitler, would destroy one another.

Though heartened by the entry of America into the war after the Japanese raid on Pearl Harbor, December 1941 brought only bad news for Churchill and Britain. The news of the loss of the battlecruiser *Repulse* and battleship *Prince of Wales* near Singapore devastated Churchill. "In all the war I never received a more direct shock. As I turned over and twisted in bed the full horror of the news sank in upon me. Over all this vast expanse of waters Japan reigned supreme, and we everywhere were weak and naked." Singapore surrendered on Christmas Day. The sinking of the cruiser *Neptune* at Malta with only one survivor and the Italian attack on British ships in the harbor of Alexandria brought Churchill to a low point.

With the Nazis dominating Europe and its Pacific possessions all but lost, Britain focused on the ongoing Battle of the Atlantic and the Mediterranean Theater. In the spring of 1942, Churchill insisted that Tobruk, in North Africa,

be held. Capturing the fortress proved difficult and became an obsession for German General Erwin Rommel. Tobruk finally fell in July. Churchill received the news while at the White House visiting President Roosevelt. Roosevelt asked, "What can we do to help?" Churchill immediately asked for and received 300 Sherman tanks, 100 self-propelled guns and several squadrons of fighters and bombers. By late 1942, the Germans would be on a 1400-mile retreat back to Tunis.

DIEPPE AND ITALY

On August 19, 1942, 5100 Canadians and 1000 British commandos and American Rangers raided the port of Dieppe, France to test defenses. The raid proved to be a debacle as almost 60% of the men who made it ashore were captured, killed or wounded. The raid did teach valuable lessons that would save many Allied lives during the 1944 invasion of Normandy.

By the time Churchill and Roosevelt met at Quebec in August 1943, the war had turned in the favor of the Allies. At this time, the two leaders agreed to accept only unconditional surrender from Italy. Though American generals wanted to invade France in 1943, Churchill convinced Roosevelt to instead focus on Italy, "the soft underbelly of Europe." The collapsing beachhead of the Anzio landing threatened to become a repeat of Churchill's Gallipoli. Exasperated at the lack of success, he told Harold Alexander, "I expected to see a wild cat roaring through the mountains — and what do I find? A whale wallowing on the beaches!" Much like at Dieppe, the Italian landings allowed the Allies to develop experience and tactics for the critical Normandy invasion.

Churchill said that at a meeting in Moscow in October 1944, he showed Stalin a piece of paper with his plan for dividing eastern and southeastern Europe between Russia and the West. Greece would fall under the influence of the West, while Romania and Bulgaria would fall under Communist influence. If the account is true, the paper essentially defined the front line of the Cold War to follow in the next four decades. After the German surrender, Churchill was even more fearful of the Soviet Union, going so far as to suggest that 700,000 Germans be kept armed in the British occupation zone.

Despite his great wartime popularity, Churchill lost an election during the Potsdam conference in July 1945. It may have been that the British people greatly respected Churchill as a war leader but did not view him as a good choice to lead in time of peace. During the conference he was replaced by the new Prime Minister, Clement Attlee. The disruption of changing leaders was one factor allowing Stalin to get much of what he wanted during the conference.

During a 1946 trip to America, Churchill lost a large sum of money in a game with President Harry Truman and gave his famous "Iron Curtain" speech at Fulton, Missouri in which he lamented the loss of Eastern Europe to Communism.

Churchill was elected to a second term as Prime Minister in 1951. He was knighted by young Queen Elizabeth II in 1953 and in the same year received a Nobel Prize for literature recognizing his numerous works. He resigned in 1955 when his health and mental capacity began to decline. He removed himself from Parliament permanently in 1964.

U.S. Naval Historic Center

A church service attended by American and British personnel is held onboard the British battleship Prince of Wales in Placentia Bay, Newfoundland during the Atlantic Charter Conference in August 1941. Seated near the tip of the left gun are Churchill and Roosevelt. The battleship Arkansas is in the background. The Prince of Wales was sunk by the Japanese four months after this photo was taken.

On January 24, 1965, Churchill passed away nine days after suffering a severe stroke. His state funeral service was attended by a great number of statesmen and heads of state. His coffin placed on a funeral train, thousands of Britons waited beside the tracks in stations and across the countryside to pay their last respects. The Famous Man who led Great Britain through its darkest days was laid to rest at St. Martin's Church, Bladon.

REVIEW QUESTIONS

1. Young Winston Churchill was captured and subsequently escaped from prison during the __Boer__ War.

2. For which of these is Churchill not well-known?
   a. writer
   b. artist
   c. army officer
   d. lawyer

The "Big Three" Allied leaders, Winston Churchill, Franklin Roosevelt and Josef Stalin, sit for photos during a conference at Yalta, Crimea. Standing behind Churchill are Admiral of the Fleet Andrew Cunningham and Marshal of the Royal Air Force Charles Portal. U.S. Navy Fleet Admiral William Leahy stands behind Roosevelt.

3. Churchill began his political career when he entered the _House of Common_ in 1901.

4. During the First World War Churchill was involved in planning the disastrous _Gallipoli_ campaign.

5. Churchill helped develop what weapon during the First World War?
   a. tank
   b. machine gun
   c. aircraft carrier
   d. grenade

6. Churchill, viewing conflict with Germany as inevitable, criticized the appeasement policies of Prime Minister _Neville Chamberlain_

7. On the day Great Britain declared war on Germany, Churchill was appointed First Lord of the _Admiralty_.

8. Churchill was named Prime Minister just hours before Germany invaded:
   a. Poland
   b. Russia
   c. France and Low countries
   d. Great Britain

9. German forces racing through the Ardennes Forest managed to trap Allied troops in the French coastal town of _Dunkirk_.

10. The evacuation of Dunkirk, Operation Dynamo, hoped to evacuate 50,000 troops. How many were ultimately evacuated?
    a. 15,000
    b. 50,000
    c. 300,000
    d. 500,000

11. Churchill's first wartime meeting with American President Franklin Roosevelt took place at:
    a. London
    b. Newfoundland
    c. Tehran
    d. Washington

12. A 1942 raid on _Tobruk_, France proved a disaster but taught important lessons for the Normandy invasion two years later.

13. Churchill persuaded American President Roosevelt to attack the European country of _Italy_ before France.

14. Despite his wartime popularity, Churchill was replaced as Great Britain's Prime Minister before the war's end while attending the _Potsdam_ conference.

Hermann Göring

Commander-in-chief of the Luftwaffe and Reichsmarschall of Nazi Germany
Born: January 12, 1893
Died: October 15, 1946

Swedish Public Domain

After Adolph *Hitler*, Hermann Göring is probably the most well-known Nazi. Controlling both the German economy and the dreaded German Air Force, the *Luftwaffe*, Göring was a friend of Hitler and first in line to take his place.

When the First World War began, Göring was serving with the Prussian infantry. After recovering from an illness, Göring was persuaded by a friend to become a pilot. An excellent pilot, he finished the war with 22 confirmed kills. He commanded the *"Flying Circus"* unit to which the Red Baron had belonged. He showed great respect for his rival pilots. After one lengthy dogfight in which he shot down an Australian pilot, Frank Slee, Göring landed and gave Slee his Iron Cross medal as a sign of respect.

Göring was one of the first men to join the Nazi party. He quickly endeared himself to Hitler. He organized the *Sturmabteilung* (Storm troopers), who helped Hitler rise to power. He may have had private reservations about Hitler but was very loyal and en-joyed the privileges of power. He amassed a great personal fortune from property seized from Jews. He wore extravagant and garish clothing and had a personal flag created that was carried by a standard-bearer at all his public appearances.

Göring was given great political and military powers. He was the driving force in the creation of the Luftwaffe in 1935. The next year, Göring was placed in charge of the German economy, which he used to aggressively arm the German military. Many of the new Luftwaffe planes were tested during the Spanish Civil War. By 1939, the Luftwaffe was arguably the world's best air force.

The Luftwaffe proved its worth in the battles for Poland, the Low countries and France. Acting as an aerial artillery in support of the *Heer* (army), Göring's planes destroyed enemy air forces on the ground, pounded defensive positions and disrupted supply columns moving toward the front.

Unlike other air forces, the Luftwaffe had its own ground forces. While most were of

Messerschmitt Bf 110

alte Postkarte

The Messerschmitt Bf 110 fighter-bomber contributed greatly to the German war effort in early campaigns but proved vulnerable to fighters during the Battle of Britain. It was converted into a night fighter, a role for which it was well suited.

Messerschmitt Bf 109

Bundesarchiv, Bild 101I-398-1794-18 / Reiners / CC-BY-SA

The primary German fighter during the Battle of Britain, the Messerschmitt Bf 109 served throughout the war in a number of roles, including ground support, bombing and reconnaissance. The 109 was the most-produced airplane during the war with more than 30,000 built during that time.

lower quality, one notable exception was the *Fallschirmjäger* (parachute elite) troops. The Fallschirmjägers were first used in Denmark and Norway with mixed results. One company was destroyed by the Norwegians at Dombás. They completed critical missions in Netherlands, Belgium and France.

BATTLE OF BRITAIN

After France surrendered, Winston Churchill addressed the House of Commons, "The Battle of France is over, I expect the battle of Britain is about to begin..." While Hitler was hopeful to arrange a peace with Great Britain, he began to make plans for an invasion of England code-named *Operation Sealion*. The superiority of the German army was unquestioned at the time, but for *Sealion* to succeed, British air and naval forces would have to be neutralized. The task was left to Göring's Luftwaffe.

The Head of Great Britain's Fighter Command was Air Chief Marshal Sir Hugh Dowding. Like Göring, he had been a pilot during the First World War. Dowding helped expand the Royal Air Force (RAF), increasing the number of fighter squadrons from 13 in 1936 to 39 in September 1939. Planning to retire in 1940, he agreed to keep working. While he is regarded as a hero today, he faced constant criticism during the war.

The future looked bleak for the RAF in the summer of 1940. During the Battle of France, the British lost 435 pilots and 959 planes. On June 8, Dowding angered Churchill by arguing to keep the remaining fighters in England rather than send them to aid France. At the start of the battle, the Germans had 2800 aircraft, of which 1050 were fighters. The British had 640 fighters, of which 199 were top line *Supermarine Spitfires* and 347 older, but capable, *Hawker Hurricanes*. The top-line German fighter was the *Messerschmitt Bf 109*.

A 1934 photo of Adolph Hitler and Hermann Göring.

Despite being outnumbered, the British held several advantages. The German fighters had a limited range, meaning they could only stay in battles for a short time. The recently broken German *Enigma* code provided a steady stream of crucial information. British pilots downed over England were recovered and soon flying again, while German pilots were taken prisoner. British factories worked feverishly to replace losses, while German factories maintained normal production because Göring did not want to alarm the populace. Finally, the British had an early, but effective, version of radar that detected when and where the Germans were heading. Un-

Dornier Do 17

The Dornier Do 17 was a light bomber designed, theoretically, to drop its payload and outrun enemy fighters. Its effectiveness was limited due to its limited range and payload.

Junkers Ju 87 Stuka

The Junkers Ju 87, better known as the Stuka, was easily recognized by its gull-shaped wings and infamous siren that instilled terror as it dived toward its intended victims. The dive-bomber attacked at angles approaching 90 degrees.

like Göring, Dowding did not have to win; he had only to survive.

On July 4, 1940, the Germans launched the first major attack when 33 *Junkers Ju 87 Stuka* dive bombers attacked the Portsmouth naval base. For most of the month of July the Germans concentrated on shipping and coastal targets where their fighters could better support their bombers. With their greater experience, the Luftwaffe initially had the upper hand.

In August, a fresh attack, code-named *Adlerangriff* ("Eagle Attack"), focused on the RAF defenses. On August 15, the Germans sent unescorted bombers from Denmark and Norway in a surprise attack against northern England. The RAF responded, and the lumbering bombers suffered heavy losses. The day saw the most Luftwaffe sorties in all during the campaign: 1786. Despite their massive numbers, the Luftwaffe lost twice as many planes on that day.

Infuriated by the losses, Göring decided to send bombers day and night. The attacks focused further inland, targeting RAF airfields, radar and infrastructure. By the end of August, damaged aircraft factories struggled to replace losses. Exhausted and worn down, RAF

TRIVIA

More than 500 pilots from a dozen nations fought against the Germans as part of the RAF during the Battle of Britain. Poland, New Zealand and Canada each contributed more than 100 pilots; seven Americans also served.

pilots appeared to be close to collapse. Hitler set September 21 as the date for *Sealion*.

Responding to small-scale British night bombing raids on German cities, Hitler and Göring switched tactics and began bombing British cities. The September 7 raid on London was unexpected and particularly damaging and demoralizing. While bombing the cities succeeded in spreading death and terror, it gave the RAF much-needed breathing room. No longer having to protect their bases, they could focus on the German bombers. The greatest German effort came on September 15, a day still celebrated as "Battle of Britain" day, when 1100 bombers and fighters swept over London. Göring hoped the attack would break the back of the British. Fifty-six German planes were shot down while many others limped back home too damaged to fly again. Others ditched in the English Channel when they ran out of gas. Only 26 RAF planes were lost on the day, and the tide of battle swung in favor of the British.

By the end of September, the Luftwaffe switched to night bombing, as daylight attacks were proving too costly. Though the attacks continued into 1941, the battle had been decided. On October 13, Hitler postponed *Sealion* until the next spring; the Germans never again seriously considered an invasion of England. In May 1941, Göring shifted his Luftwaffe planes eastward to prepare for the invasion of Russia. By 1942, it was the Allies who were sending hundreds of bombers every day to bomb Germany.

Luftwaffe at Crete and Stalingrad

Göring's Luftwaffe was active in 1941 bombing British shipping in the Mediterranean Sea and supporting Rommel's advances in North Africa. The Luftwaffe played a crucial role in the capture of the island of Crete in May. Despite success, the high rate of casualties among the Fallschirmjäger troops led German leaders to never again use them in an offensive.

Göring tried unsuccessfully in 1941 to persuade Hitler not to invade Russia. During *Operation Barbarossa,* the Luftwaffe experienced great success against the inferior Russian Air Force. The tide of war turned against the Germans as they moved deeper into Russia. In December 1942, more than 200,000 German troops of the 6th Army were trapped at Stalingrad. Göring boasted that the Luftwaffe could support the 6th Army by delivering 500 tons a day by air. The Luftwaffe never delivered more than 100 tons on any given day; the 6th Army was destroyed.

As the war progressed, the Luftwaffe's dominance faded. On April 29, 1945, Hitler, believing that Göring was negotiating with the Allies, kicked him out of the Nazi party. Hitler named Karl Dönitz as his successor. Göring surrendered to the Allies on May 9, 1945 in Bavaria.

Tried at the war crimes trial in Nuremberg, Göring claimed he had not supported the *Holocaust*. During the trial, he was confronted with orders he signed for the murder of Jews and POWs. Convicted of Crimes Against Humanity and sentenced to be hanged, Göring appealed to the court to be shot like a soldier, not hanged as a common criminal. The court denied his request. Göring ended his life the night before his execution by swallowing a cyanide capsule.

U.S. National Archives

British children sit outside their home destroyed by German bombers during the 1940 Battle of Britain.

REVIEW QUESTIONS

1. Who was the most well-known Nazi after Adolph Hitler? _Hermann Göring_

2. Göring was an accomplished _____ during the First World War.
   a. sniper
   b. general
   c. sailor
   d. pilot

3. Göring helped organize the _Sturmabteilung_ who were instrumental in Hitler's rise to power.

4. Göring created the _Luftwaffe_, Germany's air force.

5. Göring was in charge of the German _____.
   a. army
   b. economy
   c. navy
   d. agriculture

6. German paratroopers were known as _Fallschirmjäger_.

7. After the fall of France Göring was tasked with destroying the _Britain_ Air Force.

8. The planned German invasion of Great Britain was code-named:
   a. Sealion
   b. Britannica
   c. Barbarossa
   d. Walrus

9. The head of Great Britain's Fighter command was _Hugh Dowding_

10. Much of the British success during the Battle of Britain was their concentration on attacking German _bombers_ as opposed to _protection_

11. German paratroopers were never used again offensively after the invasion of which island?
    a. Malta
    b. Rhodes
    c. Crete
    d. Cyprus

12. After his conviction of Crimes Against Humanity at the Nuremberg trial, Goring:
    a. was shot
    b. committed suicide
    c. went to prison
    d. escaped

Erwin Rommel

Field Marshall German Wehrmacht
Born: November 15, 1891
Died: October 14, 1944

Erwin "The Desert Fox" Rommel is one of the most widely recognized generals to fight during the Second World War. Unlike most German generals, Rommel was not born into an aristocratic family. He was born into the family of a school headmaster in Heidenheim in 1891. He began his military career in 1910 by joining an infantry division.

Rommel served during the First World War as a lieutenant. Wounded four different times, he once captured 8000 Italian troops with a small group of mountain soldiers. For that action, he was awarded the *Pour le Mérite* (Blue Max), Prussia's highest military order. Though his military success came against a weak Italian army in full retreat, the experience instilled in him the belief that audacity led to success.

During the 1920's, Rommel served as commander of a rifle company in Germany's small army. Like many German army officers, he latched on to the Nazi cause not because of ideology, but sensing it was a vehicle to restore Germany to military greatness. He viewed German youths as weak and believed that Nazism could restore Germany to its rightful place. In 1936, he was placed in charge of Hitler's escort at the Nuremberg rally. He never did join the Nazi party.

A NATIONAL HERO

Rommel was to become well-known to both friend and foe. Winston Churchill used Rommel to give the war a personal "face" to the enemy. Rommel was also trumped up by the German propaganda machine. He was a personal favorite of Hitler. His weakness was a consuming ambition that led to an unwillingness to acknowledge logistical or strategic limitations. Fellow German army commanders considered him a renegade whose actions were impulsive and not well thought out. He had few interests outside of the army — being a soldier was his life.

On the field of battle, Rommel was a risk taker. He liked to lead from the front, often placing himself in the middle of danger. Frontline soldiers loved how he was willing to endure hardships along with them. He sought to send the enemy into disarray and keep pushing forward, creating more confusion. He exhibited a high level of personal behavior, avoiding the butchery that was so common on the Eastern Front and elsewhere. He went as far as to ignore orders to execute members of a captured Jewish brigade. Units under his command were never accused of war crimes.

Rommel commanded Hitler's mobile headquarters during the invasion of Poland. When plans were being made to invade France, Rom-

88mm Flak gun

The German 88mm gun was designed as an antiaircraft gun. While adequate in that role, the 88 earned its reputation as a superb antitank gun during the North Africa Campaign. The Panzer VI Tiger tank sported an 88mm gun.

General Erwin Rommel plans his next step during the 1940 invasion of France and the Low countries.

mel used his influence with Hitler to obtain command of the 7th Panzer Corps.

With Rommel in the lead, the 7th Panzer raced into France, crossing the Meuse River in just three days. In a tank battle at the French village of Denée, Rommel's forces destroyed 65 tanks while only losing 30. In early June, in a daring move, he led his unit across the Somme River on two railroad bridges. During a period of three weeks, Rommel captured 100,000 POWs while losing less than 50 tanks. Hitler was very excited about Rommel's success. Nazi propaganda treated him like a movie star, using him to re-enact events in France in the propaganda film "Victory in the West."

ITALIAN DEFEAT IN NORTH AFRICA

The Germans appeared unstoppable in Europe in 1940, but trouble was brewing in North Africa. Hitler desired to stay out of the Mediterranean Theater, preferring to leave it to his Italian counterpart, Benito Mussolini. However, it was apparent that the Italians needed help.

Warfare in North Africa involved battles in wide open spaces, some flat and easy to cross, others rocky and impassable. Sand, blown by strong winds, was everywhere, invading each

soldier's clothing, hair, food and weapons; 1500 miles separated Italy's headquarters in Tunis and the British headquarters in Cairo, Egypt. The campaign had swung back-and-forth as one army, moving forward, became increasingly vulnerable to counterattacks as its supply line was stretched.

In 1940, 36,000 British and Commonwealth forces opposed 250,000 Italians on the Egyptian border with Libya. Despite having greater numbers, the Italian army was poorly equipped and trained. In September, Marshal Rodolfo Graziani led Italian troops into Egypt, capturing a coastal town and constructing a string of seven fortified camps.

In December, Major-General Richard O'Connor launched *Operation Compass*, a planned five-day raid on the Italian positions. O'Connor's British, Indian and New Zealand forces snuck between an undefended opening in the fortified camps, attacked from the rear and rolled over the Italians. The raid quickly turned into a rout. Within weeks, the Commonwealth forces had advanced 500 miles, capturing all of Cyrenica, while taking 130,000 prisoners. The Italians lost 38,000 men, the Commonwealth forces less than 1000.

THE DESERT FOX

In February 1941, German forces led by Rommel began to disembark at Tripoli. The new force was given the name *Deutsches Afrika Korps* (DAK). The German forces included the Panzer III and the highly capable Panzer IV tank. The German mission was intended to prop up the Italian army and take a defensive posture that could be held until the war had been won in other theaters. Rommel's plan was more ambitious.

Despite being outnumbered, Rommel disobeyed orders and went on the offensive. British troops, worn out by the long campaign across Cyrenica, desperately needed to rest and refit their equipment. In addition, their ranks were reduced because troops had been sent to defend Greece. Rommel's forces quickly retook Cyrenica. A number of Commonwealth soldiers sought refuge in the port city of Tobruk. During the offensive, O'Connor got lost in the desert with Lt. Gen. Philip Neame, and they were captured by the Germans. Rommel soon arrived at Tobruk. Both Churchill and Admiral Andrew Cunningham demanded that Tobruk be held.

Rommel's first assault on Tobruk on April 11 with 20 tanks (all he had) supported by lightly armed German and Italian troops was easily repulsed. A larger assault two days later targeted the 9th Australian Division. Allowing Panzers to rumble through gaps in the defensive line, the Australians trapped the tanks inside without supporting infantry. Twenty-five-pounder antitank guns and dug-in tanks lit up the German tanks. For their tenacity, the 9th Australian division gained the reputation as the "Rats of Tobruk." Later attacks by the 132nd Italian Ariete Armored Division were also repulsed with a loss of 90% of its tanks. The Australian general, Leslie Morshead, in charge of Tobruk when told of an Australian newspaper's headline "Tobruk Can Take It," replied, "We're not here to take it, we're here to give it."

Pushed into action by Churchill, General Archibald Wavell launched *Operation Battleaxe* on June 15, 1941. The battle ended after three days of inconclusive fighting. The Germans had a number of powerful 88mm guns defending the imposing Halfaya escarpment. The British tanks were helpless against the 88's. Rommel was promoted by Hitler to full general over the *panzergruppe* (tank group) that included the DAK, along with several other Italian and German divisions. The Afrika Korps was placed under General Ludwig Crüwell. Churchill replaced Wavell with Sir Claude "The Auk" Auchinleck.

Auchinleck organized his forces into what was thereafter known as the Eighth Army and prepared for a new offensive. Older British tanks were replaced with newer Valentines, and U.S. Lend-Lease Stuarts and Grants. British intelligence was much improved and learned that Rommel's forces were desperately short of supplies, as Italian convoys often were intercepted by British naval forces and bombers flying out of Malta. One Italian convoy never arrived because all seven ships were sunk.

Commonwealth forces began *Operation Crusader* on November 18. The DAK initially repulsed the attack and pursued the retreating British back into Egypt. Confusion characterized the battle as units from both sides roamed the desert uncer-

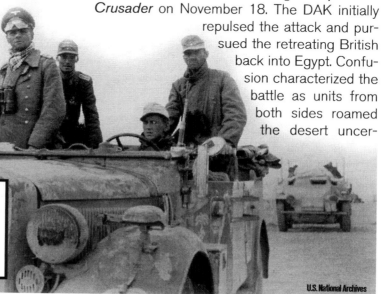

Gen. Erwin Rommel with the 15th Panzer Division in North Africa during 1941. Rommel was known as the "Desert Fox" for his skill and cunning in desert warfare tactics.

U.S. National Archives

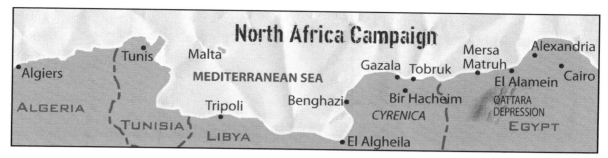

North Africa Campaign

Algiers · Tunis · Malta · MEDITERRANEAN SEA · Gazala · Tobruk · Mersa Matruh · Alexandria · Cairo · El Alamein

ALGERIA · TUNISIA · Tripoli · Benghazi · Bir Hacheim · QATTARA DEPRESSION · EGYPT

LIBYA · CYRENICA · El Algheila

tain whether they were next to friend or foe. The tide of battle eventually swung in favor of the Commonwealth forces. At Tobruk, Polish, British and Scottish "The Black Watch" soldiers broke out, linking up with the 2nd New Zealand Division. In early December, the Germans retreated west, eventually stopping in El Agheila. A surprise counterattack by Rommel on January 21, 1942 pushed the British to Gazala, where both sides spent the next several months regrouping.

In early 1942, *Luftwaffe* forces made a concerted effort to regain control of sea lanes through intensive bombing of Malta. As a result, more supplies, including tanks and gasoline, began to reach Rommel. On May 26, 1942, the Battle of Gazala began. The British had constructed a defensive line extending from the Mediterranean southward into the desert. Rommel used his Italian troops to attack and "hold" the northern end of the line, while 10,000 vehicles of 15th Panzer, 21st Panzer and 90th Light divisions swung south of the southernmost post at Bir Hacheim and turned north toward Tobruk.

The fighting was fierce, with both sides taking heavy losses. Rommel concentrated his forces in a hotly contested area that became known as "The Cauldron." After two weeks of fighting, the Germans prevailed. On June 20, in cooperation with the Luftwaffe, Rommel once again assaulted Tobruk. Tobruk's defenses had not been repaired from the siege the year before, and the garrison consisted mainly of green new arrivals. Rommel easily took Tobruk. More than 30,000 Commonwealth troops were taken prisoner, along with five generals. Churchill wrote that receiving news of the fall of Tobruk was "one of the heaviest blows I can recall during the war … a bitter moment."

Held up by the 2nd New Zealand Division for a time at Mersah Matruh, German troops heading east were finally stopped just 60 miles short of Alexandria at a railroad station, El Alamein. The Commonwealth forces had lost about half their troops and almost all their armor.

For the capture of Tobruk, Rommel was promoted to Field Marshal. It was the pinnacle of his career and secured his reputation as the "Desert Fox." Rommel anticipated the conquest of Egypt. An overjoyed Mussolini sent his white horse to Tripoli in expectation of riding it in a victory parade through Cairo.

EL ALAMEIN

The El Alamein defensive line extended 40 miles from the Mediterranean Sea to the Qattara Depression, an impassible area. Both ends were secure and could not be flanked as had occurred in other desert battles. There was inconclusive fighting for the next several months as both sides dug-in and created minefields. During this time, a relatively unknown officer, Bernard Law Montgomery, took command of the British Eighth Army. He began to rigorously train his troops in preparation for an offensive. "We will finish Rommel once and for all," he promised his troops.

An M3 Grant tank rumbles through the desert near the Kasserine Pass in Tunisia.

At 9:40 p.m. on October 23, 1942 900 British guns unleashed a barrage of an intensity that had not been seen since the First World War. Commonwealth troops, with sappers clearing paths through the mine fields, moved forward. A lack of working mine detectors slowed the advance. Both sides took heavy losses as the battle developed.

Rommel committed his reserves in order to prevent a major breakthrough. Montgomery's officers pleaded with him to withdraw. Undaunted, Montgomery pressed the attack. Rommel, outnumbered two-to-one in both tanks and men, realized by early November that he had been defeated. Defying a defend-at-all-costs order by Hitler, Rommel ordered his troops to begin a 1400-mile retreat to Tunis. Mussolini never rode his horse through Cairo.

On November 8, American forces began to land in Morocco and Algeria as part of *Operation Torch*. It would be six more months before all Axis forces in North Africa surrendered in Tunisia. Rommel would inflict heavy losses on green American troops at Kasserine Pass, but the Axis could only delay the inevitable; the Battle of El Alamein was a major turning point during the war.

In March 1943, Rommel, due to health concerns, gave up command in North Africa.

THE ATLANTIC WALL

Rommel was in Northern France in 1944 supervising the construction of the Atlantic Wall, the seacoast defense against an Allied invasion. He discounted the possibility of an invasion on June 6 because of weather and took leave to visit his family. He believed the landings at Normandy were a diversion and withheld reserves in Pas-de-Calais, giving the Allies precious time to build and consolidate their hold. He personally oversaw the fierce struggle for the city of Caen. On July 17, 1944, he suffered a head wound when his staff car was strafed by a Canadian Supermarine Spitfire.

As defeats began to pile up in 1944, opposition to Hitler increased. Three of Rommel's close friends invited Rommel to join a plot to kill Hitler. The support of the popular field marshal would help their cause. Rommel reluctantly agreed, though he preferred that Hitler be arrested and brought to trial. An assassination, he feared, might lead to civil war. A bomb attack on July 20, 1944 failed to kill Hitler, though it injured him and even blew his trousers off. In all likelihood, he survived only because the briefcase containing the bomb was unwittingly moved under a heavy table, deflecting the blast.

Anyone who had even a remote connection with the plot was arrested and executed. On October 14, 1944, Rommel was visited by representatives of Hitler. For his connection in the plot to kill Hitler, he was given two choices: commit suicide or face the humiliation of a military trial that would result in his execution and harm to his family. He chose to swallow a poison capsule. German propaganda told the German public that he died of wounds suffered in combat.

REVIEW QUESTIONS

1. Erwin Rommel's nickname was _Desert Fox_.

2. Rommel became a national hero when a propaganda film chronicled his contribution in which campaign?
   - **a. Poland**
   - b. Norway
   - c. France
   - d. North Africa

3. Operation _Compass_ resulted in the rout of the Italian Army in North Africa in December 1940.

4. Which nation was not part of the Commonwealth forces in North Africa?
   - a. Australia
   - **b. Canada**
   - c. New Zealand
   - d. India

5. Commonwealth forces nicknamed Rommel the _Desert fox_

6. In April 1941, Rommel unsuccessfully attempted to capture the fortress of _Tobruck_

7. The 9th Australian Division gained the nickname of the " _Rats of Tobruck_

8. In November 1942, Operation _Crusader_ pushed the Germans back to El Agheila.

9. Rommel finally captured Tobruk during the Battle of _____.
   - **a. Gazala**
   - b. Benghazi
   - c. Alexandria
   - d. Bir Hachiem

10. Led by Bernard Montgomery, which battle was the turning point in the fight for North Africa? _El Alamein_

11. Which fortification was Rommel in charge of building in 1944?
    - a. Siegfried Line
    - b. the Reichstag
    - c. Hitler's bunker
    - **d. The Atlantic Wall**

12. Rommel committed suicide after being linked with a plot to kill _Hitler_ rather than subject his family to harm and disgrace.

Andrew Cunningham

Admiral and First Sea Lord of the Royal Navy
Born: January 7, 1883
Died: June 12, 1963

British Admiral Andrew Browne Cunningham was born in Scotland in 1883. He enrolled in a naval school at the age of 10 and at age 14 served as a cadet on the training ship *Britannia*. As captain of the destroyer *Scorpion* during the First World War, he once demonstrated aggressiveness by charging four destroyers against 13 German destroyers. He only turned back when poor weather conditions made targeting impossible.

Cunningham assumed command of the battleship *Rodney* in 1929, and the Royal Navy promoted him to Rear-Admiral three years later. He was knighted for his 40 years of service in 1939 and named Commander-in-Chief of the Mediterranean Fleet. His ability to delegate earned the respect of his fellow officers, though he lacked a common touch with everyday sailors.

The British controlled both outlets of the Mediterranean Sea. On the western end stood a fortress, the Rock of Gibraltar, a British possession since 1713. On the eastern end of the Mediterranean, the Suez Canal sliced 12,000 miles off the journey around the continent of Africa. Italian surface ships could not exit, and German ships could not enter. Another factor affecting the campaign was that, unlike an ocean, the Mediterranean was under the cover of land-based aircraft.

Cunningham's first crisis occurred shortly after the defeat of France. When France surrendered in June 1940, the French Navy was still at large. The British were fearful that the French fleet would fall into the hands of the Axis. The proud French did not want either side to have their ships. The British initiated a plan, *Operation Catapult*, to seize or neutralize the French ships. At Mers-El-Kébir in Algeria, French Admiral Marcel-Bruno Gensoul refused to disarm, scuttle or turn his ships over to the British fleet. The British opened fire, sinking the battlecruiser *Dunkerque* and battleships *Provence* and *Bretagne*. More than 1200 French sailors died

Mediterranean Campaign

in the tragic engagement. Only the battlecruiser *Strasbourg*, along with several smaller ships, escaped. At Alexandria, Cunningham engaged in a tense confrontation with his friend, French Admiral René-Emile Godfroy. Knowing that Godfroy felt honor-bound to fight, Cunningham appealed to the French officers and men for a peaceful rebellion. The French honored his plea and disarmed their ships.

THE ROYAL NAVY VERSUS THE REGIA MARINA

With the French fleet out of the picture, the *Regia Marina* (Italian Navy) with six battleships, 20 cruisers, more than 60 destroyers and more than 100 submarines suddenly had an advantage in numbers over the Royal Navy. Most of the Italian ships were faster than their British equivalent, but speed came at the cost of thinner armor. Though superior in numbers, the *Regia Marina* had many shortcomings. The fleet suffered from poor leadership. A lack of fuel limited its time at sea. Italian subs had limited range and submerged slowly. Italian light cruisers were brittle and their destroyers small enough to be swamped in rough seas. A lack of proper depth charges and antiaircraft weapons hampered convoy duties. Italy had no aircraft carriers, as all air power was separate from the navy. With no flashless powder, illumination rounds, night optics or radar (the Italians rejected the concept as "futuristic" in 1936), night fighting proved almost impossible.

One important advantage for the British was Malta, a tiny speck of an island in the center of the Mediterranean. The key location of this British possession allowed the British to wreak havoc with Italian convoys delivering troops and supplies to North Africa and provided air cover for British convoys between Gibraltar and Alexandria.

Cunningham itched for a fight once the Italians entered the war in June 1940. On July 9, a

HMS WARSPITE

Imperial War Museum / A 11787

Affectionately referred to by Admiral Cunningham as "The Grand Old Lady," the British battleship *Warspite* was one of the most glamorous and fortunate ships in the history of the Royal Navy. Launched in 1913, the ship survived the First World War despite taking 15 hits during the Battle of Jutland.

In early 1940, *Warspite* supported operations in Norway, sinking the German destroyer *Z13 Erich Koellner*. In the summer of 1940 she participated in the Battles of Calabria and Cape Matapan. *Warspite* was sent to the U.S. for repairs and to replace her 15" guns after suffering damage from German bombers while covering troop evacuations off the coast of Crete.

In January 1942, she sailed for the Indian Ocean, serving as flagship of the Eastern Fleet. In 1943, she was once again in the Mediterranean, supporting the invasion of Sicily. Three German *Fritz-X* radio-controlled bombs struck the *Warspite* while off the coast of Salerno. Although heavily damaged, only nine men were killed in the attacks.

Warspite returned to Great Britain for more repairs, returning to action in time to help support the Normandy landings. *Warspite's* career ended when it struck a mine off Harwich on June 13, 1944. After plans to make her a museum ship fell through, the decision was made in 1946 to scrap the Royal Navy's proud warrior.

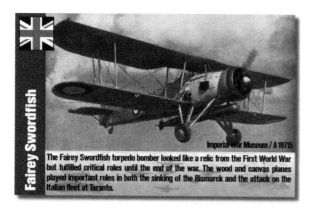

Fairey Swordfish

Imperial War Museum / A 19715

The Fairey Swordfish torpedo bomber looked like a relic from the First World War but fulfilled critical roles until the end of the war. The wood and canvas planes played important roles in both the sinking of the Bismarck and the attack on the Italian fleet at Taranto.

British convoy fleet engaged an Italian convoy in the Battle of Calabria. Cunningham ran ahead of his slower battleships *Malaya* and *Royal Sovereign* in his command battleship, the *Warspite*. Seven minutes after the Italian battleship *Giulio Cesare* opened fire, the *Warspite* hit the *Cesare* at 26,000 yards (more than 15 miles!) in what is probably the longest-ranged naval artillery success in history. The damaged *Cesare* slipped away behind a destroyer smoke screen. Several ships on each side were damaged but none sunk.

On July 19, 1940, the Australian light cruiser *Sydney* and British destroyers *Havock*, *Hyperion*, *Hasty*, *Ilex* and *Hero* engaged two Italian cruisers in the Battle of Cape Spada. The Italian light cruisers *Giovanni dalle Bande Nere* and *Bartolomeo Colleoni* pursued the destroyers, who led them toward the *Sydney*. The *Colleoni*, hit hard by the *Sydney*, lost her

steering and was finished off by the British destroyers. The *Sydney* disengaged after running out of ammunition.

On October 23, Hitler met with Spain's dictator Francisco Franco. Hitler hoped to bring Spain into the war on the side of the Axis to assist with an assault on Gibraltar. The Germans were unwilling to give into Franco's demands for weapons and large areas of France's Africa holdings in exchange for Spain's assistance. Hitler scrapped his plan to attack Gibraltar.

TARANTO

A critical point in the Mediterranean war came on November 11, 1940 when the British attacked the Italian fleet anchored in a harbor at Taranto. The bold plan could easily have ended in disaster. Launched from the carrier *Illustrious*, 21 canvas-covered biplane *Fairey Swordfish*, equipped with special torpedoes designed to run under defense nets, flew to Taranto and made their bombing runs at less than 35 feet. The battleships *Conte di Cavour*, *Littorio* and *Duilio* were hit and knocked out of action for most of the war. Only two of the Swordfish were lost. That success of the attack had several consequences. As a result, the Italians moved their remaining ships north and refused to meet the British in battle. The attack also inspired Japanese Admiral Isoroku Yamamoto to plan the devastating raid on Pearl Harbor one year later.

Private Archive of Burzagli Family

The Zara was the lead ship of her class. Launched in 1931, the Italian cruiser weighed more than 14,000 tons when full and could make 33 knots. She was sunk while attempting to rescue her sister ship, the Pola, during the Battle of Cape Matapan.

The raid on Taranto had other consequences. With the Italian fleet unwilling to risk its remaining ships, Italian convoy ships on their way to Africa were more vulnerable. Hitler took notice and decided to take action.

On January 10, 1941 Cunningham watched with concern from the *Warspite* as 36 *Junkers-88* and *Junkers Ju-87 Stuka* bombers appeared overhead. Thirty bombers concentrated their attacks on the *Illustrious*. The bombers dropped their bombs at 1200-800 feet and continued their dives, spraying the deck with machine gun fire. Cunningham could see flames and smoke rise as multiple bombs hit the unfortunate carrier. *Illustrious* eventually limped back to Alexandria before sailing south around Africa and to America for repairs.

As Cunningham's fleet was left with only one aircraft carrier, the outdated *Eagle*, control of the central Mediterranean switched back to the Axis after one seven-minute attack. Rommel's army began to receive much-needed supplies while Malta endured under several months of intensive bombing.

THE BATTLE OF CAPE MATAPAN

Under pressure from Germans, who were planning to invade Greece, Vice Admiral Angelo Iachino steamed to attack British convoys between Alexandria and Greece. The Italian fleet included the battleship *Vittorio Veneto*, six heavy cruisers and 19 smaller ships. The British forces included the newly arrived carrier *Formidable*, the battleships *Barham*, *Valiant* and *Warspite*, and 24 smaller ships.

Italian cruisers attempted to lure the British cruisers within range of the battleship *Vittorio Veneto*. The British battleships soon joined the fray, forcing the overmatched *Veneto* and her escorts to turn away. A *Fairey Albacore* torpedo bomber from the *Formidable* slowed the

Vittorio Veneto with a torpedo hit to her propeller. The damaged *Veneto* shot down the Albacore before it could retire. Albacores flying out of Crete found and hit the heavy cruiser *Pola*, leaving her dead in the water. The Italian cruisers *Zara* and *Fiume* were dispatched with four destroyers to rescue the *Pola*.

The pursuit went on into the night. The British and Italian fleets arrived at the *Pola* at the same time. With no radar and their main guns disarmed, the Italian ships were completely surprised. The destroyer *Greyhound* switched on her searchlight, and *Warspite* and *Valiant* opened fire. The sky lit up with flames and whole turrets flew into the air. Both Italian cruisers soon sank. Only two Italian destroyers escaped the Battle of Cape Matapan; the *Vittorio Alfieri* and *Giosué Carducci* sank. The Italian losses were greater than 2300, while the British lost only a single bomber with a crew of three. In an act of compassion and true professionalism, Cunningham sent word to the Italians of the location of the battle so they could send hospital ships to pick up survivors.

INVASION OF CRETE

The next month, after a daring raid to bomb Axis facilities in Tripoli, Cunningham's fleet successfully evacuated nearly 50,000 British, Com-

Imperial War Museum / E 3265E

German Fallschirmjäger paratroopers make their descent to Crete after jumping from Ju-52's on May 20, 1941.

monwealth and Greek soldiers from mainland Greece to the island of Crete. After a streak of successes, Cunningham's Mediterranean fleet soon faced its biggest challenge.

On May 20, 1941, the Germans launched *Operation Mercury*, the invasion of Crete. British and Commonwealth forces on the island fought courageously in the hopeless battle. Cunningham called on his fleet once more to evacuate troops. During 10 days of evacuations German and Italian air attacks claimed three cruisers and six destroyers. Two battleships, one carrier, two cruisers and two destroyers required repairs before they could fight again. Fewer than 16,000 of the 50,000 troops who were originally evacuated to Crete had been saved. Those who were rescued showed their gratitude by showering the British Navy with gifts.

Despite the losses, submarines based at Malta continued to sink Italian convoy ships at an alarming rate. Hitler sent 10 U-boats that together with small Italian torpedo boats quickly began to take their toll on British convoys. The U-boats also claimed several capital ships including the carrier *Ark Royal* and battleship *Barham*. Italian commandos entered Alexandria harbor and disabled the battleships *Queen Elizabeth* and *Valiant*. It appeared the British might be forced to abandon the Mediterranean.

In early 1942, the Germans mercilessly bombed Malta by day while the Italians bombed at night. *Operation Hercules*, the planned invasion of Malta, was scheduled for July 1942. Grand Harbor in Valetta had become a ship graveyard. Submarines were successful in delivering critical supplies, but food became scarce and the Maltese were placed on strict rationing. Some Maltese died from malnutrition, while others endured a diet of watery stew made of dirty, poorly cooked vegetables flavored with horse meat.

U.S. Naval Historic Center

The Royal Navy carrier Ark Royal steams forward during a 1939 journey while Fairey Swordfish biplanes fly overhead.

On April 15, King George VI awarded the *George Cross*, for bravery, to the entire Maltese population.

In August, Great Britain organized a desperation attempt to deliver supplies to Malta. Sixty warships, including four carriers, escorted 14 convoy ships in *Operation Pedestal*. During a four-day period, the convoy endured massive air and sea assaults. Only four of the convoy ships survived, but their precious stores breathed new life into the weary island. Despite Allied losses, the Axis admitted that the defiant island would not fall. Benito Mussolini's power fading and Hitler distracted by the epic struggle in Russia, *Operation Hercules* was canceled and most German planes relocated to support other areas. The Allies were in the Mediterranean to stay.

In April 1942, Britain sent Cunningham to Washington in order to coordinate war efforts with American admirals. The Americans liked his straightforward style. Dwight Eisenhower named him Allied Naval Commander to cover the *Operation Torch* landings in North Africa in November. Soon after the landings, the Royal Navy promoted him to First Sea Lord (Admiral of the fleet). He spent the remainder of the war directing the overall strategic effort of the Royal Navy.

Eisenhower said of him, "He was the Nelsonian type of admiral. He believed that ships went to sea to find and destroy the enemy." Cunningham retired shortly after the war. He died in 1963 and, as fitting the great seaman, was buried at sea.

REVIEW QUESTIONS

1. Great Britain controlled the Rock of ___Gibraltar___ and the ___Suez___ Canal, the only two entrances to the Mediterranean Sea.

2. Why did the British Navy attack their former ally, the French, at Mers-El-Kébir?
They didn't want the axis to gain control of the French ships

3. How did Admiral Cunningham avoid bloodshed with the French fleet at Alexandria?
   a. Brought in reinforcements
   b. appealed to French sailors
   c. sabotaged their ships
   d. allowed them to leave

4. The name of the Italian Navy was the ___Regia Marina___

5. Which was NOT a weakness of the Italian Navy?
   a. lack of ships
   b. lack of fuel
   c. no aircraft carriers
   d. no radar

6. Which island in the central Mediterranean served as a key British base?
   a. Cyprus
   b. Crete
   c. Malta
   d. Gibraltar

7. Which British battleship hit the Italian battleship Giulio Cesare at a range of 15 miles during the Battle of Calabria?
   a. Vanguard
   b. Malaya
   c. Royal Sovereign
   d. Warspite

8. Hitler attempted to persuade Spanish dictator _Francisco Franco_ to join the war on the side of the Axis in order to assault the Rock of Gibraltar.

9. What successful carrier-based British raid inspired Japanese Admiral Isoroku Yamamoto to plan the devastating raid on Pearl Harbor?
   a. Taranto
   b. Dieppe
   c. Alexandria
   d. Messina

10. The cruisers Zara and Fluime and 2300 Italian sailors were destroyed during the Battle of _Cape Matapan_

11. The German paratrooper assault on the island of Crete was code-named Operation _Mercury_.

12. For enduring months of constant Axis bombing, Great Britain's King George awarded the George Cross to the entire island of _Malta_.

13. Cunningham oversaw the Allied landings in _____.
   a. France
   b. Italy
   c. Iwo Jima
   d. North Africa

Benito Mussolini

Il Duce, Prime Minister of Italy
Leader National Fascist Party
Born: July 29, 1883
Died: April 28, 1945

Benito Mussolini was born in 1883 in Romagna, Italy to a family of modest means. As a boy, Mussolini worked in his father's blacksmith shop. His Catholic mother sent him to a boarding school run by monks, where he was expelled after a series of misbehaviors. As a young man, he held various jobs, including stone masonry, teacher and secretary of an Italian workers' union. Even as a young adult, his socialist views were becoming apparent. In 1908 he became a political journalist, supporting workers' rights, and in 1914 he started his own newspaper, *Il Popolo d'Italia*, which espoused his Fascist ideas until 1943.

During the First World War, Mussolini spent nine months fighting in frontline trench warfare. His wartime service ended when a mortar bomb accidentally exploded, leaving Mussolini with at least 40 shards of metal in his body. He returned to work at his newspaper.

The First World War destroyed Italy's economy. During the war years, inflation increased prices 500%. The unrest caused by economic trouble resulted in strikes by workers and the birth of many political parties. In 1919, Mussolini announced in his newspaper a meeting to organize a new party. About 100-200 men showed up for the meeting. The group would take its name from the *fasces*, bundles of rods with an axe head, that were carried as a symbol of power by ancient Roman *lictors* (guards) who protected the emperor. Within two years, the Fascist party of Italy boasted 300,000 members.

MUSSOLINI'S RISE TO POWER

In 1922, the Italian government struggled just to provide basic services. Mussolini ordered his Fascist followers to step in and keep the trains, mail and factories running. Mussolini won the admiration of the grateful people of Italy with his decisive action. Desiring greater power, several months later he demanded, "Either they give us the government or we shall take it by marching on Rome." In no position to bargain, the king of Italy, Victor Emmanuel III, allowed Mussolini to become prime minister and create a new government.

Mussolini, known as *Il Duce* (leader), projected a hypnotic, larger-than-life public presence with his flaming oratory and extravagant ways. Italy prospered during the early days of his rule. Italians revered Mussolini so much that they often put up photos of him in their homes. Unfortunately, he had a gambler's temperament and often defied common sense. He would ultimately ruin Italy and him-

Macchi MC.202

Regia Aeronautica

The Italian Macchi MC.202 "Thunderbolt" is considered one of the more elegant fighters of the Second World War. With a top speed of 372 mph the Macchi MC.202 was a deadly dogfighter despite carrying just two machine guns.

Bundesarchiv, Bild 101I-175-1270-36 / Teschendorf / CC-BY-SA

A German Panzer IV tank rumbles through the occupied city of Athens, Greece in 1943.

self. Like Hitler, he disliked Jews. In 1941, he forbid newspapers to mention Christmas, as the observance "...only reminds one of the birth of a Jew." He projected a public image of being a devoted family man but was unfaithful to his wife.

The Fascists came to power in Italy a full decade before the Nazis in Germany. Hitler, still relatively unknown when Mussolini came to power, was inspired by what had been accomplished in Italy. Hitler borrowed many of Mussolini's ideas, including youth indoctrination camps and the Fascist salute.

Mussolini dreamed of creating a new Roman empire encompassing the Mediterranean Sea. In 1933, Mussolini began an aggressive plan to arm Italy, focusing on air and naval power. Naval ships were designed for speed in order to dominate the Mediterranean. The Air Force produced more than 1000 planes a year. Coveting the empires of France and Great Britain, Mussolini plotted to establish Italian colonies. In 1935, he sent troops to invade Ethiopia. On May 5, 1936, General Pietro Badoglio led conquering Italian troops into Addis Ababa. The conquest marked the high point of Mussolini's reign.

TRIVIA

Mussolini's body was buried in an unmarked grave in Milan. His remains were moved to a family burial vault in 1957.

In a speech at Milan on Nov. 1, 1936, Mussolini said, "This vertical line between Rome and Berlin is not a partition but rather an axis round which all European states animated by the will to collaboration and peace can also collaborate." This is considered to be the first use of the term "Axis" that would subsequently describe Italy, Germany, Japan and their minor allies during the Second World War.

MUSSOLINI PUSHES ITALY INTO WAR

Mussolini looked on jealously as Poland and other European countries toppled into Hitler's hands at the beginning of the Second World War. Though he desired a share of the glory, Italy simply was not ready for war. The Italian people had little interest in the conflict between Germany and the Allies. Italy suffered many material shortages necessary for supporting a war, including oil, coal, cotton and iron. The shortages were made more acute as Mussolini insisted that public works projects continue during the war.

While the *Regia Aeronautica* (Air Force) and *Regia Marina* (Navy) showed promise, the Italian Army was woefully unprepared. The soldiers were ill-equipped, ill-trained and skeptical of Mussolini's Fascist propaganda. Italy claimed to have more than 8000 planes of all kinds, but less than half were fighters and bombers, and most were inferior to Allied planes. One-sided victories in Ethiopia and Spain against weak opponents spoiled the Regia Aeronautica. Italian pilots mistakenly believed that slower, but more agile, biplanes were superior to faster single-wing planes. The Regia Marina lacked leadership, radar, the capability to fight at night and airplanes (all air power was given to the Regia Aeronautica).

U.S. National Archives

Benito Mussolini talks with Adolph Hitler during a meeting in Berlin in 1940.

Though Hitler and Mussolini were allies, they were also rivals. When it became evident that France would soon fall, Mussolini decided he could no longer remain idle. To gain prestige and a share of the loot that Germany had already won, he declared war on France on June 10, 1940. The small-scale invasion was a big-time disaster and brought a declaration of war from Great Britain. During the summer of 1940, the Regia Marina skirmished with the Royal Navy a number of times with inconclusive results. The devastating British raid on Taranto in November 1940 intimidated the Regia Marina into hiding for most of the remainder of the war.

After Hitler brought Romania under German influence, a jealous Mussolini impulsively decided to take Greece before Hitler had the chance. On October 28, 1940, Italy declared war on Greece under pretense of the Greeks aiding British naval and intelligence units. Mussolini expected a quick, easy victory. General Pietro Badoglio said he needed three months to prepare an attack. Mussolini gave him only 11 days.

Once again, the Italian lack of preparation was their undoing. General Sebatiano Visconti-Prasca led a force of 87,500 men in Albania across the Greek border. The Greeks, under General Alexander Papagos, met the Italians with 150,000 men. The rainy season had begun and temperatures dropped as the Italians fought their way into mountainous Greece. Many of the raw Italian recruits were without winter boots. The Greeks, with help of the British Royal Air Force, pushed the hapless Italians back into Albania. In December, believing he had no other choice, Hitler sent in German troops. Greece surrendered to Germany in April 1941. An estimated 54,000 Greek Jews, 75% of the population, were killed as part of Hitler's *"Final Solution."*

Humiliated in Greece, Mussolini suffered another disgraceful defeat when a December 1940 British raid in North Africa turned into a rout with more than 130,000 Italian soldiers taken prisoner. In February 1941, Hitler sent Erwin Rommel and the *Afrika Korps* to rescue the flagging Italian effort in North Africa. Several months later, the British completed the liberation of Ethiopia. Emperor Haile Selassie re-entered Addis Ababa riding in an Italian-made limousine. In June, desiring to show the world that Italy could still fight, Mussolini sent 60,000 troops to Russia for *Operation Barbarossa*. Expecting the campaign to last no longer than three months, Italy experienced initial success in Russia but was unprepared for the bitter winter of 1941-42.

In August 1941, as Italy's woes were growing, Mussolini suffered a personal loss from which he never really recovered. His son Bruno, a pilot, died in a crash while test-flying a *Piaggio P.108B bomber.*

In the summer of 1942, the number of Italian soldiers in Russia was increased to

200,000. That summer, 600 Italians of the *Savoia* Cavalry routed 2000 troops of the Siberian 812th Infantry Regiment in the Ukraine in the last great cavalry charge of the war. The winter of 1942 devastated Italian forces on the Eastern Front. In an epic retreat, half the Italian 8th Army was lost to the elements and the Russian Army.

THE FALL OF MUSSOLINI

As military disasters multiplied, members of the government and military began to discuss how to remove Mussolini and pull Italy out of the war. In early 1943, strikes swept across Italy. The Germans, sensing Mussolini's weakness, began to infiltrate Italy in anticipation of taking over the country. The end in North Africa came in May when German General Jürgen von Arnim surrendered all Axis forces in North Africa. In July, the Allies invaded Sicily. Italy could no longer defend herself. Which side would gain control over Italy?

On July 25, 1943, Mussolini met with the King and was asked to resign. He was taken into protective custody — a nice way of saying he was under arrest. Badoglio took over as prime minister. On September 8, Italy announced its surrender to the Allies. The Germans activated their plan to disarm and occupy Italy. Allied forces landing on the Italian mainland the next day and expecting to be welcomed as liberators were instead met by determined German troops.

After seven weeks in custody, Mussolini was freed by 90 German troops, who in a daring raid landed in gliders on the mountaintop ski resort hotel where Mussolini was being held. Mussolini formed a new Italian Fascist party and created a phantom government known as the Saló Republic. Serving as Hitler's puppet, Mussolini's government had little influence. The Holocaust

Italian Public Domain

The Piaggio P.108B was Italy's only four-engine bomber during the Second World War. The bomber had a top speed of just 267 mph and only 35 were manufactured. The Germans used nine as transports after the Italian surrender.

arrived in Italy with German control. In October, 1000 Jews in Rome were sent to the death camp at Auschwitz. Only 16 survived. A total of 9000 Italian Jews were killed during the war.

On April 27, 1945, Mussolini attempted to escape Italy along with his current mistress. He posed as a German soldier in a *Heer* (German Army) uniform and hid in the back of a truck. He and his mistress were executed the next day after they were discovered by Italian Communist partisans. A political career that started with so much promise ended in tragedy for both Mussolini and Italy.

REVIEW QUESTIONS

1. *Which job did Benito Mussolini not try as a young man?*
   a. journalist
   b. lawyer
   c. teacher
   d. stone mason

2. As a consequence of the First World War, Italy experienced:
   a. workers' strikes
   b. inflation
   c. new political parties
   d. all of the above

3. Mussolini founded the _____ party, named for the bundles of rods with an axe head that were carried as a symbol of power by ancient Roman lictors.

4. Mussolini became prime minister of Italy in the year _____.

5. Mussolini's nickname was _____.

6. Italy entered the Second World War when it invaded _____ in June 1940.

7. Hitler had to bail out Mussolini and Italy after the failed invasion of _____ in fall 1940.
   a. Greece
   b. Romania
   c. Turkey
   d. Austria

8. Hitler sent the _____ to bail out Mussolini after the Italian effort faltered in North Africa.

9. About how many Italian troops fought on the Eastern Front against Russia?
   a. 10,000
   b. 100,000
   c. 200,000
   d. 400,000

10. In 1943, Mussolini was replaced as prime minister by _____.

11. After he was rescued in a daring raid Mussolini established the _____ government.
   a. Neo-Roman
   b. Saló Republic
   c. Italian Republic
   d. Duce democracy

12. How did Mussolini die?
   a. Executed by orders of the Italian king.
   b. Suicide.
   c. Assasinated by partisans.
   d. Assasinated by own bodyguards.

Erich von Manstein

Field Marshall German Wehrmacht
Born: November 24, 1887
Died: June 9, 1973

Born in 1887, Erich von Manstein was the 10th child of a Prussian artillery general. Manstein's mother's younger sister and Georg von Manstein adopted him. Considering that four of Manstein's relatives were Prussian generals, it is not surprising that he became one of the greatest generals of the Second World War. Manstein's military career began when he joined the Third Foot Guards Regiment in 1906.

During the First World War, Manstein served on both the Eastern and Western fronts. Injured in Poland early in the war, he afterwards served as a staff officer. He began serving on the general staff in 1927. In 1935, he proposed an idea for motorized assault guns. The result was the *StuG* series. Essentially tanks with fixed guns, the StuGs proved to be useful and inexpensive weapons during the war.

Manstein is generally considered to be one of Germany's best commanders of the war. He assisted General Gerd von Runstedt in preparing the plan of attack for the defeat of Poland. He devised the bold move through the Ardennes Forest in the Battle of France that trapped Allied soldiers in Belgium and Netherlands, necessitating the Dunkirk evacuation. Manstein personally led a corps during the Battle of France. He was Hitler's choice to lead *Operation Sealion*, the invasion of England that was never undertaken.

For all of his early war accomplishments, Manstein's greatest impact was on the Eastern Front. In the spring of 1941, Adolph Hitler planned his most ambitious attack: *Operation Barbarossa*. Named after a 12th-century German king, the massive invasion hoped to bring the Soviet Union to its knees in a matter of weeks.

In all likelihood, the Second World War was decided on the Eastern Front. The fight between Germany and the Soviet Union was an epic, brutal struggle involving millions of men fighting throughout the vast expanse of eastern Europe. Josef Stalin and Hitler attempted to will their armies to victory, disregarding the suffering and loss it cost the people of both nations. The numbers are staggering. In a little less than four years, upwards of 25 million people lost their lives on the Eastern Front. Almost nine out of 10 German soldiers killed during the war died on the Eastern Front. By some estimates, 75 Russians, mostly civilians, perished for every American death in the war.

BARBAROSSA

In June 1941, Hitler looked back on an impressive string of victories: Poland, Belgium, Norway, The Netherlands, France, Yugoslavia and Greece. Emboldened by past success, Hitler made the fateful decision to invade the Soviet Union. Not only would he crush Communism,

StuG III Assault Gun

The Sturmgeschütz (assault gun) was simply a gun mounted (it could not rotate) on a tank chassis. The StuGs proved invaluable in supporting infantry attacks and destroying enemy armor. The StuG IIIG pictured here is near Stalingrad in September 1942.

he would turn Russia into a slave state, exploiting its natural resources and securing land for German expansion.

The Red Army was large but suffered from a lack of coordination, radios, staff cars and transportation. It boasted 12,000 planes, most of which were obsolete. Thirty cavalry divisions, comprising 210,000 men, would prove useful in the bitter Russian winter, but otherwise were ineffective. Of Russia's 24,000 tanks, all but 1500 were obsolete. Even after the 1939 war with Finland revealed problems, the Russians remained overconfident — training manuals talked only of offensive actions, not defensive.

Barbarossa began at 3 a.m. on June 22, 1941 when 6000 German guns bombarded Russian defense posts along the border; 110 divisions, 3200 tanks, 10,000 guns, 500,000 trucks and 300,000 horses surged into Soviet territory along a 980-mile front. Border posts were quickly overrun, and much of the Soviet Air Force was destroyed on the ground as the Germans quickly advanced. Stalin was slow to accept the fact that the attack was genuine and did not officially allow Russian soldiers to fight back until 7:15 a.m.

The German attack was divided into three army groups: North, Center and South. Manstein was in charge of *LVI* (56) *Corps* as part of *Army Group North* (AGN). His units advanced more than 100 miles during the first two days. AGN's goal was to capture the important city of Leningrad. The unskilled Russians lost 185 of 300 tanks in one frontal assault in Lithuania. Soviet resistance stiffened as they were pushed out of Poland and the Baltic States and into their homeland. Manstein learned quickly that the wooded terrain near Leningrad did not allow for quick tank attacks. Stalin demanded that Leningrad, the birthplace of communism, be held at any cost. Half a million Leningraders constructed fortifications that slowed the German advance. On September 12, 1941 Hitler ordered a halt to the attack on Leningrad in order to prepare for *Operation Typhoon*, the attack on Moscow.

Army Group Center (AGC), led by Field Marshal Fedor von Bock, Heinz Guderian and Hermann Hoth, attacked Belorussia (modern-day Belarus). Albert Kesselring's 1000 *Luftwaffe* planes spread fear and confusion among the Red Army. Poorly trained soldiers, driven by political commissars, pointlessly attacked in human waves. By June 26, AGC was 185 miles inside Russia. The next day, the Germans surrounded (enveloped) a Russian Army near Minsk, trapping many Russian soldiers. By July 3, 290,000 Russian prisoners had been taken and 2500 tanks captured or destroyed. Three weeks later, after capturing Smolensk, AGC troops heading toward Moscow were diverted toward Kiev, likely missing their one realistic chance to capture the city. Another 300,000 Russian troops were killed or captured in the Smolensk area.

Army Group South (AGS) attacked into the Ukraine with the goal of capturing Kiev. Many Ukrainians welcomed the Germans as liberators from communist rule. Little did they know

German troops fight Russians on the Eastern Front in 1941. The soldier on the right is preparing to toss a Model 24 "potato masher" grenade.

that Hitler planned to turn the Ukraine's agricultural lands into the "bread basket" of the Third Reich. Heinrich Himmler's *Einsatzgruppen* (Task Force) death squads moved in the newly conquered areas and began to systematically exterminate Jews, including 7000 in Lvov. An estimated 1.25 million Jews in the Soviet Union would die before the end of the war.

BATTLE OF MOSCOW

The weeks turned into months and summer into fall. Frustrated with the lack of progress, Hitler turned his attention toward capturing Moscow, the capital of the Soviet Union. Like most East Front battles, the Battle for Moscow comprised numerous smaller actions covering a wide area over a period of months.

Weather cooperated for the launch of *Operation Typhoon* on October 2. Guderian's troops advanced 150 miles in four days. Kes-selring threw 1500 airplanes into the effort. Mass panic overtook Moscow as the Germans drew near. Many fled the city while those left behind began to hoard. Police and essential government functions ceased to operate. The fall of Moscow appeared imminent as several German units pushed within sight of the spires of the Kremlin and Saint Basil's Cathedral.

Then it began to rain and the roads turned into mud. Since the 69 German divisions approaching Moscow only had three major roads on which to travel, infantry was often forced to march across the countryside. South of Moscow in a battle near Tula, panzer losses were greater than Russian for the first time as T-34 tanks showed what they were capable of when used in numbers.

The Germans, cold and tired after months of fighting without a break, suffered without adequate winter clothes. Some troops were forced to wear women's coats or even silk underwear in order to try to keep warm. As the temperature dropped in mid-November, German generals wanted to go on the defensive and wait for spring. Hitler, refusing all logical arguments, pushed them forward.

The German generals stopped the offensive when it became obvious the troops were unable to continue. As a result, Hitler sacked 30 generals, including Rundstedt, Guderian and Bock. Manstein would later write that it was his opinion that if Hitler had not meddled and left Russia to the generals, the Soviet Union would have been conquered.

SIEGE OF SEVASTOPOL

While the Battle of Moscow was reaching its climax, Manstein was placed in command of the 11th Army and tasked with the capture of the Crimean Peninsula. Manstein's German and Romanian troops were outnumbered but succeeded in capturing the peninsula in November 1941. Only the port of Sevastopol held out. Factories built underground continued to produce mines and other ammunition as Manstein besieged the city. The Germans steadily pounded Sevastopol and even repulsed a poorly planned counterattack in April 1942 when the Russians reinforced the Crimean peninsula with 250,000 men and 200 tanks.

In June, after a five-day, non-stop barrage, including huge siege guns, Manstein launched the final assault on Sevastopol. The Russians used every ship available to evacuate troops. Rather than be captured, Soviet commissars blew up one huge factory, killing themselves and several thousand civilians. Near the end of the battle, teenage girls of the Communist Youth picked up weapons from dead soldiers and continued the fight. The 250-day siege finally ended on July 4. Manstein was promoted to Field Marshal for his efforts but was left with a greatly weakened army.

German troops struggle to pass through muddy conditions common during the Russia Rasputitza during the fall. Rasputitza literally means "The time of year when the roads are impassable."

GERMAN RETREAT

In December 1942, Manstein attempted to break through to the trapped 6th Army in Stalingrad. His troops were stopped 30 miles short of their goal. Manstein encouraged the 6th Army commander, Friedrich Paulus, to break out but was unwilling to give the order knowing that Hitler had forbidden it. Paulus held his position and by February 1943 the doomed army ceased to exist.

As head of the new Army Group South, Manstein successfully recaptured the city of Kharkov in February 1943 with clever strategy. He set a trap by first evacuating the city. When the Russians overextended themselves, he counterattacked and pushed them back. His plan is often considered the most successful German counterattack of the war.

In July, he led the southern pincer in an effort to entrap Russian troops at the Battle of Kursk. Manstein achieved most of his goals, causing more casualties than he took. However, the attack proved to be a failure and the last great offensive for the Germans in Russia. Manstein protested when Hitler called off the attack, believing that victory was near.

By 1944, the Germans were on the defensive. Manstein proved adept in delaying tactics,

SIEGE WEAPONS

Polish public domain

Three 540 mm Karl mortars fight from behind the front lines in Poland in 1944. The tracked vehicle on the right is a Munitionsträger that provided ammunition for the gigantic mortars.

The most powerful siege weapons ever made were brought in to break Sevastopol. Siege cannons Dora and Schwerer Gustav featured barrels 107 feet long and fired 800 mm (31.5-inch), 7-ton shells. Mounted on railroad tracks, the weapons took 1500 crewmen 20 minutes to prep and fire. No fewer than 60 railroad cars were required to transport parts of the guns. They lobbed shells from 19 miles away. One shell bored through 90 feet of solid rock before destroying a Russian ammunition dump. It took six weeks to prepare the cannons for action.

winning a number of smaller battles. In February, he saved many German lives by ordering surrounded troops in the Korsun pocket to breakout. Hitler belatedly agreed to giving the order after the breakout had begun. Manstein was sacked the next month, when he suggested that Hitler leave the military to professionals.

Manstein retired and returned to Germany. He was approached by conspirators who wanted to kill Hitler. Manstein, fearing the death of Hitler would spark a civil war, declined to join the conspiracy. In January 1945, he moved his family to western Germany. He surrendered to British General Bernard Montgomery in August.

Under pressure from the Soviets, the British put Manstein on trial in 1949 for war crimes. He faced 17 charges, including taking food from Russian citizens and leaving them to starve. He was only convicted of two charges: not protecting civilians and using scorched earth tactics. Though he had vilified Jews in a 1941 order, he claimed to have been ignorant of the *Holocaust*. He served four years of his 18-year sentence.

In his later years, Manstein served as advisor to the West German army and helped with its incorporation into NATO. He died in 1973 of a stroke. As he was never a member of the Nazi party, he was allowed to be buried with full military honors.

REVIEW QUESTIONS

1. Erich Von Manstein is considered to be one of _____ best commanders of the Second World War.

2. Manstein devised the successful plan to attack France with a bold move through the _____ Forest.
   a. Ardennes
   b. Black
   c. Meuse
   d. Pas-de-Calais

3. The German invasion of Russia was named after this 12th-century German king:
   a. Frederick the Great
   b. Blücher
   c. Barbarossa
   d. Wilhelm

4. The German invasion of Russia was expected to last:
   a. Several days
   b. One month
   c. A matter of weeks
   d. A year

5. For every American who died in the Second World War, about how many Russians perished?
   - a. 1.5
   - b. 5
   - c. 25
   - d. 75

6. During Operation Barbarossa, Manstein was part of:
   - a. Army Group North
   - b. Army Group Center
   - c. Army Group South
   - d. The Sixth Army

7. In early July 1941, Army Group Center successfully enveloped and captured 290,000 Russian troops near _____.

8. In September 1941, Hitler halted the advance on Leningrad in order to attack the Russian capital city of _____.

9. Which was not a major factor in stopping the German advance on Moscow?
   - a. Rain and mud
   - b. Lack of roads
   - c. Soviet Air Force
   - d. Cold winter temperatures

10. In late 1941, Manstein was charged with capturing the port of _____ on the Crimean Peninsula.

11. Manstein attempted unsuccessfully to rescue the trapped 6th Army in _____.

12. Manstein is widely credited with the greatest German counterattack of the Second World War when he recaptured the city of _____ in 1943.
    - a. Moscow
    - b. Leningrad
    - c. Stalingrad
    - d. Kharkov

13. Heinrich Himmler's Einsatzgruppen (Task Force) death squads followed victorious German Wehrmacht troops across the Soviet Union. About how many Soviet Union Jews were killed as part of the Holocaust?
    - a. 12,500
    - b. 125,000
    - c. 1.25 million
    - d. 12.5 million

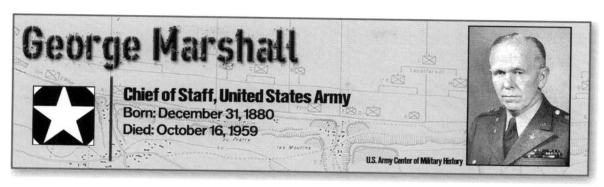

George Marshall

Chief of Staff, United States Army
Born: December 31, 1880
Died: October 16, 1959

U.S. Army Center of Military History

When the Second World War began, the American Army, with less than 200,000 men, was smaller than the armies of 19 other nations. By the end of the war, that number grew 40-fold to more than 12 million. At the height of the war, four divisions a month were heading to Europe and the Pacific. The man most responsible for the greatest American military buildup in history was George Marshall.

Marshall was born to a middle-class family in Union, Pennsylvania in 1880. Though he struggled as a student, Marshall determined to graduate from the Virginia Military Institute to prove his worthiness to his father and brother. His first assignment after graduation was to serve under Arthur MacArthur, father of Douglas MacArthur, in the Philippines.

During the First World War, Marshall was director of planning and training for the 1st Infantry Division. He worked closely with mentor General John Pershing, the leader of American forces in Europe. Between the wars, Marshall taught and trained officers in modern warfare tactics in the War Department and the Army War College.

Marshall was sworn in as Army Chief of Staff on the same day the Germans started the Second World War by invading Poland. For some time, Marshall had sensed that America would soon be involved in another war. He kept a little black book in which he wrote names of officers he thought could be counted on to lead. He encouraged leaders under him to take initiative and make important decisions. He delegated authority and tolerated disagreement.

Marshall made many decisions that ultimately affected the outcome of the war. He attended every major conference of the Allied leaders. He placed Dwight Eisenhower, a soldier with a perfect blend of administrative, strategic and diplomatic skills, in charge of Europe. While he had disagreements with the head of the Navy, Ernest King, they found ways to get things done.

A draft was instituted that required all American men ages 21 to 35 to register. Marshall understood that a democracy using a drafted army could only fight for so long. He felt that the quickest way to end the war would be a direct strike at Germany through an invasion of France. He called for a limited invasion of France, *Operation Sledgehammer*, in 1942. The British, wary of an European invasion but wanting to help ease the pressure on the Russians, pushed to attack North Africa first. President Franklin Roosevelt finally decided with the British. Marshall began to prepare plans for *Operation Torch*.

MARSHALL'S MILITARY BUILDUP

American military manpower

July 1940	464,000
July 1941	1,807,000
July 1942	3,918,000
July 1943	9,240,000
July 1944	11,689,000
July 1945	12,355,000
Jan 1946	6,907,000
July 1946	3,004,000

Source: U.S. Census Bureau

INVASION OF NORTH AFRICA

Marshall selected Eisenhower to lead the invasion of North Africa, *Operation Torch*, with 107,000 American and British soldiers taking part in the largest amphibious assault in history up to that time. On November 8, 1942, the Allies began a three-pronged attack, landing at Casablanca, Oran and Algiers. All the landings were on colonial land owned by the Vichy French. It was hoped that the French would not fight back and quickly join the Allies.

Eisenhower, watching the invasion from Gibraltar, wrote, "A most peculiar venture. ... We were invading a neutral country to create a friend. However, there was concern that there might be backlash against the British for their actions against the French Navy at Mers-El-Kébir in 1940. American troops were told not to fire unless first fired upon. Even British planes were marked to look American so as not to upset the French.

No naval bombardment preceded troops going ashore at Casablanca, as the Allies desired not to provoke the French. When French coastal guns began to fire and planes took to the air to attack troops already ashore, American na-

U.S. National Archives

A Grumman F4F Wildcat taking off from the American carrier Ranger in support of the Operation Torch landings in North Africa in November 1942.

val guns and carrier-based planes responded. The battleship *Massachusetts* quickly disabled the only working turret of the French battleship *Jean Bart*. Fighter planes from the carrier *Wasp* engaged and bested the French airplanes. The French fleet was all but eliminated, but not before destroying almost half of the 347 American landing craft. North of Casablanca, the French held the Kasba fortress and even managed to

U.S. National Archives

American troops land near Algiers during Operation Torch. On the left is an American flag flown in hopes of persuading French soldiers not to fire.

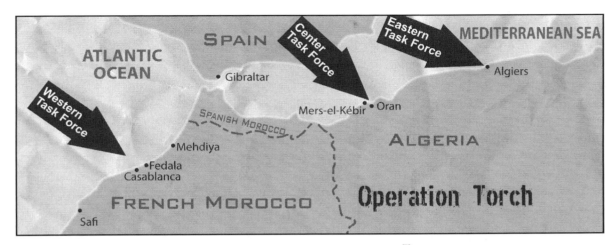

launch an armor counterattack that was blunted by American M3 Grant tanks. Casablanca did not surrender until the 11th.

At Oran, Algeria, the French response was mixed. Several landing ships were damaged in shallow water. A Jeep belonging to the assault commander, Major General Lloyd Fredenhall, was dumped in eight feet of water. In Oran Harbor, one French motor boat hunted injured Americans while others tried to save them. American mortar troops fired traditional red/white/blue fireworks showing the Stars and Stripes. Oran surrendered the day after the invasion.

At Algiers, 400 French Resistance fighters staged an early morning coup, capturing key targets that made the American invasion much easier. The only fighting to occur at Algiers took place in the harbor. Before dawn, the British destroyers *Broke* and *Malcom* attempted to land commandos at Algiers Harbor in order to prevent port facilities from being destroyed. Both destroyers were heavily damaged by French fire. The few commandos who landed were soon captured. However, the action caused enough delay that the port defenders were captured before the port could be destroyed. Algiers surrendered on the first day.

TUNISIA AND BEYOND

After the landings, the Allied forces were to head east into Tunisia. The day after the invasion began, Germany airlifted troops into Tunisia. The initial invasion was a success, but it would be six more months before the Germans would finally be driven from North Africa.

Marshall argued against the 1943 invasions of Sicily and Italy, still preferring an invasion of northern France. In both cases, he was overruled. Despite the fact that victory in the Mediterranean did not mean the surrender of Germany, attacks in the Mediterranean Theater paved the way for a successful invasion of France. The Allies were able to season their tactics and troops and discover who their best leaders were. While

M3 "Grant" tank

U.S. Army

The crew of an M3 tank belonging to the 1st Army Division rests at Souk el Arba, Tunisia. Named the "General Grant" after the famous Civil War general, the Grant served admirably in the early part of the war but was pulled from duty in favor of the M4 Sherman.

the 1944 D-Day was far from easy, there was a certain inevitability about it. A 1942 or 1943 invasion of France likely would have ended in catastrophe.

Marshall often left Washington to visit commanders and troops in the field. His most extensive trip was in October 1944. He visited all the European army commanders (including Eisenhower, Bernard Montgomery, George Patton and Omar Bradley). He visited frontline troops, gauged their morale, asked about their needs and awarded combat medals.

Marshall also understood personally what many American families were going through, as his beloved stepson was killed in action in Italy the week before D-Day. On December 16, 1944, Marshall was the first American general promoted to five-star rank as General of the Army.

The Marshall plan

In November 1945, the war over, Marshall left his post as Army Chief of Staff to become the American Ambassador to China. His mission was to end the Chinese civil war. A Chinese truce was signed in early 1946, but it did not hold. Chiang Kai-Shek soon moved his forces to Formosa (Taiwan). Today, mainland China claims the island country of Taiwan as its own.

In 1947, President Harry Truman appointed Marshall as Secretary of State. Much of Europe was still in a desperate state as it attempted to rebuild after the six-year war. Marshall realized that the Soviet Union's communist influence was growing and threatened to engulf Europe unless the United States took action. He proposed that vast financial assistance be given to rebuild Europe. The *European Recovery Program*, more commonly known as the "Marshall Plan," was born. The United States spent billions modernizing European industry and business practices. The effort contributed to a period of great prosperity in Europe in the 1950's and '60's.

U.S. Army

A salvage crew dismantles a German Heinkel He 111 bomber in Egypt in 1942. In the background is a German Messerschmitt Vf 109 and a British Hawker Hurricane.

Marshall was twice named *Time* Magazine's "Man of the year." Winston Churchill credited him as the organizer of American victory. Harry Truman said about Marshall, "I don't think in this age in which I have lived, that there has been a man who has been a greater administrator; a man with a knowledge of military affairs equal to General Marshall." Marshall died in 1959 and was buried at Arlington National Cemetery.

Review Questions

1. *George Marshall was instrumental in increasing the size of American military forces from 200,000 at the start of the Second World War to _____ by the end of the war.*
   a. 1 million
   b. 2 million
   c. 10 million
   d. 12 million

2. Marshall served under _____, leader of American forces in Europe during the First World War.

3. What major event took place the same day Marshall was sworn in as Army Chief of Staff?
   a. Germany invaded Poland
   b. First atomic bomb detonated
   c. America entered the Second World War
   d. Winston Churchill named prime minister

4. Marshall kept a _____ in which he tracked officers he thought could be counted on to lead.
   a. manifesto
   b. little black book
   c. chalkboard
   d. wall chart

5. Marshall's counterpart in the U.S. Navy was _____.

6. The Allied invasion of North Africa was known as Operation _____.

7. The Allied invasion of North Africa took place in colonies owned by what country?
   a. Germany   b. Italy
   c. Vichy France   d. Spain

8. Which future president and leader of the 1944 D-Day invasion did Marshall select in 1942 to lead the invasion of North Africa?
   a. Harry Truman
   b. Dwight Eisenhower
   c. John Kennedy
   d. George H. Bush

9. Marshall called for an invasion of northern France as early as _____.
   a. 1941
   b. 1942
   c. 1943
   d. 1944

10. Marshall was the first American general promoted to _____ rank as General of the Army.

11. The European Recovery Program, better known as _____, helped rebuild Europe after the Second World War.
    a. The Marshall Plan
    b. Roosevelt's Rebuilding Program
    c. The Truman Plan
    d. The European Union

Georgii Zhukov

Marshall of the Soviet Union
Hero of the Soviet Union
Born: November 19, 1896
Died: June 18, 1974

Russian Public Domain

Who was the greatest general of the Second World War? Was it George Patton? Bernard Montgomery? Erich von Manstein? Erwin Rommel? No debate would be complete without the consideration of Georgii Konstantinovich Zhukov. No Russian played a greater role in the Allied victory. Stalin counted on Zhukov to restore the situation in every military crisis the Soviet Union faced during the war. Zhukov's name is associated with many of the great Russian victories of the war, including the defense of Moscow, Stalingrad, Kursk and the capture of Berlin.

Zhukov was born December 2, 1896 in a small village outside of Moscow. As a young child, Zhukov worked as an apprentice furrier. Despite the long hours, he continued his studies at night. At the age of 19, he was conscripted into the Czar's army. He was badly wounded during the First World War. During the Russian Civil War, he fought on the side of the Communists as a cavalry officer.

In 1939, Zhukov successfully planned and led an offensive that drove Japanese invaders back to the Mongolian-Manchurian border. For his action, he was recognized as a *Hero of the Soviet Union* and came to the attention of Josef Stalin as a man who could get things done. Zhukov was tough, decisive and willing to take heavy losses to gain success on the battlefield. His coarse personality made him unpopular with many of his fellow officers whom he often bullied and insulted with sarcasm and profanity.

LENINGRAD

During the war, Zhukov planned grand strategy at the Kremlin and also managed to be present to control the action at almost every major battlefield. Zhukov was chief of the General Staff when Germany invaded the Soviet Union in June 1941. While symbolically the head of the Red Army, all major decisions had to pass through Stalin's Central Committee. In

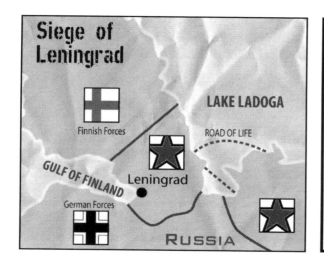

Siege of Leningrad

LAKE LADOGA

Finnish Forces

ROAD OF LIFE

GULF OF FINLAND

Leningrad

German Forces

RUSSIA

LENINGRAD "BREAD"

This recipe for "bread" was used by one baker during the siege of Leningrad.

Defective rye flour 50%

Salt 10%

Cottonseed cake 10%

Cellulose 15 %

Soya flour, reclaimed flour dust, sawdust 5%

Source: Salisbury, Harrison E. The 900 Days: The Siege of Leningrad.

Women and elderly citizens construct defenses to protect the city of Moscow from the German advance in 1941.

July 1941, Zhukov had a falling out with Stalin. He was reassigned to Smolensk, where he led the Russians to their first successful counterattack of the war.

In September 1941, with the Germans closing in on Leningrad, Zhukov was appointed to prevent the fall of the city bearing the name of the Soviet Union's founder, Vladimir Lenin. Zhukov constructed a deep zone of defenses in the suburbs. Antiair guns were converted to antitank use. Snipers, booby traps and a constant barrage wore down the *Wehrmacht*. The Germans advanced into the suburbs but were stopped. Hitler decided to subdue the city through a siege.

The winter of 1941-42 was the coldest ever recorded and the citizens of Leningrad began to starve as food became scarce. January 1942 was the bleakest month. Many people died in their homes and in the streets. Children's sleds were used to pull bodies to the city limit where they were stacked in great piles. In February, engineers drove wood piles through the ice of Lake Ladoga. Trucks drove across the 3-foot-thick ice "Road of Life." Two-thousand tons of food were delivered every day, while thousands were evacuated, helping to alleviate the food

shortage. In the spring, Leningraders planted gardens in every available open area to ease the food crunch.

The Germans never captured Leningrad, but it would be 900 days before the siege officially ended. Ten times as many civilians died in Leningrad during the war than were killed by the atomic bomb in Hiroshima. The official death toll arrived at by the *Extraordinary State Commission* was 641,803. Counting the surrounding areas, it is likely that more than 800,000 perished.

With the Germans stalled in front of Leningrad, Zhukov moved to Moscow, where the situation was so grim that the Soviet government had been evacuated to Kuibyshev. A German breakthrough encouraged Hitler to claim that a German parade would be held in Moscow's Red Square on November 7, the Soviet Union's equivalent of the 4th of July.

Hundreds of thousands of old men, women and children were recruited to build a defense that included 60 miles of antitank ditches, 5000 miles of troop trenches and 177 miles of barbed wire. Zhukov rushed 400,000 troops in from Siberia after Stalin gained the assurance that the Japanese would not attack.

The hastily constructed defenses held. In November, the Germans, having received fresh troops, went back on the attack. Soviet soldiers resisted fiercely despite having very high casualties. The German offensive

T-34 tank

No tank during the war proved as dependable and versatile as the Russian T-34. Its sloping armor deflected all but the largest shells, and its 76mm gun (later 85mm) brewed up many German tanks. The power of the T-34 was magnified by its sheer numbers. Almost 50,000 were produced by the end of the war.

sputtered as the temperatures dropped. On December 2, Germans entered the suburb of Khimki, only six miles from Red Square. They would get no closer.

Zhukov organized a winter offensive that sent 50 unsuspecting German divisions reeling backwards. The offensive lasted until March but was limited in scope. The Soviets, while better fit for the winter weather, were not immune to it.

BATTLE OF STALINGRAD

As winter gave way to spring in 1942, Hitler once again planned to take the offensive. The result was *Operation Blau* (Blue), a plan overambitious to an extreme. Hitler's plan envisioned driving to Stalingrad and holding it while troops surged southwards to capture oil centers in the Caucasus mountains. In this fanciful scenario, the troops would eventually link up with Erwin Rommel's forces arriving from the west through Persia.

Stalingrad was a thin ribbon of city stretching 30 miles along the Volga River. The city was self-named by Stalin in 1925 in "honor" of his efforts to defend it in the Russian Civil War. Though capturing Stalingrad would cut off resources to Moscow, the Battle of Stalingrad was out of all proportion to its strategic value.

The city would be the scene of some of the fiercest fighting in all of history as the inflated egos of two of the most evil men who ever lived sought to impose their will. Obsessed with the city, Hitler refused to admit the attack was a mistake. Stalin wanted "his" city held no matter the cost in human lives. The legacy of Stalingrad would be the deaths of more than 1 million people and the destruction of 99% of the city.

On August 23, 1942, the German 6th Army, under General Friedrich Paulus, assaulted Stalingrad. The *Luftwaffe* pounded the

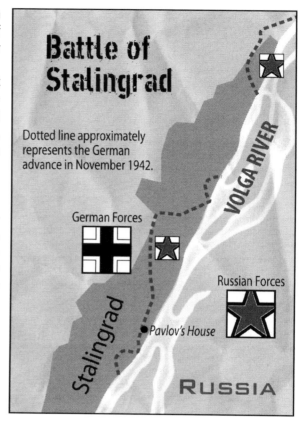

Battle of Stalingrad

Dotted line approximately represents the German advance in November 1942.

German Forces

VOLGA RIVER

Russian Forces

Stalingrad

Pavlov's House

RUSSIA

city but in the process created vast rubble that benefitted the Russian defenders. On August 27, Zhukov was placed in charge of the defense of Stalingrad.

On September 13, Zhukov and General Alexsandr Vasilevsky met with Stalin. They proposed a plan to crush the weak Romanian units protecting the German flanks, thus trapping the 6th Army in Stalingrad. The Russians patiently waited two months in order to build up strength, allow the ground to freeze to give tanks a firm footing and for the Allied invasion of North Africa to pin down German reserves.

Meanwhile, by October most of southern and central Stalingrad was in German hands, with only the stubborn factory quarter holding out. Pockets of Russians held out for long periods of time. One sergeant, Yakov Pavlov, held

Russian State Military Archive

Red Army Sergeant Yakov Pavlov commanded a platoon of the 13th Guards Rifle Division that successfully held out in this building for nearly two months against daily German attacks. Pavlov was awarded the title of Hero of the Soviet Union for his bravery. The building today is known as "Pavlov's House."

out with his troops in a house for 58 days. The house is known today as "Pavlov's House." On October 14, Paulus launched what he hoped would be the final offensive. The attacks captured much of the tractor factory and Red October plant. Losses were very heavy on both sides. In early November the Germans held 90% of Stalingrad.

On November 19, the planned Russian counterattack began; 3500 guns pounded the hard-pressed Romanians with resistance dissolving within several hours. Two days later, two Red Army forces met, sealing off the 6th Army; 95,000 Axis troops were killed and 72,000 captured, though at a cost of 100,000 Russian casualties.

Hitler believed that the 6th Army could be supplied by air. Not having the required resources, the Luftwaffe delivered only one-fifth of what was minimally needed. General Erich von Manstein attempted to break in from the southwest. Zhukov sent in fresh re-

inforcements to blunt the attack. On December 16, the Italian Eighth Army was overrun. German troops attempting to relieve Stalingrad were pulled back before they, too, were trapped. Paulus, heeding Hitler's irrational order to hold at all costs, did not attempt to break out.

The situation began to quickly deteriorate for the Germans. In mid-December, the Volga froze over thick enough for the Russians to bring supplies in via horse-drawn carts. On Christmas Day, more than 1000 German soldiers died of frostbite, exposure and starvation. As a Christmas gift, Paulus ordered 400 horses slaughtered to be served to the troops.

On January 9, 1943, the Russians demanded that the 6th Army surrender. Paulus refused. The next day, a Russian attack began to tighten the circle around the 6th Army. The once proud army of 300,000 men was doomed. On January 30, Hitler promoted Paulus to Field Marshal. The promotion was not an honor, but a charge; as no German Field Marshal had ever been taken alive Hitler expected Paulus to commit suicide rather than surrender. The next day Red Army troops burst into Paulus' headquarters. He and several thousand surviving troops went in captivity. For his effort at Stalingrad, Zhukov was awarded the *Order of Suvorov 1st Class.*

TRIVIA

Russians officially refer to the Second World War not as World War II, but as the "Great Patriotic War of the Soviet people against Fascist Germany."

KURSK: THE GREATEST TANK BATTLE

In early 1943, hoping to salvage the flagging effort in Russia, Hitler planned a new offensive. He identified a concentration of Russian troops in a bulge around the city of Kursk, 280 miles south of Moscow. The plan called for simultaneous attacks from the north and south, trapping Red Army troops inside the bulge. Originally planned for mid-April, Hitler delayed

Red Army soldiers inspect a German Panther tank destroyed during the Battle of Kursk.

Operation Zitadelle (Citadel) in order to await the production of more new Panther and Tiger tanks. Time favored the Red Army — only 50 Panthers and 25 Tigers were rolling off the assembly line each month, while the Soviets were producing 1000 T-34's.

Intelligence alerted Zhukov well in advance of the Germans' plan. Zhukov resisted Stalin's pleas for an offensive, instead preparing defensive positions upon which to blunt the German attack. Once exhausted, the Red Army would counterattack. Hitler's delays allowed Zhukov to pour reinforcements into the bulge, turning it into a fortress.

Zitadelle began on July 5, 1943. General Walter Model attacked from the north, gaining six miles on the first day. The stout Russian defenses only yielded an additional six miles during the next seven days. At the peak of battle, more than 1200 tanks and 3000 artillery pieces were involved in the northern attack.

Manstein was tasked with attacking from the south. His strategy was to form wedges in the Soviet defenses with the large Tiger tanks followed by the smaller Panthers and Panzer IV's. Many tanks were destroyed in minefields

during the initial assault, but the Russians were driven back.

A week after the offensive began, with the Germans bogged down in the deep defenses, Zhukov gave the order for the counterattack. At Prokhorovka, the largest tank battle ever took place; 850 Russian tanks, mainly T-34's, and more than 700 German tanks advanced over open ground. The tanks were soon intertwined with no order or formation. Smoke from guns and burning tanks, combined with dust thrown up by tank tracks, added to the confusion. The close-range fighting allowed the T-34s to pierce the armor of the heavily armored Tiger tanks. Overhead, another battle raged between

German Tiger tanks advance during the 1943 Battle of Kursk.

German and Russian air forces. Both sides lost more than 300 tanks. At the end of the day, the German 2nd SS Panzer Corps held the ground while the Russians pulled back to regroup. The next morning both Germans and Russians were prepared to resume the battle.

The Germans had received reinforcements overnight and might well have prevailed at Prokhorovka. However, on that date, July 13, Hitler called off the attack. The Allies had invaded Sicily, and with the Italians fighting poorly, Hitler pulled two armies from the Kursk battle to reinforce the Balkans for an invasion that never materialized. By July 23, the Germans had been pushed back past their starting lines. The retreat to Berlin began in earnest. The Germans never again mounted any major offensives in the east.

On to Berlin

By late 1943, more than half the land occupied by the Germans had been recaptured. In January 1944, Zhukov planned and successfully trapped 60,000 German troops at Korsun. In late 1944, Zhukov raced up and down the frontline observing troops and honing tactics.

On April 16, 1945, under pressure to reach Berlin, Zhukov ordered an unusual attack against German positions on the Seelow Heights. Before dawn, 140 antiaircraft lights switched on to light up and blind the enemy. The results were mixed. In a week Zhukov linked up with Ivan Konev's troops, surrounding Berlin.

The Germans fought bravely to the end, inflicting 300,000 casualties on the Red Army in the final defense of Berlin. The city surrendered to the Soviets on May 2. Zhukov presided over the German surrender ceremony on May 9, a date that is today observed as a national holiday in Russia.

After the war, Zhukov served as supreme Military Commander of the Soviet Occupation Zone in Germany. Stalin, ever paranoid of Zhukov's popularity, reassigned him to an insignificant

Farm Security Administration

Allied generals (from LEFT) Bernard Montgomery, Dwight Eisenhower and Georgii Zhukov celebrate the end of the war at Eisenhower's headquarters in Frankfurt, Germany.

command. After Stalin's death in 1953, Zhukov was promoted to Minister of Defense. The four-time recipient of the title of *Hero of the Soviet Union* passed away in 1974. He was given full military honors and a Red Square parade. His ashes were placed in a wall of the Kremlin.

Review Questions

1. *At which famous battle was Georgii Zhukov not present?*
   a. Battle of Moscow
   b. Battle of the Bulge
   c. Battle of Kursk
   d. Battle of Berlin

2. *Zhukov was recognized as a Hero of the Soviet Union for driving back the _____ across the Mongolian-Manchurian border in 1939.*

3. *Zhukov led the first successful counterattack of the war at _____ in the summer of 1941.*

4. The Russian city of Leningrad was named for _____, the founder of the Soviet Union.

5. The grueling siege of Leningrad lasted _____ days.
   a. 20
   b. 300
   c. 900
   d. 983

6. What dangerous action did the Russians take to supply Leningrad during the winter?
   a. Raided German camps
   b. Drove supply trucks over a frozen lake
   c. Delivered supplies using zeppelins
   d. Airlifted food via plane

7. What actions did Zhukov take to protect Russia's capital, Moscow, from the advancing German armies?
   a. Constructed defensive trenches and antitank ditches.
   b. Brought in reinforcements from Siberia
   c. Launched a counteroffensive to push back the Germans
   d. All of the above

8. Hitler's summer 1942 offensive was named Operation _____.

Katyusha Rocket

Russian State Archives

The Katyusha rocket was first fired on July 14, 1941. A metal launching framework mounted on the back of a truck could launch 16 rockets at a time. The Germans so feared the screaming rockets that they made it known to the Russians that any soldier caught near a Katyusha would be not be taken alive.

9. Situated on the Volga River, the Battle of _____ was the deadliest battle of the Second World War.

10. The Battle of Stalingrad resulted in _____.
    a. a great German victory
    b. the death of Georgii Zhukov
    c. the destruction of the German 6th Army
    d. All of the above

11. The largest tank battle in history was fought near Prokhorovka during the Battle of _____.

12. In 1945, Zhukov led troops in capturing the German city of _____ that resulted in Nazi Germany's surrender.

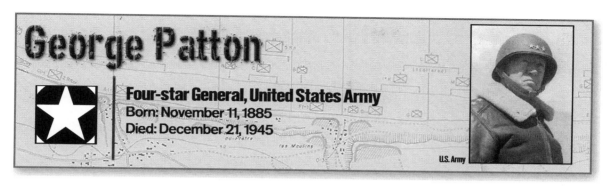

George Patton

Four-star General, United States Army
Born: November 11, 1885
Died: December 21, 1945

U.S. Army

Raised in a family with a long military heritage George Smith Patton felt destined for greatness. Born in San Gabriel, California in 1885, Patton did not begin formal schooling until the age of 12. John "the Gray Ghost" Mosby, the Confederate leader of Mosby's Raiders during the Civil War, was a family friend of the Pattons. As a child, Patton's imagination was fueled by the stories told by his father and Mosby. Patton developed a love of reading classics and military history.

Patton graduated from West Point in 1909. He was a member of the 1912 U.S. Olympic team in Stockholm, Sweden. Competing in the modern pentathlon (combining horse riding, shooting and running), Patton finished fifth overall. During the Pancho Villa expedition in

U.S. Army Signal Corps

Lieutenant Colonel George Patton standing before a Renault light tank in France during the summer of 1918. Patton served in the U.S. 1st Tank Battalion during the First World War.

1916-17, Patton shot two of Villa's men, killing one, in an old-west style gunfight using his ivory-handled revolvers.

During the First World War, Patton was assigned to lead a new tank corps. Signs that Patton would prove to be one of the most aggressive leaders in the history of the U.S. Army were already apparent, as he often frustrated his superiors by "bending" orders to take advantage of opportunities in the field. Wounded by a bullet in the hip during the Battle of Saint-Mihiel, he convinced his ambulance driver to take him to headquarters instead of the hospital. After dictating a report, he passed out and was shipped, without objection, to the hospital.

After the war, Patton met Dwight Eisenhower while both men were stationed at Fort Riley, Kansas. Sharing a love of tanks, they disassembled and rebuilt a French Renault tank. One day while observing a tank being towed up a hill, the connecting cable snapped and flew within a foot of their heads before cutting down nearby brush. The two men barely escaped certain death.

TUNISIAN CAMPAIGN

Patton was a striking figure, often parading around displaying his prized pearl-handled pistols while sporting a polished helmet, shiny boots and campaign ribbons. Despite a reputation of being tough on subordinates, he only fired one general during the war. In September 1941, large war games were held in Louisiana. Patton's forces won by executing an all-night forced drive using gas personally purchased by the general.

Patton led the amphibious assault at Casablanca on November 8, 1942 as part of *Operation Torch*. He watched the naval battle of Casablanca from the heavy cruiser *Augusta* before going ashore. Patton's assault troops quickly moved inland, but support troops were not unloading supplies. Once onshore, Patton stormed up and down the beach swearing at support troops in foxholes to get out and start unloading ships. The Vichy French government at Casablanca surrendered three days later.

By early 1943, German General Erwin Rommel had linked up with Jürgen von Arnim's forces in Tunisia. Reinforcements, including the powerful Panther and Tiger tanks, were rushed to the front. Bernard Montgomery's Eighth Army drove from the east while Free French, British and American units hemmed in the Germans from the west. In February, Rommel, seeking to take advantage of the green American troops, sent his battle-hardened troops against the American lines commanded by General Lloyd Fredenhall.

> ### TRIVIA
>
> The captain of the British monitor *Abercrombie* tilted his ship by intentionally flooding one side in order to lob 15-inch shells 21 miles inland, hitting an Axis headquarters, during *Operation Husky*.

One American battalion lost all but four of 58 tanks in an ill-advised counterattack at Sbeïtla. On February 19, Rommel's main attack struck at Kasserine Pass. The pass was guarded by 2000 Americans armed with a number of French 75mm guns. With the help of dive bombers, the Germans broke through the American lines, destroying more than 200 tanks. Fredenhall proved incapable of handling the situation. American and British reinforcements rushed to fill the gaps. Despite success, Rommel retreated in order to deal with Montgomery's forces that were threatening to break through the Mareth line.

After the American disaster at Kasserine Pass, British General Harold Alexander took command over all Allied forces in North Africa. Ironically, the British looked down upon American soldiers, despite having suffered several defeats themselves before finding success. Patton replaced Fredenhall as the commander of II (Second) Corps.

Patton set about rebuilding the shattered American unit. Strict discipline was instituted, dress regulations enforced, training focused on weak areas and field kitchens moved closer to front lines so troops could have hot meals. II Corps made steady, if unspectacular, progress, though its greatest contribution was drawing away German troops from Montgomery's offensive.

As the campaign in North Africa drew to a close, Patton handed over command of II Corps to Omar Bradley. Patton began to prepare for the invasion of Sicily.

The situation for the Germans in Tunisia began to deteriorate in April 1943 as their flow of supplies dwindled. On April 18, the "Palm Sunday Massacre" occurred in which Allied fighters shot down 51 Luftwaffe transports loaded with supplies and 16 fighters in just 10 minutes.

U.S. National Archives

General George Patton (left) oversaw the initial stages of the amphibious assault of Casablanca from the heavy cruiser Augusta. Second from left is Rear Admiral H. Kent Hewitt.

German General Erwin Rommel's experienced troops routed green American forces in the first major encounter between German and American forces of the war at the Kasserine Pass in Tunisia. Here American soldiers reoccupy the pass shortly after Rommel removed his troops.

On May 12, with Army Group Africa's ammunition exhausted and equipment destroyed, von Arnim surrendered all Axis forces in North Africa. More than 238,000 Germans and Italians were taken prisoner, more than had been captured several months previously at Stalingrad.

INVASION OF SICILY

Operation Husky was the largest amphibious invasion in history. *Operation Overlord* (northern France) would boast the largest number of ships, but seven divisions landed in Sicily, as opposed to five in France. The Italians had 200,000 troops stationed on the island while the Germans had about 60,000 in the Hermann Göring and 15th Panzer Grenadier divisions.

The plan was for Patton's 7th Army to land on the western side of the island and hold Italian and German troops while Montgomery's Eighth Army landed on the southeast corner and drove to the north. The secondary role in the campaign upset Patton. The rivalry between Montgomery and Patton began in earnest.

The landings took place on July 10, 1943. While Allied troops were able to quickly establish a beachhead against the demoralized Italian coastal defenders, not all went well. The Americans preceded the landing with airborne drops while the British used gliders. The pilots were not well-trained and had trouble finding their drop zones in the dark. Troops were scattered everywhere with many British gliders landing in the sea.

The Germans also introduced an effective new weapon. Undetected remote-controlled *Fritz X* glide-bombs struck several Allied ships. The British battleship *Warspite* and American cruiser *Savannah* were among those damaged by glide bombs.

The Americans also introduced a new weapon — the *DUKW*. Many Allied troops came ashore on the six-wheeled vehicle that could travel on land or water. Once on shore, Patton

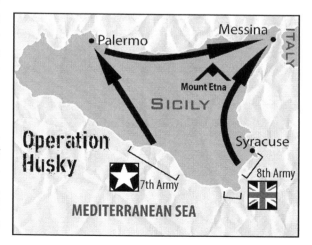

U.S. National Archives

General George Patton talks with Lt. Colonel Lyle Bernard, 30th Infantry Regiment, near Brolo, Sicily.

pushed his men to start moving inland. In one memorable encounter, he chewed out several soldiers digging a foxhole between two large piles of ammunition.

Patton's troops moved quickly, capturing Palermo on July 22. The race was on to see whether Monty or Patton would capture Messina. The steep, narrow and winding roads in mountainous northeastern Sicily favored the defenders. The remaining Axis soldiers, foreshadowing the bitter fighting that would characterize the Italian campaign, used the rugged terrain to slow the Allied advance.

On August 8, Albert Kesselring ordered the Germans to begin their own Dunkirk, evacuating 40,000 troops plus many vehicles, tanks and supplies to mainland Italy. Patton succeeded in beating Monty to Messina on August 16, showing that American capability to fight the Germans was improving.

Patton's career almost ended as a consequence of his anger during the Sicily cam-

paign. While visiting troops in a hospital, Patton slapped one soldier suffering from battle fatigue and told him to return to his unit. The incident might have passed without notice, but just a week later Patton came upon another soldier in a hospital exhibiting no outward sign of injury. "It's my nerves, I guess. I can't stand shelling," the soldier said. Infuriated, Patton cursed the man, calling him a "coward" and then hit him in the head twice, sending his helmet flying while shocked nurses and doctors watched. Patton believed that he was doing both men a favor, shocking them out of what he thought was cowardice so they could return to combat and "fight like men." Few men of Patton's generation understood that soldiers exposed to long periods of combat developed the real illness of battle fatigue.

SUMMER 1944

Eisenhower realized that Patton's ability to command was irreplaceable. However, in order to give the slapping incidents time to fade from public memory, Eisenhower reprimanded Patton and made him publicly apologize. In addition, it was Bradley, not Patton, who led the American invasion force during Overlord. Patton participated in name by being placed over a phantom army created to confuse the Germans. Even after D-Day the Germans awaited the arrival of Patton's phantom army. It was a month before they were convinced that Normandy was the main invasion.

Once the Allied beachhead was established, Patton was placed over the U.S. Third Army under Omar Bradley. Patton's army advanced and fought well, taking advantage of close air support much like the Germans had during their early Blitzkriegs. Patton focused his effort on getting to Germany as quickly as possible. The task of supplying the growing number of Allied troops in Europe became increasingly difficult throughout the summer of 1944. In late August, Patton's army literally ran out of gas. To the dismay of Patton, Eisenhower gave priority of supplies to Monty's army.

RELIEF OF BASTOGNE

Patton's Third Army played an important role during the Battle of the Bulge in December 1944. Patton's intelligence officer, Oscar Koch, worried for some time about a German buildup against the U.S. First Army to the north. Patton asked that plans be prepared to respond to the threat on the chance the Germans attacked.

After the Germans attacked in mid-December, Eisenhower held a conference. Asked what he could do to help, Patton claimed he could turn his Third Army to the north and attack within 48 hours. This surprised the other Allied officers, who did not know that Patton had already set his emergency plans into motion. Patton's forces opened a corridor into the besieged town of Bastogne on December 26. Patton received all the headlines, much to the displeasure of the 101st Airborne Division, which had bravely held off the Germans.

During the spring of 1945, German resistance began to quickly fade. When Patton crossed the Rhine River, the last natural defensive barrier in Germany, he paused long enough to urinate in its water. Patton's army liberated a number of prisoner of war (POW) and concentration camps on their way across Germany and into western Czechoslovakia and then south into Austria, where he was on *VE-Day* (Victory in Europe).

After the war, Patton returned home for a short time. In California, 100,000 people turned out to give him a hero's welcome. He returned to Germany, where he was military governor of Bavaria for a short time. Patton was paralyzed from the neck down after hitting his head during a car accident near Mannheim, Germany on December 9, 1945. Thirteen days later, Patton died from complications due to the accident. George "Blood and Guts" Patton was buried in Luxembourg alongside fallen members of the Third Army, fulfilling his wish to "be buried with his men."

U.S. National Archives

African-American privates George Cofield and Howard Davis man an antiaircraft gun overlooking the Rhine River during the latter days of the war.

REVIEW QUESTIONS

1. *What Civil War general did George Patton know as a child?*
   a. Robert E. Lee
   b. John Mosby
   c. George Meade
   d. Jeb Stuart

2. *Patton competed in the 1912 Olympics in the modern* _____.

3. *What was not a part of Patton's usual military attire?*
   a. Pearl-handled pistols
   b. Shiny helmet
   c. Silver cape
   d. Campaign ribbons

4. *Patton led a* _____ *corps in the First World War.*

5. During Operation Torch, Patton led the amphibious assault on _____.
   a. Mers-El-Kébir
   b. Algiers
   c. Oran
   d. Casablanca

6. Patton took command of II Corps after the disastrous battle at _____ Pass.

7. German General Jürgen von Arnim surrendered all Axis forces in North _____ on May 12, 1943.

8. Operation _____ was the largest amphibious invasion in history based on the number of men put ashore.

9. Patton developed a rivalry with the famous British General _____.
   a. Bernard Montgomery
   b. Harold Alexander
   c. Douglas Haig
   d. Archibald Wavell

10. Which Allied general reached Messina first: Patton or Montgomery?

11. Patton's army career almost ended after _____ two soldiers.

12. Soldiers exposed to long periods of combat often develop an illness called _____.

13. Where was Patton on D-Day?
    a. Sword Beach
    b. Omaha Beach
    c. Utah Beach
    d. England

14. Patton's forces opened a corridor into the besieged town of Bastogne during _____.
    a. the Battle of the Bulge
    b. the Battle of Pas-de-Calais
    c. Operation Market Garden
    d. the Battle of Paris

15. Approximately _____ people turned out to give Patton a hero's welcome in California after the war.
    a. 10,000
    b. 100,000
    c. 150,000
    d. 200,000

16. What unfortunate event happened to Patton on December 22, 1945?
    a. He was relieved of command
    b. He died of complications due to an auto accident
    c. His wife passed away
    d. He died in a plane crash

Albert Kesselring

Field Marshall, German Luftwaffe & Wehrmacht Commander-in-Chief South (Mediterranean)
Born: November 30, 1885
Died: July 16, 1960

One of the Second World War's most versatile soldiers, Albert Kesselring led *Wehrmacht* forces, including the *Heer* (army) and *Luftwaffe* (air force), on every major front contested by Germany. The son of a Bavarian schoolmaster, Kesselring joined the German Army when he was 19. A stint as a balloon observer in 1912 hinted at his future in aviation. However, he focused on artillery for the next two decades. During the First World War, he was awarded an Iron Cross for stopping the British at the Battle of Arras.

Albert Kesselring chats with the head of the Luftwaffe, Hermann Göring. From left, Kesselring, Kesselring's chief of staff Wilhelm Speidel and Hermann Göring.

In 1933, at the age of 48, Kesselring learned how to fly. In 1936, he was appointed chief of staff of the fledgling Luftwaffe under Herman Göring. He oversaw the development of new planes and expanded the power of the air force. Kesselring made a critical decision, later regretted by the Germans, to cancel development of large long-range bombers.

German troops gave Kesselring the affectionate nickname of "Uncle Albert." The Allied press gave him the nickname of "Smiling Al" because he had an optimistic outlook and, unlike most generals, often smiled for photographs. During the war, he flew on a regular basis and was shot down five times.

LUFTWAFFE LEADER

Kesselring was given many important duties throughout the war. Kesselring's air fleets supported the advancing German armies during the invasions of Poland, France and the Low Countries. On July 19, 1940, Kesselring was promoted to Field Marshal for his gallant service. During the summer and fall of 1940, he directed bombing raids on southeastern England and London during the Battle of Britain.

In 1941, Hitler launched *Operation Barbarossa*, the invasion of Russia. Kesselring's *Luftflotte 2* (Air Fleet 2) was assigned to work with *Army Group Center*. Kesselring's pilots destroyed more than 2500 Soviet planes, most of which were caught on the ground, in the opening weeks of the attack. Luftflotte 2 also supported *Operation Typhoon*, the drive on Moscow.

Albert Kesselring, sitting in a a Siebel Fh 104, became an accomplished pilot despite not learning how to fly until he was 48.

THE MEDITERRANEAN

Kesselring arrived in the Mediterranean in November 1941. Italian convoys were struggling to get men and weapons to Erwin Rommel in North Africa. The key to success was to neutralize Great Britain's "unsinkable" air base, the tiny island of Malta. Kesselring organized intense bombing of the island, intent to catch and destroy British planes on the ground. On February 7, 1942, 16 Axis raids pounded the island. Convoys successfully delivered supplies to Rommel's Afrika Korps that allowed him to mount an offensive, the Battle of Gazala, that sent the Allies reeling.

During the summer of 1942, the Axis powers stood at the pinnacle of their power. By late fall, an entire Russian army was surrounded at Stalingrad. In North Africa, Rommel was being pushed toward Tunisia by Bernard Montgomery's Eighth Army, and American troops pressed from the west out of Algeria. With armies approaching from east and west, Kesselring successfully deployed enough troops into Tunisia to prevent its easy capture by the Allies. Kesselring knew he could no longer hold North Africa, but as a result of his swift response, Allied forces were held up for six months and forced

to postpone the invasion of Northern France until 1944.

During the summer of 1943, the Allies made an amphibious assault, *Operation Husky*, on the Italian island of Sicily. Kesselring was disappointed as the invaders, though somewhat disorganized, quickly defeated the Italian coastal divisions. The German divisions on the island fought hard, taking advantage of Sicily's rugged terrain and foreshadowing the bitter fighting to come in Italy. After touring the battlefield, it was clear to Kesselring that the only option was to delay the Allies long enough to withdraw to the Italian mainland; 40,000 German troops were successfully evacuated to Italy.

GERMANY OCCUPIES ITALY

When Italians deposed Mussolini in July 1943, the Germans realized the Italians were serious about getting out of the war. Kesselring formed a plan, *Operation Achse*, to occupy Italy when necessary. German divisions moved quietly into Italy. On September 8, the day preceding *Operation Avalanche*, the Allied invasion of Italy, news reached Allied troops offshore that Italy had surrendered. Many soldiers thought there would be no fighting when they landed. The Germans activated *Operation Achse*, quickly disarming Italian troops and occupying the country. Allied forces landing the next morning were met by determined German troops.

Montgomery's Eighth Army crossed the Strait of Messina and landed on Italy's "toe." Mark Clark, at 47 the youngest lieutenant general in American history, landed with the U.S. Fifth Army at Salerno, a rounded flat plain surrounded by hills occupied by 17,000 German troops. Allied troops surged off the LST's (American troops jokingly called the Landing Ship - Tanks *"Large Stationary Targets"*) and gained a foothold. Their goal to move north and capture the Italian capital, Rome, was immedi-

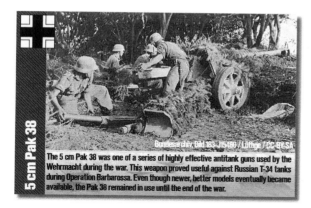

The 5 cm Pak 38 was one of a series of highly effective antitank guns used by the Wehrmacht during the war. This weapon proved useful against Russian T-34 tanks during Operation Barbarossa. Even though newer, better models eventually became available, the Pak 38 remained in use until the end of the war.

5 cm Pak 38

ately put on hold as the 16th Panzer Division poured in fire on the exposed beaches from the surrounding heights.

On September 13, Kesselring ordered General Heinrich von Vietinghoff to attack the beachhead. As the German panzers advanced with guns blazing, the situation became so desperate that Clark contemplated evacuation. After decimating an entire battalion, only a few infantry and the 105mm guns of 189th and 158th Field Artillery Battalions stood between the Germans and the sea. Cooks, mechanics and clerks stopped what they were doing and took up weapons.

Morale jumped after 1300 paratroopers of Matthew Ridgeway's U.S. 82nd Airborne Division landed in the shrinking Allied perimeter. As the Germans advanced into open ground, the 105mm guns, firing up to eight rounds a minute, chewed up the advancing German tanks. The advance was stopped.

DEFENSIVE WARFARE

Kesselring showed his genius in defensive warfare, establishing a succession of fortified lines that slowed the Allied advance. The winding, twisting roads, viaducts and tunnels of mountainous Italy challenged

transportation even under normal conditions. When the Germans mined the roads and paths, destroyed bridges, set booby traps, embedded strong points in the side of mountains and covered all approaches with machine gun nests, vehicles and tanks became useless. The Allies rounded up all available donkeys and handlers. Engineers who could fix bridges and clear minefields were invaluable. Kesselring said the Italian mountains were "God's gift to gunners." The Allies would pay with their blood for every foot of ground in Italy.

Because of the terrain, the Allies were forced to go through Cassino in the Liri Valley. Sitting above the valley was Monte Cassino, a monastery founded by St. Benedictine in 529 A.D. The Allies, hampered by the miserable winter weather, tried unsuccessfully for three weeks to take the mountain. During January 20-22, 1944, the U.S. 36th Division, made up of Texas National Guard units, attempted to cross the Rapido River in the Liri Valley. The river was only 25 to 50 feet wide but was icy, fast-moving and 10 feet deep. The Germans cleared trees on both sides of the river's marshy mile-wide

ITALY
• Rome
• Anzio • Cassino

Allied Italian Landings

Salerno

Taranto

January 22, 1944
VI Corps - Lucas

September 3, 1943
5th Army - Clark

September 3, 1943
8th Army - Montgomery

September 9, 1943
1st Airborne - Hopkinson

MEDITERRANEAN SEA

• Messina

SICILY

The mountainous terrain of Italy aided the German defense and greatly slowed the Allied advance. Here, the 370th Infantry Regiment moves through Prato, Italy on April 9, 1945.

floodplain. Despite the murderous fire, several thousand soldiers managed to cross the river only to be killed, wounded or captured. Clark refused to take responsibility, instead blaming the commanders on the scene.

One unit that seemed to embrace the challenge was the French Expeditionary Force under General Alphonse Juin, who had already proved himself in restoring the front in Tunisia by calming green American commanders. He made generous use of mules that were superior to vehicles in the mountains. Many of the French troops were natives of North Africa, able to scale the difficult routes and capture strategic positions high in the mountains.

Prodded by Winston Churchill, the Supreme Allied commander, Dwight Eisenhower, authorized *Operation Shingle*, an amphibious landing at Anzio to cut off the Germans and break up the deadlock at Monte Cassino. The landing in January met initial success. Only 13 soldiers were killed, as 50,000 piled onshore within 24 hours. However, General John Lucas, armed with vague orders and a fear of overextending his position, failed to advance. The Germans moved in reinforcements and contained the beachhead.

On February 15, in a controversial decision by Mark Clark, the Monte Cassino monastery was leveled by Allied bombers. Kesselring had avoided military occupation of the monastery in order to protect the historical building. The Allies were convinced it was occupied. The next day, German troops under General Eberhard von Mackensen launched an offensive at Anzio. The Germans relented after suffering heavy casualties — the beachhead survived. Kesselring later blamed himself for not crushing the Anzio beachhead. For

Mark Clark

the next several months, the beachhead resembled the trench warfare of the First World War as Allied troops dug in deep to defend against the constant German artillery bombardment.

In early May, the firing of 1600 guns along a 25-mile front signaled an Allied offensive. The Allies fooled Kesselring into believing he was only facing six divisions, not 15, as was the case. On May 17, Polish troops finally captured the ruins of Monte Cassino. A week later, US II and VI Corps met up, connecting Anzio with Allied troops moving up from the south.

The Germans declared Rome an open city and began to retreat north. On June 4, to the great joy of the Romans, Allied troops entered the city. It was the final noteworthy Allied victory in Italy — Allied troops landed in northwestern Europe two days later and the conflict in Italy became an afterthought. The Italy campaign proved to be the longest continual campaign for the Allies, as the Germans continued their delaying tactics throughout the rest of 1944 and into 1945. In October 1944, Kesselring was injured in an auto accident, suffering head and facial injuries that required him to return to Germany.

Some historians view the Italian campaign as a huge mistake on the part of the Allies. It was based on optimistic assumptions about how the Italians and Germans would react, was continually short of supplies and tied down two Allied armies in a region with little to gain. However, it contributed to wearing down the Wehrmacht and pinned 50 divisions across the Adriatic Sea in the Balkans waiting in vain for an Allied invasion that never came. Those troops could have been better used in defending France or fighting the Russians.

KESSELRING ON THE WESTERN FRONT

In January 1945, Kesselring was assigned to the Western Front. His optimism never flagged, as he believed that despite Allied advances the front could be held until Russia surrendered. Shortly after the Germans surrendered in early May, Kesselring surrendered himself to U.S. troops in Austria.

Though highly respected by Allied forces, Kesselring's name was synonymous with terror and oppression to Italian citizens. In 1947 he was charged with war crimes of inciting to kill civilians. In one 1944 incident, Kesselring was accused of allowing 335 Roman citizens to be executed in retaliation for a partisan bomb that had killed 32 German soldiers. Kesselring was found guilty and sentenced to death by firing squad. His sentence was reduced in 1947 after Churchill and others complained it was too harsh. He was released in 1952 after he became ill with cancer. He died in West Germany in 1960.

U.S. National Archives

A 240mm howitzer of Battery 'B', 697th Field Artillery Battalion prepares to fire on German positions near Mignano, Italy.

REVIEW QUESTIONS

1. *During the war Albert Kesselring led German forces in the _____.*
   a. Luftwaffe
   b. Wehrmacht (*or* Heer)
   c. Kriegsmarine
   d. Both a and b

2. *German troops gave Kesselring this upbeat nickname.*
   a. Smiling Al
   b. Uncle Albert
   c. The Flying General
   d. Iron Man

3. *In which campaign did Kesselring not help lead Luftwaffe forces?*
   a. Invasion of Poland
   b. Invasion of Norway
   c. Invasion of France
   d. Battle of Britain

4. The Axis powers reached their pinnacle of success in _____.
   a. Summer 1942
   b. Fall 1939
   c. Spring 1944
   d. Summer 1941

5. Kesselring successfully evacuated 40,000 troops from the island of _____ in 1943.

6. Operation Achse was the German plan to occupy _____.

7. The U.S. Fifth Army landed at _____ on the Italian mainland.
   a. Rome
   b. Venice
   c. Salerno
   d. Monte Cassino

8. The leader of the American forces in Italy was General _____.

9. In Italy, Kesselring's forces showed a genius for _____.
   a. offensive warfare
   b. defensive warfare
   c. air operations
   d. armored tactics

10. The Allies found _____ better suited to Italy's mountainous terrain than tanks and vehicles.

11. In a controversial decision, Mark Clark decided to bomb the _____ monastery founded by St. Benedictine in 529 A.D.

12. The Allies made a second amphibious landing near Rome at _____, Italy that quickly bogged down.

13. Allied forces entered Rome on June 4, 1944, just two days before the D-Day invasion of _____.
    a. Pas-de-Calais, northeastern France.
    b. Southern France
    c. Normandy, northern France
    d. Belgium

14. Despite criticism that the Italian campaign was an Allied mistake, it did provide what benefit?
    a. Hastened the surrender of Italy
    b. Cut off Germany from North Africa
    c. Pinned 50 German divisions in the Balkan states
    d. Wore down the Luftwaffe

Dwight Eisenhower

Five-star General, United States Army and Supreme Commander of Allied Forces in Europe
Born: October 14, 1890
Died: March 28, 1969

U.S. Army

Dwight David "Ike" Eisenhower was born in Denison, Texas in 1890 shortly before his family moved to Kansas. After graduating from high school he worked as a night foreman for two years to support his brother Edgar's schooling. He entered the Army military academy at West Point, graduating in the 1915 class known as "the class the stars fell on" because so many of the graduates eventually achieved high rank. He was a good football player, once tackling the legendary Jim Thorpe in a game.

During the First World War, Eisenhower trained tank crews in Pennsylvania but never saw combat. As the years passed after the First World War, he became frustrated over never getting a chance to lead in combat. In 1933, Eisenhower became Douglas MacArthur's chief military aide. Dealing with MacArthur's strong-willed personality was difficult, but he admired Mac's dedication. MacArthur recognized Eisenhower's ability to organize and plan. MacArthur took Eisenhower with him to the Philippines in 1935, and Eisenhower returned to Washington in 1939.

EISENHOWER GIVEN COMMAND

In the summer of 1941, Eisenhower drew up plans for a series of large-scale war games to be held in Louisiana. His plans proved so successful that the Army Chief of Staff George Marshall took notice. Eisenhower moved to Washington, D.C. where he joined Marshall's *War Plans Division* (WPD). While Eisenhower knew his new role as a planner was very important, he could not help but notice that many of his fellow officers were already commanders of combat units. In 1942 Eisenhower wrote in his diary, "I'd give anything to be back in the field."

Marshall knew that to conquer the Axis would require a coalition of forces. Though many countries would participate, Great Britain would be America's main partner. The partnership required a leader who could balance the needs of two nations' military structures, each with three distinct services (air, land, naval) and their strong-willed leaders. Marshall saw in Eisenhower a rare combination of strategic, diplomatic and organizational skills. On June 11, 1942, Eisenhower was named as *Commander of U.S. Forces, European Theater of Operations.*

Like Marshall, Eisenhower wanted to confront the Germans directly through an invasion of France. The British disagreed. They wanted to start campaigning in the Mediterranean Theater in order to draw away German forces fighting against the besieged Russians. The British, who had already been fighting for several years, were concerned that green American troops would be ineffective. The final decision

Sherman Duplex Drive

Imperial War Museum / MH 3660

The Sherman DD (Duplex Drive) amphibious tank was equipped with waterproof canvas float screens. Before entering water, the float screen was raised. Special propellers mounted on the rear provided thrust.

U.S. Air Force

Douglas A-20 Havoc attack aircraft fly over France in 1944.

called for Eisenhower to command an invasion of North Africa against the Italians and the Germans led by Field Marshal Erwin "The Desert Fox" Rommel.

BAPTISM BY FIRE IN NORTH AFRICA

Operation Torch was the code name for the invasion of North Africa. The invasion got off to a good start, but soon the fears of the British concerning the untested American soldiers were confirmed. Though the Germans had recently lost the critical battle of El Alamein, they were battle-hardened and fought hard under the inspired leadership of Colonel General Jürgen von Arnim and Rommel. Pinned in Tunisia between the British 8th Army on the east and a

coalition force on the west, Rommel attempted to smash through the fresh American troops. At the Battle of the Kasserine Pass, the Americans proved to be undisciplined and poorly led. Eisenhower reached a low point. Instead of sulking, he removed commanders who had performed poorly and replaced them with ones, such as George Patton, who brought discipline and determined leadership. The American forces fared much better in the remainder of the North Africa campaign.

The next Allied target was the Italian island of Sicily. During the Sicily campaign, a rivalry blossomed between Patton and Bernard Montgomery, causing Eisenhower much annoyance as the two men competed for resources to

U.S. National Archives

General Dwight Eisenhower gives words of encouragement to paratroopers in England shortly before the beginning of Operation Overlord.

Planning and preparation for *Operation Overlord* were monumental in scale. To bring in supplies after the landings, floating harbors known as mulberries were built. Montgomery's brother-in-law, General Percy Hobart, devised a number of new weapons (nicknamed *"Hobart's funnies"*) that included crab tanks with chain flails to destroy mines and bobbin tanks that could unfurl a thick roll of canvas over barbed wire. Duplex Drive (DD) tanks were developed that could "swim" ashore. Allied troops spent months waiting and training in England.

The Germans knew an invasion was inevitable; they just did not know when or where. Generals Gerd von Runstedt and Rommel were in charge of constructing coastal defenses. To force the Germans to spread out their troops, Allied intelligence created a fake army, led by George Patton. Using fake radio traffic and a spy network, the Allies kept Hitler guessing. As a result, many German troops were thinly distributed along the 3000-mile *"Atlantic Wall."*

As the planned time for the invasion drew near, Eisenhower was gravely concerned about the unusually stormy weather. The operation required a full moon for air operations and advantageous tides. Weather forced the postponement of the invasion on June 5. That evening, Allied meteorologists predicted a 48-hour window of clear weather would soon open. Eisenhower made the momentous decision to proceed: "I am quite positive we must give the order. ... I don't like it, but there it is. ... I don't see how we can possibly do anything else."

To protect the flanks of the troops coming ashore and cut off German reinforcements, paratroopers were dropped behind the coastal defenses during the night before the invasion. British airborne units were to hold the eastern

fight the war their way. When Patton slapped enlisted men in two separate incidents, Eisenhower considered relieving him of duty. However, much fighting remained and gifted leaders were rare; Patton was disciplined but not sent home. Eisenhower oversaw the invasion of the Italian mainland and the surrender of Italy. Serving under him was British General Harold Alexander, who was responsible for the detailed planning and execution of the Italian campaign.

D-DAY: OPERATION OVERLORD

Their was much speculation that George Marshall would be given command of the invasion of France. However, the work Marshall was doing in Washington was also very important. On August 6, 1943, Roosevelt promoted Eisenhower to *Supreme Headquarters Allied Expeditionary Force* (SHAEF) as *Supreme Commander of Allied Forces in Europe.*

TRIVIA

Bangalore torpedoes were long tubes containing explosives that could be connected and extended from relative safety to blow up barriers. Bangalores proved invaluable on D-Day to Allied troops pinned on the beaches.

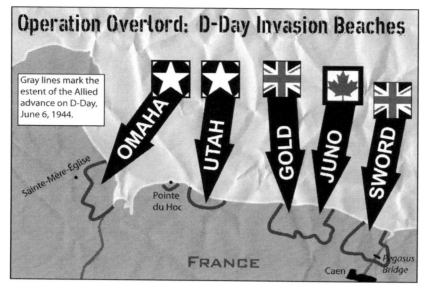

Operation Overlord: D-Day Invasion Beaches

Gray lines mark the estent of the Allied advance on D-Day, June 6, 1944.

OMAHA   UTAH   GOLD   JUNO   SWORD

Sainte-Mère-Église

Pointe du Hoc

FRANCE

Caen   Pegasus Bridge

key bridges, preventing German reinforcements from reaching the coast.

Early on the morning of June 6, 1944 the largest armada in history, more than 5300 ships strong, appeared off the Normandy coast. Though Eisenhower was in charge of Overlord, the basic premise of a five-division landing was the brainchild of Montgomery. Each division landed on a different beach. The British landed on *Sword* and *Gold*, the Canadians on *Juno* and American divisions under Omar Bradley on *Omaha* and *Utah*. In case the invasion failed, Eisenhower had written a note that he kept in his pocket, personally claiming all responsibility. Hitler slept through most of the invasion. When Rundstedt called with the news, Hitler's aides refused to wake him up. Hitler did not wake until 3:40 in the afternoon.

At 5 a.m., the fleet, led by 600 warships, including the battleships *Texas*, *Nevada* and *Warspite*, unleashed a deadly rain of shells and rockets along a 50-mile front. Allied bombers, protected by squadrons of fighters, attacked the coastal positions. On D-Day, the Allies flew 13,000 missions while the *Luftwaffe* managed only 100.

British soldiers came ashore on Gold Beach at 7:25 a.m. Initial resistance was strong but quickly overcome with the help of DD tanks brought directly to shore rather than having to "swim." By early evening, troops had pushed six miles inland.

The British 2nd Army landed on Sword Beach. Six Commando linked up with the paratroopers at the Pegasus Bridge by early afternoon. Behind the beaches, the 21st Panzer Di-

flank, while U.S. units seized the western. Many planes lost their way or came under heavy antiair attack. Many paratroopers landed far from their planned drop zones. Some, encumbered by heavy packs, drowned in areas flooded by the Germans. Residents of Sainte-Mére-Église, under the supervision of German soldiers, were putting out fires when U.S. paratroopers missed their drop zone and instead descended into the town. Illuminated by flames from the fire, the paratroopers of the 82nd Airborne were easy targets for the German soldiers. One paratrooper, John Steele, survived by pretending to be dead after his parachute caught on the spire of the town church.

On the eastern flank, Major John Howard and 181 men of the British 6th Airborne embarked on six *Airspeed Horsa* gliders. The gliders were released over the Bénouville bridge on the Orne River near Caen. Five gliders landed within 100 yards of the bridge. The Germans were completely surprised, and the bridge was captured intact within 10 minutes with only two British fatalities. The bridge was renamed *Pegasus Bridge* in honor of the symbol of the 6th Airborne. Other airborne units captured or blocked

The Pegasus Bridge on the Caen Canal in Benouville, France. Three days after its capture from the Germans, a Horsa glider still rests in the background.

vision launched the one German counterattack of the day. Armed with 50 Panzer IV and 80 light tanks, the 21st reached the beach. Late in the day, afraid that they would be cut off, the Germans retreated. The British 3rd Division objective, the city of Caen, was not captured until July 9. British losses on Sword Beach were less than 700 men.

The 3rd Canadian Division started landing on Juno Beach at 7:55 a.m. About one-third of the landing craft were destroyed by rough seas and underwater defenses. The entire division was onshore by 2 p.m., but fighting remained fierce as the Canadians tried to expand their beachhead.

The U.S. First Army landed at Utah Beach at 6:30 a.m., accidentally landing 2000 yards from their planned position. The mistake proved providential, as the planned beach was more heavily defended. Major General Theodore Roosevelt, Jr., who at 57 was the oldest man to come ashore on D-Day, landed at Utah Beach. U.S. casualties were about 200. The troops

from Utah linked up with the 101st Airborne before dark.

By far the most difficult landing was at Omaha Beach. Omaha was overlooked by bluffs rising up to 150 feet in places. Expertly crafted fortifications easily withstood the Allied air and naval bombardment. The German 352nd Infantry Division manning the defenses was of better quality than the troops defending other beaches. Of 32 DD tanks launched, only five reached the shore. Infantry, already fatigued by the rough three-hour trip to shore, were met by a hail of bullets as the doors opened on their landing craft. Many soldiers were let out on sand bars several hundred yards from shore and forced to wade to shore. Some soldiers hid behind German beach obstacles while others huddled at the bottom of the bluffs.

One company of the 116th Regiment suffered 96% casualties out of 197 men. Resistance was so strong that U.S. commander Omar Bradley almost called for a retreat. Eventually,

American soldiers are forced to wade onto shore from their landing craft while under heavy fire from German soldiers in fortified positions during D-Day, June 6, 1944.

assault leaders began to organize the men. Working their way through the defenses with grim determination, infantry reached the crest by 9 a.m. and began clearing the German positions. By the end of the day, the beach was secure. An estimated 2500 Americans died on D-Day.

On June 7, all five invasion beaches were linked up to form a front that the Germans would never seriously threaten. Runstedt and Hitler continued to believe Normandy to be a diversion and withheld reserves for several weeks. Rommel had said before the invasion that "... the first 24 hours of the invasion will be decisive ... the fate of Germany depends on the outcome ... for the Allies, as well as Germany, it will be the longest day."

In late 1944, Eisenhower became frustrated that the Allies still did not have a sufficient manpower advantage over the Germans. Rather than punch through German lines, he sought more of a wide front, reducing German positions one-by-one with superior artillery and air support.

At one point in his career, Eisenhower spent 15 years as major. On Dec. 16, 1944 (the same day the Battle of the Bulge began), he was promoted to five-star general, his sixth promotion in just three-and-one-half years.

MAGIC CARPET RIDES

For many of the Famous Men of the Second World War, the war was the height of their careers. After the war, they returned to their homelands and slipped out of public view. This was not the case with Eisenhower. When George Marshall retired as Army Chief of Staff in late 1945, Eisenhower took his place. Eisenhower would oversee the most complex and rapid demobilization of an army in history.

When the war ended, more than 8 million Americans soldiers were scattered across the globe. The War Shipping Administration was tasked with bringing them home in *Operation Magic Carpet*. Three-hundred *Liberty* and *Victory* ships were converted into transports. Carriers stripped of their planes provided "Magic Carpet" rides for thousands of troops. The first ships left Europe in June 1945, and the last troops returned from the Pacific in September 1946.

PRESIDENT EISENHOWER

In 1948, Eisenhower became the President of Columbia University. He soon reached the conclusion that running a university required even more administrative detail than running an army.

Fearing that the spread of Communism might totally engulf Europe, the United States and European nations led by Great Britain, France and Italy formalized a mutual defense known today as the *North Atlantic Treaty Organization* (NATO). President Truman offered Eisenhower the opportunity to be the first supreme commander in Europe. Eisenhower jumped at the offer. As NATO's first leader, he built a command structure designed not to fight a war, but to prevent one.

Eisenhower was elected as the 34th President of United States in 1953. Serving two full terms, he championed the Interstate Highway System that bears his name as necessary for national defense and economic growth. Eisenhower was instrumental in the addition of the words "under God" to the Pledge of Allegiance and "In God We Trust" as the motto of the United States. In his later years, he retired to Gettysburg, Pennsylvania. Eisenhower died in 1969 of heart failure. He was buried in a small chapel on the grounds of the Eisenhower Presidential Library in Abilene, Kansas.

TRIVIA

Eisenhower loved paint-by-numbers. In 1953, while President, he gave his staff paint-by-numbers as Christmas presents. The novel gifts set off a national craze that greatly increased the popularity of paint-by-numbers.

REVIEW QUESTIONS

1. *Dwight Eisenhower was born in Texas but grew up in _____.*
   a. Hawaii
   b. Kansas
   c. Pennsylvania
   d. Oklahoma

2. *In the 1930's, Eisenhower served in the Philippines as an aide to which Famous Man?*
   a. Douglas MacArthur
   b. George Patton
   c. Franklin Roosevelt
   d. Chester Nimitz

3. *Success during the 1941 Louisiana war games brought Eisenhower to the attention of Army Chief of Staff _____.*

4. *Eisenhower's first command role in the Second World War was the invasion of _____.*
   a. France
   b. Sicily
   c. North Africa
   d. Spain

5. *In 1943, Eisenhower was promoted to _____.*
   a. Field Marshal
   b. Three-star General
   c. Commander of Allied Forces in the Mediterranean
   d. Supreme Commander of Allied Forces in Europe

6. *What was the name of the complex and critical invasion of Northern France?*
   a. Operation Barbarossa
   b. Operation Sledgehammer
   c. Operation Overlord
   d. Operation Husky

USS Texas (BB-35)

Launched in 1912, the battleship USS Texas served in both World Wars. The dreadnaught-era ship participated in Operation Torch, Operation Overlord, the Battle of Cherbourg and Iwo Jima. Today the Texas is a museum ship at the San Jacinto Battleground in LaPorte, Texas.

U.S. National Archives

7. *Which was not a tool or weapon developed for the invasion of France?*
   a. Fritz-X glide bombs
   b. Mulberry floating harbors
   c. Chain flail tanks
   d. Duplex Drive tanks

8. *German Generals Gerd von Runstedt and Erwin Rommel constructed the 3000-mile long _____ _____ to repel an Allied invasion.*

9. *Eisenhower's greatest concern in the days leading up to the invasion concerned the _____.*
   a. weather
   b. lack of ships
   c. Luftwaffe threat
   d. lack of training

10. *Paratroopers were dropped behind the Normandy beaches to secure the _____ of the invasion force.*

11. *The Bénouville bridge on the Orne River near Caen successfully captured by British paratroopers in gliders was renamed the _____ Bridge.*

12. Operation Overlord was supported by the largest such armada in history. About how many ships were in the fleet?
    a. 1200
    b. 2600
    c. 5300
    d. 8100

13. While Eisenhower was in command of Operation Overlord, the idea of a five-division landing is credited to _____.
    a. George Patton
    b. Bernard Montgomery
    c. Harold Alexander
    d. George Marshall

14. Name the five Normandy D-Day invasion beaches.

15. Which beach suffered the most casualties on D-Day?

16. After the Second World War ended, Army Chief of Staff Eisenhower oversaw Operation _____, the demobilization of the wartime U.S. Army.

17. In 1953, Eisenhower was elected as the 34th _____ of the United States of America.

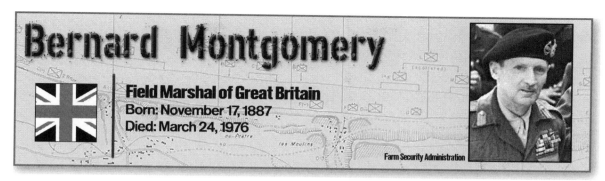

Bernard Montgomery

Field Marshal of Great Britain
Born: November 17, 1887
Died: March 24, 1976

Farm Security Administration

One of the most famous, and controversial, men of the Second World War was Bernard Law "Monty" Montgomery. A diminutive man with an elfish look about him, Monty was more comfortable wearing a casual sweater than a traditional uniform. The British people hailed him as a national hero, while American commanders often found his imperious ways to be insufferable. It was his rivalry with American General George Patton that would dominate the Allied war effort in Europe.

Monty was the fourth of nine children. His father, an Anglican priest, moved the family to Tasmania. With his father away as long as six months at a time and a very strict mother who was quick to punish, Monty often misbehaved by bullying other children. While attending the Royal Military Academy, he was almost expelled once for setting a classmate on fire with hot pokers during a fight.

A near-death experience in the First World War profoundly shaped Monty's view of himself. During the Battle of Ypres in 1914, Monty was shot through the lung by a bullet. The wound was serious enough that a grave was dug in the expectation that he would soon die. Instead, he recuperated and went on to serve in other major battles, including the Somme, Arras and Passchendaele. The incident convinced Monty that it was his destiny to one day save his country.

Monty's conservative nature, harboring resources until he felt victory was certain, helped preserve Britain's limited manpower. Though he often flustered his fellow officers, Monty had an ability to connect with the common soldier.

Both British and American soldiers loved him. Once, while visiting the U.S. 2nd Armored Division, he asked the soldiers to remove their helmets. After pausing a minute, he said, "All right, put them back on. Now next time I see you, I shall know you."

At the beginning of the Second World War, Montgomery was in charge of the British 3rd Division, part of the *British Expeditionary Force* (BEF) in Belgium. Montgomery perceived that disaster loomed for the BEF. He trained his troops in defensive tactics that allowed them to retreat to Dunkirk and evacuate with minimal casualties in May 1940. Monty was one of the last men to leave Dunkirk.

Hero of El Alamein

Monty found fame and glory when General Harold Alexander placed him in charge of the Eighth Army in North Africa. The Desert Fox, General Erwin Rommel, had recently captured the fortress of Tobruk and advanced to within 60 miles of Alexandria, Egypt, threatening all of Great Britain's Middle East possessions. Monty was ordered to attack.

Monty did not attack immediately but instead methodically attended to every detail impacting the impending battle. There was a time during the battle when things began to look bad for the Commonwealth forces; however, Monty stuck to his plan. Steady pressure eventually broke the Germans, sending Rommel and his men into retreat. The Battle of El Alamein was the last battle fought by British and Commonwealth forces without the participation of Americans. Despite the fact that

Rommel escaped, it was a political and morale boost for the British and made Monty a hero in Great Britain.

After El Alamein, Monty was knighted and promoted to full General. Monty's Eighth Army chased Rommel westward into Tunisia. When Monty's troops met heavy resistance at the Mareth Line, a series of fortifications in southern Tunisia originally constructed by the French, he trapped the defenders by sweeping around the end of the line and attacking from the rear.

During the invasion of Sicily, Monty's Eighth Army was given the primary role of landing at Syracuse. However, American General George Patton turned the campaign into a race, entering the final Axis-held city of Messina shortly before Monty.

While Dwight Eisenhower is the general most-often associated with D-Day, the basic plan of the invasion was Monty's idea. He came up with a five-division assault on five beaches, with three airborne drops to secure rearward areas. Monty's troops landed on Sword Beach with the objective to capture the French city of Caen.

U.S. National Archives

Bernard Montgomery watches his troops advance in North Africa in November 1942.

Monty said his men would take the town on the first day. It took 33 days of hard fighting to capture Caen, though the British efforts succeeded in blocking German forces that would otherwise have attacked Allied troops to the west.

OPERATION MARKET GARDEN

In late August 1944, the Germans were in full retreat across France and the Low countries. The Allies were unable to take full advantage, as many seaports were still in German hands. Most supplies were still being delivered from the Normandy invasion beaches, 400 miles from the front. Monty was criticized for capturing the port at Antwerp but not clearing German defenses along the 60-mile long estuary connecting Antwerp to the sea. Montgomery was promoted to Field Marshal on September 1.

In early September, while Eisenhower struggled with how to keep all Allied forces moving, Montgomery suggested a bold and daring plan that had the potential to end the war in 1944. Instead of heading east into Germany through the Siegfried Line, Monty proposed that Allied forces dash up through the Netherlands, turn right, cross the Rhine River and capture the industrial Ruhr Valley, thus threatening Berlin. It was believed the few German troops in the area were of lower quality, made up mostly of inexperienced boys and old men. Eisenhower, under pressure to put the new First Allied Airborne Army into action and convinced that German troops in the area were near collapse, gave his approval.

The plan was given the name *Operation Market Garden*. The "Market" aspect was Lt. General Lewis Brereton's First Allied Airborne Army, which was assigned the capture of key bridges along the route of attack. The "Garden" element was the Second Army XXX (pronounced "thirty") Corps under Lt. General Brian Horrocks. *Market Garden* was the largest airborne operation of all time.

Bernard Montgomery and George Patton bid one another farewell before leaving the Palermo, Sicily airport.

Market Garden began on September 15 as thousands of Allied planes took to the sky. Despite the 4700 aircraft involved on the first day, the plan was so ambitious that it would require airborne drops on three different days. Bombers flew ahead of the troop planes to attack antiaircraft and troop positions and 2000 troop planes were escorted by 1500 fighters and fighter-bombers. People in England were in awe at the sight and deafening sound of the great air armada heading for the Netherlands.

The U.S. 101st Airborne was dropped closest to the frontline between Eindhoven and Veghel. The 101st captured four of five bridges, meeting little resistance. Paratroopers were within sight of the Wilhelmina Canal bridge at Son when the Germans blew it up, an act that ultimately delayed the Allied advance by 36 hours.

North of the 101st, the U.S. 82nd Airborne was dropped between Grave and Nijmegen. The 82nd captured the Grave bridge, but two of the three bridges across the Maas-Waal canal were destroyed. The third bridge was held by the 9th SS Reconnaissance Brigade. The Allies had not expected any frontline units to be in the area.

Sixty-four miles behind enemy lines, the British 1st Airborne "Red Devils" Division attempted to capture the bridge over the Rhine River at Arnhem. In a controversial decision, the troops were dropped six miles from the bridge in order to avoid antiaircraft guns. The 9th and 10th SS Panzer divisions, powerful German units that were believed to be elsewhere, were refitting at Arnhem. Less than 1000 paratroopers, led by Lt. Colonel John Frost, reached the north end of the bridge. The remainder of the British paratroopers, led by Major General Roy Urquhart, were cut off to the west in and around the village of Oosterbeek.

C-47 Dakota transport planes in England loaded with paratroopers of the First Allied Airborne Army prepare to take off for Holland on September 17, 1944 during Operation Market Garden.

While paratroopers were landing on Dutch soil, XXX Corps pounded the German front line in preparation for the long journey north. The plan was for XXX Corps to reach Arnhem and relieve all airborne units within 48 hours. From the start, progress was slowed by unexpectedly strong German resistance.

XXX Corps relieved the 101st Airborne at Eindhoven the next day but had to wait while engineers constructed a new bridge across the Wilhelmina Canal. On the third day of the operation, the 82nd Airborne welcomed XXX Corps to Grave. The 82nd still had unfinished business, as the Waal River bridge in Nijmegen was still under German control.

In a daring plan to capture both ends of the bridge at the same time, tanks from XXX Corps laid down a thick smoke screen as 27-year-old Julian Cook led paratroopers on a daylight river crossing in small assault boats. Under heavy fire, only half the boats reached the far

Paratroopers of the First Allied Airborne Division land in the Netherlands during Operation Market Garden.

shore, but the surviving paratroopers fought tenaciously and quickly captured the bridge.

As the first British tanks rolled onto the bridge, German General Heinz Harmel ordered it destroyed. An engineer pushed down the plunger on the detonator. For reasons that remain a mystery to this day, the explosive charges under the bridge did not explode. The American paratroopers, knowing the British paratroopers in Arnhem were in trouble, were furious when, after capturing the bridge, XXX Corps halted in Nijmegen for 18 hours to allow their infantry to catch up.

Eleven miles away in Arnhem, the 1st Airborne was in a desperate fight for survival. John Frost's small band held the Arnhem bridge for four days as the Germans systematically destroyed every building near the approach. Wounded, Frost and a few survivors were taken prisoner. In Oosterbeek, Urquhart's men were pressed into an ever-shrinking thumbnail-shaped area on the bank of the Rhine River. Few canisters from the daily air supply drops reached the paratroopers, with most landing in German-held areas. Food, water, ammunition and medical supplies reached critically low levels.

Delayed for days by bad weather, the Polish Parachute Brigade, led by the fiery and outspoken Major General Stanislaw Sosabowski, dropped on the south side of the Rhine across from Urquhart's position on September 22. Sosabowski's fears of a slaughter were realized when his paratroopers were met with heavy fire, with many dying before reaching the ground. The paratroopers who survived set up defensive positions after learning that the ferry they hoped to use to

U.S. Army

The bridge at Nijmegen was successfully captured by paratroopers of the 82nd Airborne Division in a daring cross river assault during Operation Market Garden.

cross the river and reinforce the Red Devils had been destroyed.

The last few miles to Arnhem were the toughest for XXX Corps. Built on exposed levees, the roads leading to Arnhem had no room to maneuver on either side. Small numbers of well-positioned German tanks and anti-tank guns were able to easily defend the roads. On the 25th, nine days after the start of *Market Garden*, the remaining British paratroopers were withdrawn by boats under the cover of darkness. Market Garden was a failure. It would be March 1945 before Allied troops once more crossed the Rhine in force. Of the nearly 10,000 British paratroopers dropped near Arnhem, only 2200 managed to escape.

Montgomery thought that the failure of the operation was not due to poor weather or the unexpected presence of frontline German troops but the lack of resources. Montgomery afterwards said, "I remain *Market Garden's* unrepentant advocate."

BATTLE OF THE BULGE CONTROVERSY

During the Battle of the Bulge, Monty took command of American units that had been cut off to the north side of the German attack. He organized them into a solid defensive line. A controversy developed when he made comments that made it sound like he was the hero during the battle. Winston Churchill smoothed over the issue when he said, "… Care must be taken not to claim for the British Army an undue share of what is undoubtedly the greatest American battle of the war, and will, I believe, be regarded as an ever-famous American victory."

Monty's 21st Army Group crossed the Rhine on March 24, 1945. They sealed off the Danish peninsula to prevent a possible Red Army move into Denmark. At the close of the war, he accepted the surrender of German forces in northern Germany, Denmark and the Netherlands.

After the war, Montgomery served for a time as Chief of the Imperial General Staff. It was a difficult time, as the position required political and diplomatic skills that he did not have. In 1951, as Eisenhower's deputy, he played an important role in the creation of the *North Atlantic Treaty Organization* (NATO). Despite their disagreements during the Second World War, Monty became one of Eisenhower's biggest supporters during his time with NATO. Monty retired from military life in 1958. He passed away at the age of 88 in 1976.

REVIEW QUESTIONS

1. What event during the First World War convinced Bernard Montgomery that he was destined for greatness?
   a. Awarded the Victoria Cross
   b. Praised by Winston Churchill
   c. A near-death experience
   d. Sole survivor of his company

2. Though he often flustered fellow officers, Montgomery was respected by the _____ soldier.

3. At the beginning of the Second World War Montgomery was in command of the _____.
   a. British Eighth Army
   b. British 3rd Division
   c. British Expeditionary Force
   d. British XXX Corps

4. Montgomery was hailed as a hero in Great Britain after victory in the Battle of _____.

5. On D-Day, Montgomery's troops landed on _____ beach.
   a. Utah
   b. Omaha
   c. Gold
   d. Sword

6. Montgomery persuaded _____ to undertake Operation Market Garden, a bold move designed to end the war in Europe in 1944.
   a. Dwight Eisenhower
   b. Winston Churchill
   c. George Patton
   d. Omar Bradley

7. Operation Garden Market was the largest _____ operation in history.

8. How many planes participated in the first day of Operation Market Garden?
   a. 2700
   b. 3700
   c. 4700
   d. 5700

9. The Operation Market Garden plan was for XXX Corps to drive 64 miles to relieve the three airborne groups within _____ hours.

10. The British 1st Airborne "Red Devils" Division was ordered to capture the final bridge over the Rhine River in _____, The Netherlands.

11. American paratroopers, led by Julian Cook, made a daring daylight raid to capture the bridge at _____.
   a. Nijmegen
   b. Arnhem
   c. Berlin
   d. Eindhoven

12. Only 2200 of the original 10,000 British paratroopers were evacuated across the Rhine River _____ days after the start of Market Garden.

13. Montgomery credited the failure of Market Garden to _____.
   a. unexpected German units in the area
   b. poor weather
   c. lack of training
   d. lack of resources dedicated to the operation

14. After the war, Montgomery played an important role in the creation of NATO. What does the acronym NATO stand for?

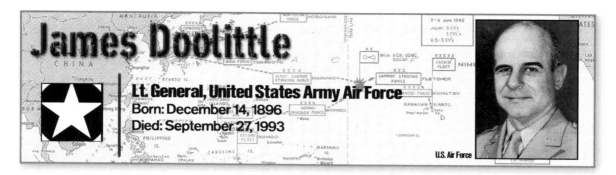

James Doolittle

Lt. General, United States Army Air Force
Born: December 14, 1896
Died: September 27, 1993

U.S. Air Force

The Second World War sparked great leaps in airplane technology. By the end of the war, slow, primitive biplanes had given way to jet aircraft. While many men and women helped mold the Allied air effort into a deciding factor in the war, perhaps no one stood higher in the public eye than James "Jimmy" Doolittle.

Born in California in 1896, Doolittle spent much of his youth in Alaska, where his father settled after failing to make a fortune in the 1897 Klondike Gold Rush. A small child, he quickly earned respect from the other children because of his skill in fighting.

In 1908 his family returned to California. In 1910 Doolittle attended the first great aviation meet in the United States held near Los Angeles. Inspired, he built his first glider at the age of 15. Jumping off a cliff, the tail of the glider hit the edge hurtling him 15 feet to the ground. Undaunted, he continued to learn all he could about aviation.

> ## TRIVIA
> Jimmy Doolittle is the only person to be awarded both of America's two highest honors, the Medal of Honor and the Medal of Freedom.

A CELEBRITY PILOT

Doolittle was enrolled at the University of California, Berkeley when the United States entered the First World War. In October 1917 he enlisted in the Signal Corps Reserve as a flying cadet. He stayed in the U.S. and served as flight instructor for the duration of the war.

Doolittle became a national celebrity during the interwar period. He set flying records for speed and endurance. While dominating the air racing circuit, he retired unexpectedly stating, "I have yet to hear of anyone engaged in this work dying of old age."

Doolittle's greatest contribution to aviation was in pioneering the development of navigational instruments that greatly increased the safety of flight. As a test pilot, he was the first to take off, fly and land a plane using only instruments.

EARLY BOMBER EFFORTS

During the early stages of the war the British developed a vision for strategic bombing of Axis industry and military targets such as U-boat bases far from the front line. While it sounds silly after the fact, at the time not everyone was convinced that airplanes could bomb effectively.

Great Britain's first "bombing" missions merely dropped leaflets urging the Germans to get rid of Hitler. The planes did not fly in formation and heavy losses forced the British to resort to nighttime raids where the dark-

Republic P-47 Thunderbolt

U.S. Air Force

The Republic P-47 Thunderbolt was an effective fighter but excelled in ground attacks. A large and heavy plane, it was nicknamed the "Jug."

U.S. Navy

One of Jimmy Doolittle's B-25s flies off the deck of the carrier Hornet on an early war mission to bomb Japan.

ness that served as protection also hindered accuracy. Winston Churchill, who said "the fighters are our salvation, but the bombers alone provide the means of victory," grounded bomber command in November 1941 when losses reached critical levels. The new German *Würzburg* radar proved effective in locating incoming bombers.

The situation began to improve soon after Air Marshall Arthur "Bomber" Harris took over in February 1942. Harris replaced precision bombing with area bombing. Planes were sent in concentrated numbers. Lead planes, manned by experienced crews, dropped flares to mark targets for the following planes. The damaging attack on a Renault plant near Paris in March marked the beginning of a period of success for the Royal Air Force (RAF).

Doolittle's Raid

While the British effort was beginning to see results in early 1942, America was still reeling from the shock of Pearl Harbor. In an effort to boost morale and show the Japanese

that they were in for a fight, Doolittle planned, trained and led a top-secret attack on the Japanese mainland.

Doolittle's men trained to do what many thought impossible: launch a medium bomber from an aircraft carrier. Without actually having tried it beforehand, 16 *North American B-25 Mitchell* bombers successfully launched from the carrier *Hornet* on April 18, 1942. The bombers targeted several Japanese cities including the capital, Tokyo.

The bombers could not land on the carrier and therefore continued westward towards friendly airfields in China. Doolittle and his crew bailed out after they could not locate their designated airfield. Most crewmen made it to safety with the help of the Chinese though several were caught and killed by the Japanese. The largely symbolic attack caused little damage but greatly embarrassed the Japanese and elevated Doolittle as a hero to an entire generation of Americans.

Bomber Barons

Around the time of Doolittle's raid, American General Ira Eaker arrived in Great Britain to set up headquarters for the Eighth Air Force bomber command. Unlike the British who had established a separate air force two decades previously, the U.S. "Army Air Corps" was part of the Army. Dwight Eisenhower referred to the air generals as "Bomber Barons."

Ira Eaker

The Americans introduced new ideas, including improved radar and the Norden bombsight that greatly increased the accuracy of bombs. The Americans preferred daylight raids believing their well-armed, sturdy *Boeing B-17 Flying Fortresses* could fend off the *Luftwaffe*. Major Curtis LeMay came up with an idea to reduce bomber vulnerability by organizing the

Boeing B-17 Flying Fortress

U.S. Air Force

Developed in the mid 1930s, the B-17 Superfortress developed a reputation for ruggedness and reliability. Though used in all major theaters during the war, the B-17 was put to greatest use in the United States Army Air Forces daylight bombing campaign against Germany. Over 12,000 B-17s were produced by the end of 1945.

planes into box-shaped formations in which they helped defend one another.

The Americans conducted their first European raid in August 1942. Progress was slow as the Eighth Air Force still only had about 100 operational bombers in March 1943. Eaker waged a campaign in Washington for more bombers. As American industry ramped up production Eaker was gratified by the promise of 944 bombers by July 1st and double that by the end of 1943.

Defense Imagery Management Operations Center

A B-17 prepares to return to England after dropping its payload. One of the first raids by the Eighth Air Force in 1943 was to bomb the Focke Wulf plant at Marienburg, Germany. Luftwaffe resistance was fierce and 80 bombers and 800 men were lost.

The Allies made a controversial decision to target German cities in an effort to demoralize the population. In July 1943 Hamburg, an older city with many wooden buildings, was destroyed by fire caused by ten days of American bombing. In November the RAF launched a series of 35 major raids averaging over 500 bombers each in what was called the "Battle of Berlin." Damage was minimized as most buildings in Berlin were brick and set apart from one another.

The Germans were not easily demoralized. Even when factories were damaged much of the machinery remained usable. The large con- scripted labor force from conquered countries manned antiaircraft guns (*flak*), and quickly repaired damage. The Germans constructed extensive decoys including a nine-mile wide plywood decoy of Berlin in the countryside. The Bomber Barons were upset when B-17 bomb- ers proved to be more vulnerable to Luftwaffe fighters than expected. The bombers had to de- fend themselves as Allied fighters did not have the range to provide escort on long missions.

Doolittle took over command of the Eighth Air Force from Eaker in March 1944. Already the sheer number of Allied planes were begin- ning to wear down the Germans, who despite increasing airplane production, were having trouble finding and training replacement pilots. Unlike Allied airmen who were pulled from duty after a set time, skilled Luftwaffe pilots kept fly- ing until they were killed or captured.

With the introduction of the longer range *Lockheed P-38 Lightning*, *Republic P-47 Thunderbolt* and *North American P-51 Mus- tang* (perhaps the best fighter of the war) Doo- little was able to extend fighter support deep into German airspace. Bomber pilots referred to their escort fighters as "little friends." In early 1944 Allied efforts turned towards knocking out the Luftwaffe in preparation for *Operation Overlord*. Their efforts were successful; on D- Day the Luftwaffe was a non-factor.

DAM BUSTERS

Imperial War Museum / CH 21121

One of the most daring raids of the war took place on May 16, 1943 when 19 British Lancasters targeted three dams on the Ruhr River. Months of special train- ing went into preparing for the mission.

The planes flew to their destinations at less than 1500 feet in order to avoid radar detection. Special bombs were developed just for the attack. Given a backspin, the barrel-shaped bombs were released at precisely 60 feet, skipping across the water and over anti-torpedo nets. Once the bombs hit the backside of the dam they began to sink. A fuse detonated the bomb at a depth of 30 feet. The resulting explosion amplified the pressure of the water on the dam.

Two of the three dams were successfully breached with water flooding 16 miles downstream. The Ger- mans repaired the damage in just three months but the effort diverted many workers from construction on the Atlantic Wall defenses that were crucial to German plans to stop an Allied amphibious invasion.

Consolidated B-24 Liberator

U.S. Air Force

With more than 18,400 built, the Consolidated B-24 Liberator was the most-pro- duced American military airplane in history. While it had a longer range, higher top speed and was capable of carrying a larger payload, the plane was difficult to fly and not as rugged as the B-17 Flying Fortress.

U.S. National Archives

Aviators of the Tuskegee Airmen 332nd Fighter Group attending a briefing in Ramitelli, Italy, March 1945.

RAIDS ON PLOESTI

The 15th Air Force based in Italy was charged with bombing what might have been the most heavily defended air target in the world, the Ploesti oil fields in Rumania. Ploesti was Nazi Germany's largest supplier of fuel. With their greater range, *Consolidated B-24 Liberator's* were given the task of knocking out Ploesti. In the first large raid in August 1943, 53 out of 177 B-24's failed to return. 40% of Ploesti's capacity was knocked out but reserve facilities kept oil flowing to Germany.

Allied bombers continued to make the dangerous journey. By the summer of 1944 German oil production was reduced by over 90%. After the Russians captured Ploesti in late summer, attacks on German synthetic fuel refineries, where coal was turned into gasoline, were

increased. Aviation fuel production plunged from 200,000 tons in May 1944 to only 7000 by October.

During the fall of 1944 1000 bomber raids became commonplace. With the help of their "little friends" the strategic bombing campaign began to take a real toll on German war efforts. By early 1945 the Allies firmly controlled the skies over Europe. In the final months of the war the Germans introduced the highly capable *Messerschmitt Me 262* jet, but they were too few in number and too late. In the final month of the war much of what was left of the Luftwaffe was shifted in a futile attempt to stop the Russian advance on Berlin. There too they were outnumbered as the Soviet Air Force boasted 7500 combat aircraft. On April 16, 1945 most of the strategic bombers were grounded for a lack of targets.

In the postwar years Doolittle continued to stay in the public eye by serving on federal boards and commissions. In 1985 Congress promoted him to the rank of full General. President Ronald Reagan assisted in pinning Doolittle's fourth star. Jimmy Doolittle died in 1993, more than 50 years after his famous raid, and was buried at Arlington National Cemetery. In his honor, a B-25 bomber performed a flyover during his funeral.

North Amer. P-51 Mustang

U.S. Air Force

The North American P-51 Mustang was designed and built in just 117 days. The workhorse fighter of the 8th Air Force by 1944, the long-range Mustang was the equal of any Luftwaffe fighter and could travel with bombers all the way to their target and back, greatly increasing their survival rate.

REVIEW QUESTIONS

1. What great contribution to aviation did James Doolittle make?
   a. Developed the jet engine
   b. Developed navigational instruments
   c. Test pilot of first supersonic plane
   d. Made first carrier landing

2. The Royal Air Force preferred to send their bombers on _____ missions.

3. In early 1942, shortly after the attack on Pearl Harbor, James Doolittle planned a raid on the _____ mainland.
   a. German
   b. Italian
   c. Japanese
   d. Russian

4. Doolittle's Raid required _____'s to be launched from the carrier USS Hornet.
   a. B-25 medium bombers
   b. F4F Wildcat fighters
   c. P-51 Mustangs
   d. SBD Dauntless dive bombers

5. The planes on Doolittle's Raid could not return to their carrier and were forced to land in _____.

6. Which American general established the Eighth Air Force in Great Britain?
   a. James Doolittle
   b. Ira Eaker
   c. Curtis LeMay
   d. Chuck Yaeger

7. The workhorse of the American strategic bombing effort in Europe was the _____.
   a. B-52 Stratofortress
   b. B-17 Flying Fortress
   c. B-26 Marauder
   d. B-29 Superfortress

8. As part of a controversial decision to target German cities in an effort to demoralize the population, the German city of _____ was destroyed by fire from American bombers in July 1943.

9. _____ increased the survival rate of Allied bombers in German airspace.
   a. A lack of Luftwaffe planes
   b. Long-range Allied fighters
   c. Radar warnings
   d. Increased bomber speeds

10. Most of the Nazi war machine ran on fuel from _____, Romania.

11. Because of the distance to Ploesti, _____ bombers were used instead of B-17s.
   a. B-24 Liberator
   b. Avro Lancaster
   c. B-25 Mitchell
   d. B-26 Marauder

12. By the fall of 1944 the Allies were capable of sending _____ bombers in a single raid.
   a. 100
   b. 500
   c. 1000
   d. 1500

13. Though a very effective weapon, the German Messerschmitt 262 fighter _____ introduced in the final months of the war was too few in numbers to impact the outcome.

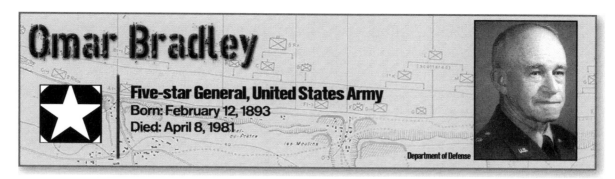

Omar Bradley

Five-star General, United States Army
Born: February 12, 1893
Died: April 8, 1981

Department of Defense

Other American generals have achieved greater fame, but it was Omar Bradley who the *St. Louis Globe-Democrat* described as "the nearest thing to Abraham Lincoln in uniform the American Army has ever produced." Often called "the soldier's general," he was known for usually saying "please" when he gave an order. He could be difficult and predictable but was a steady leader throughout the war in northwest Europe and in later service during the Cold War.

Bradley was born in 1883 in rural Missouri. Growing up in a family he described as "desperately poor," he loved to play baseball, read and shoot. While at West Point he was considered one of the best college baseball players in the country. His 1915 graduating class is known as "the class the stars fell on" because it contained many future leaders. In August 1918 he was scheduled for European deployment, but an influenza pandemic prevented his departure before the armistice. In the 1920s he taught math at West Point before working under George Marshall at the War Department.

In 1943, Bradley, who was George Patton's aide at the time, took over Patton's II (Second) Corps and directed the final battles in Tunisia in North Africa. Bradley next led II Corps in *Operation Husky*, the invasion of Sicily. When it came time to name commanders for the D-Day invasion of France, Bradley was chosen over Patton, who was being disciplined for slapping two soldiers.

BREAKOUT FROM NORMANDY

On D-Day, Bradley watched from aboard the heavy cruiser *Augusta* as his troops struggled to secure Omaha Beach. He contemplated withdrawal before his troops finally secured the beachhead. Eight weeks later, preceded

U.S. National Archives

After spending two months fighting in the hedgerows on Normandy, American troops of the 28th Infantry Division bask in the glow of a victory parade as they march down the Champs Elysees in Paris on August 29, 1944.

by heavy strategic bombing, Bradley planned and led *Operation Cobra*, an offensive in which Allied forces broke out of the restrictive terrain of Normandy. Bradley was criticized for allowing 240,000 German troops to escape through the Falaise pocket, but the offensive proved that the Allies were in Europe to stay.

On August 1, 1944, Bradley was placed over the 12th Army Group. At 900,000 strong and consisting of four field armies, it was the largest group of soldiers ever placed under one American field commander. The French capital, Paris, was liberated on August 25. During the late summer, American forces pushed forward quickly enough that they ran ahead of their fuel and supplies.

The Germans were further pressured on August 15 when American and French forces landed in the Cannes-Toulon area of southern France as part of *Operation Anvil*. American General Luscian Truscott led all assault troops (VI Corps) while Jean de Lattre headed Free French forces. Toulon, home to the French fleet, was soon captured, and within weeks forces from *Anvil* linked with Allied troops in the north.

The summer of 1944 was devastating for the Germans: 1.2 million soldiers were killed, wounded or missing. Fifty-two divisions were destroyed in the east and 28 in the west. Romania and Bulgaria defected to the Russians while 555 Soviet divisions moved toward Germany. On the Western front German resistance stiffened as they were pushed back into their homeland. The fall Battle of Hürtgen Forest cost the Allies 24,000 casualties. With the onset of winter, the Allies decided to dig in, rest and prepare for a spring offensive to finish Germany.

THE BATTLE OF THE BULGE

On September 16, 1944, Hitler shocked his generals by announcing a grand offensive against the Allies in northwestern Europe. His generals pleaded, to no avail, to abandon the

American troops pass the Arc de Triomphe in their M8 Greyhound armored car after the liberation of Paris in August 1944.

plan and give priority to stopping the Russian push from the east. Hitler's plan was to drive through the Ardennes Forest in Belgium and recapture the port city of Antwerp. Seizing Antwerp would cut the Allied armies in two, deprive them of a supply port and stir up political indecision amongst Allied leaders, allowing Germany to turn its full strength against the Russians. Hitler personally planned the attack — called *'Wacht am Rhein'* — Watch on the Rhine.

The November date for the attack was pushed back to December. Hitler counted on bad winter weather to ground the superior Allied air force. The winter of 1944 was especially cold. Winter gear for American forces was rare until January 1945. Bradley stated, "I had deliberately bypassed shipments of winter clothing in favor of ammunition and gasoline." Bradley's

12th Army Group covered a front stretching 200 miles south of Bernard Montgomery's 21st Army Group and north of Patton's 3rd Army. The thinly spread American forces were content to spend the winter resting and rearming. When Major General Troy Middleton complained about the thin lines, Bradley told him, "Don't worry, Troy, they won't come through here." Little did Bradley know the largest battle of the war to be fought in Western Europe was heading their way.

Four German armies, made up of 20 divisions, 300,000 men and almost 1000 tanks, began their attack on December 16 with a predawn artillery barrage. Otto Skorzeny, whom German radio labeled "The Most Dangerous man in Europe," was in charge of generating confusion behind the lines. His 2000 commandos, outfitted with American uniforms, captured Shermans and disguised German tanks, appeared to be an American unit fleeing to the rear. Skorzeny's men succeeded in spreading confusion by changing signs to redirect American traffic, blocking roads with white tape (indicating mine fields) and spreading rumors that convinced American units to retreat.

Defense Imagery Management Operations Center

American soldiers belonging to the 289th Infantry Regiment march toward St. Vith-Houffalize in Belgium during the Battle of the Bulge. The winter of 1944-45 was bitterly cold.

On the north (right) shoulder of the attack, the 6th SS Panzer Army, led by Sepp Dietrich, advanced. Among his units was a regiment led by 29-year-old Lieutenant Colonel Joachim Peiper. Leading 5000 men and 42 King Ti-

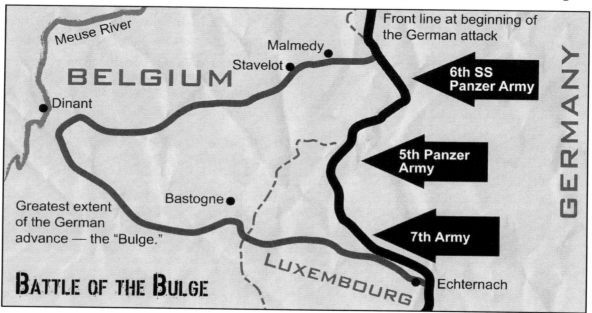

Meuse River

Malmedy

Stavelot

BELGIUM

Dinant

Front line at beginning of the German attack

6th SS Panzer Army

5th Panzer Army

GERMANY

Bastogne

Greatest extent of the German advance — the "Bulge."

7th Army

LUXEMBOURG

Echternach

BATTLE OF THE BULGE

ger tanks, Peiper had already earned a reputation on the East Front for aggressiveness and ruthlessness, having burned down entire villages. Peiper's unit progressed quickly at first, overrunning a number of American positions.

Soldiers of the 44th Armored Infantry, working with armor of the 6th Armored Division, attack German troops surrounding Bastogne, Belgium on December 31, 1944 during the Battle of the Bulge.

Near Malmedy, SS troops herded more than 100 American prisoners into a field and opened fire, murdering 84 men. The few survivors who escaped told of the massacre, strengthening the resolve of other American troops who no longer saw surrender as an option. American engineers frustrated Peiper's advance several times, once blowing up a bridge right in front of him. A small number of engineers held up Peiper at Stavelot, forcing him to postpone an attack until the next day. Short on fuel and stymied time after time, the 6th SS never came close to its objective, Antwerp.

On the south (left) shoulder, General Erich Brandenberger led the Seventh Army. Their goal was to make a limited advance and form a defensive line to protect the main thrust as it swung north toward Antwerp. With only four infantry divisions and no armor, the advance soon stalled. American units held up the Germans at Echternach for five days until a solid defensive line could be built to the west.

Only the 5th Panzer Army in the center under General Hasso von Manteuffel made marked progress. On the first day, Manteuffel sent in infantry to neutralize American tank destroyers. After nightfall, tanks began to move, using artificial light from spotlights bounced off low clouds. Manteuffel's forces destroyed the American 106th Division and broke the 28th Division, but lost much precious time doing it.

On December 19, Eisenhower met with his commanders. Bradley commanded General Courtney Hodges to drive from the north and Patton from the south. On the 20th, with sever-

al of Bradley's northern units cut off by the German progress, Eisenhower temporarily placed the units under Montgomery. That same day elements of the U.S. 101st Airborne and 10th Armored were encircled at Bastogne. Shaking off the initial shock, American forces switched to the offensive. Within four days of the start of the battle, a half-million soldiers were at or on their way to the front.

COURAGEOUS STAND AT BASTOGNE

Bastogne was of strategic importance as numerous roads lead out of the town like the legs of a spider. On the 21st, Manteuffel's troops attempted to take Bastogne. The next day, Germans holding a white flag approached soldiers of the 101st. At first the Americans were

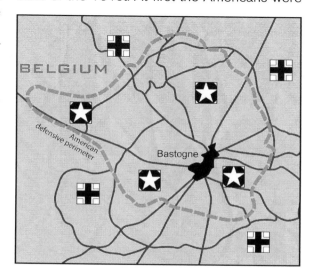

hopeful that the Germans wished to surrender. Led to General Anthony McAuliffe, acting commander of the 101st, the Germans demanded that the Americans surrender. McAuliffe's first words were "Aw, nuts!" An aide gave him the idea to use that as his reply:

> *"To the German Commander:*
> *Nuts!*
> *The American Commander"*

On December 23, the weather cleared up, allowing the Allies to fly 2000 sorties, including 241 cargo planes that dropped critical supplies into Bastogne. Fighter bombers armed with rockets proved to be especially handy in dealing with the large Tiger and Panther tanks.

On Christmas Day, 2nd Panzer reached its furthest point, 60 miles from the start, near Dinant. The same day Germans pushed through the northwest perimeter of Bastogne. The 101st, helped by tank destroyers and artillery, rebuilt their lines and repelled the invaders. On the 26th, Patton's 4th Armored, having traveled more than 100 miles in 48 hours, arrived at Bastogne. Fighting at Bastogne would continue into the new year, but the Germans never again seriously threatened the town. Soldiers of the 101st were annoyed that the Allied camp had been so worried about them. McAuliffe said, "We're in fine shape: we're ready to take the offensive."

HITLER RETREATS

On the 28th, Hitler officially called off the offensive. German troops began a slow defensive withdrawal. On January 1, most of what remained of the weakened *Luftwaffe* was sent in to relieve pressure on the retreating troops in what Hitler fancifully called "The Great Blow." More than 200 Allied aircraft were destroyed but at a cost of 300 German planes. The Luftwaffe never again took to the sky in appreciable numbers. By early February, all the German gains had been recaptured by Allies.

The German offensive merely created a "bulge" in the American lines, giving the battle its name. The offensive was doomed from the start because of a lack of fuel, rough terrain and lack of air support. Defiant American troops, though often outnumbered, fought well enough to delay the Germans until help arrived. The net result was only to delay the inevitable German defeat for a couple of weeks. Nineteen-thousand Americans lost their lives, while 100,000 Germans were killed, wounded or captured.

CROSSING THE RHINE RIVER

As winter waned, the Rhine River stood as the last major obstacle between the Allies and the heart of Germany. In Germany, all bridges spanning the river had been destroyed with the exception of the Ludendorff Bridge at Remagen. Members of the U.S. 9th Armored Division

Eight thousand Allied troops crossed the Rhine River via the Ludendorff Bridge before the Germans suceeded in destroying it.

Field Marshal Wilhelm Keitel, representing the Nazi government, signs surrender documents in Berlin, Germany in May 1945.

were the first to cross the bridge, while under heavy fire, on March 7, 1945. Eight-thousand troops were rushed across before the bridge collapsed from German bombing.

Controlling a swath of the eastern shore, American engineers were able to construct more than 50 temporary bridges. Bradley aggressively pushed his Army group against the disintegrating German forces. American forces met up with Russian forces near the Elbe River in mid-April. Per terms agreed to at the Yalta Conference, the Russians were allowed to capture Berlin. The Allies accepted the unconditional surrender of Germany on May 8, 1945. Millions of citizens in Allied countries took to the streets in celebration.

LAST OF THE FIVE-STAR GENERALS

Bradley's sense of duty to his men continued after the conclusion of the war. He headed up the Veterans Administration, working to improve health care for veterans. He was named Army Chief of Staff in 1948 and the next year became the first Chairman of the Joint Chiefs of Staff. He earned his fifth star

when was promoted to General of the Army in 1950.

As Chairman, he oversaw the American war effort during the Korean War. He retired from the military in 1953 but remained in the public eye throughout the years, attending sporting events, parades and advising President Lyndon Johnson. The last surviving five-star general, Bradley passed away in 1981 and was buried in Arlington National Cemetery.

REVIEW QUESTIONS

1. In 1943, Omar Bradley was serving as an aide to General _____.

2. Bradley oversaw the struggle to capture _____ Beach on D-Day.
   a. Sword
   b. Juno
   c. Utah
   d. Omaha

3. Bradley planned and led Operation _____, an offensive in which Allied forces broke out of the restrictive terrain of Normandy.

4. A key moment in the Allied war effort was the liberation of _____ on August 25, 1944.

5. The often-overlooked invasion of southern France on August 15, 1944 was code-named _____.
   a. Operation Anvil
   b. Operation Winepress
   c. Operation Toulon
   d. Operation Bagration

6. While German troops were in full retreat in September 1944, Hitler shocked his generals by announcing an offensive though the Ardennes Forest to capture the port city of _____.

7. *Hitler's offensive, code-named 'Wacht am Rhein' – Watch on the Rhine – is known to the Allies as* _____.
   a. the Battle of Antwerp
   b. the Battle of Bastogne
   c. the Battle of the Ardennes
   d. the Battle of the Bulge

8. *The winter of 1944-45 in northern Europe was* _____
   a. wet and muddy
   b. late in arriving
   c. very cold
   d. All of the above

9. *Four German armies, made up of 300,000 men and 1000 tanks, began their attack against thinly spread American forces on* _____.
   a. November 1, 1944
   b. December 16, 1944
   c. December 25, 1944
   d. January 1, 1945

10. *Led by Otto Skorzeny, 2000 commandos caused trouble behind American lines by* _____.
   a. wearing American uniforms
   b. changing road signs to redirect reinforcements
   c. disguising German tanks to look like American units
   d. All of the above

11. *American prisoners captured at* _____ *were slaughtered by SS troops under Lieutenant Colonel Joachim Peiper.*

Panzer IV "Tiger"

The Tiger I tank was a 57 ton behemoth armed with a deadly 88 mm gun. Designed to counter Soviet heavy armor, it saw action in all German theaters. The tank was expensive and difficult to produce; only 1347 were produced. The tank shown here was captured by Allied forces in Tunisia.

U.S. Army

12. *When German troops demanded that General Anthony McAuliffe, acting commander of the 101st, surrender the village of Bastogne, McAuliffe's reply was* _____.
   a. "I have not yet begun to fight!"
   b. "Come and take it!"
   c. "Nuts!"
   d. "I demand that you surrender!"

13. *What was the name of Hitler's desperate attempt to relieve pressure on troops retreating from the Battle of the Bulge?*

14. *In March 1945 Allied troops crossed the Rhine River, the last great natural barrier in Germany, using the Ludendorff Bridge at* _____ .

15. *Omar Bradley was the last surviving* _____.
   a. Purple Heart recipient
   b. five-star general
   c. veteran of the First World War
   d. American field marshal

Josef Stalin

Premier of the Soviet Union
Born: December 18, 1878
Died: March 5, 1953

Library of Congress

The epic scale of the conflict between Germany and the Soviet Union during the Second World War is unequaled in history. The strong-willed leaders of these two nations, Josef Stalin and Adolph Hitler, rank as two of the most evil men in history. Ultimately, it was Josef Stalin, who through patriotic appeals and brute force, willed his country to victory.

Josef Stalin in 1902

Born in Gori, Georgia in 1879, Stalin's father, a shoemaker, was an alcoholic who abused his wife and son. Stalin's father wanted his son to forsake education in order to become a shoemaker. Beatings from his mother were also common, though she made certain that he received an education.

Growing up in Gori, though, was rough, with gangs and fighting an everyday part of life. Stalin seemed to thrive on the violence. At an early age, it became apparent that Stalin always sought to be the leader and to undermine those who had authority over him. Despite his violent tendencies, he was an intelligent student, excellent singer and a published poet.

At the age of 16, Stalin entered a Georgian Orthodox seminary in Tiflis, Georgia. Despite a stifling atmosphere similar to that of a prison, Stalin did well in his studies. During this time, he developed a love for forbidden books, including writings by Communist Karl Marx. He found a role model in the fictional book *The Parricide* (Father killer) by Alexander Kazbegi. In the book, a Georgian outlaw named Koba leads a struggle against the czar. Inspired, Stalin asked his friends to call him "Koba." The rebellious child began to transform into a revolutionary. Shortly before graduation, Stalin was expelled.

BOLSHEVIK REVOLUTION

In 1903, Stalin joined Vladimir Lenin's Bolsheviks. He first met Lenin at a meeting in Finland in 1905. Lenin sent Stalin back to Georgia to recruit and train revolutionary terrorists to help overthrow the czar. Stalin robbed banks to raise money to fund revolutionary activities and was arrested 10 times by the czar's police.

In the midst of his revolutionary activities, Stalin fell in love and was married in 1906. His

Wikipedia Commons

Josef Stalin, right, talks with Vladimir Lenin, founder of the Soviet Union.

wife, Ekaterina, died of pneumonia in 1907. Some sources report that, at her funeral, he told a friend that "with her died any human feeling in him." They had one son, Yakov.

In 1912, Lenin promoted Stalin to the Bolshevik Party Central Committee. The next year, Stalin was captured by police and sent to Kureika, Siberia, north of the Arctic Circle. There he spent four years in exile. The First World War accelerated the collapse of the Russian Empire. As the war went poorly against the Central Powers, the Russian people began to revolt. On March 2, 1917, Czar Nicholas II stepped down. Ten days later, Stalin arrived in St. Petersburg. In October, the Bolshevik Red Army, under Lenin, seized power and began to implement its Communistic agenda. Quickly negotiating a peace with Germany, the Red Army turned its attention to dealing with the remnants of Russian unrest.

During this time known as the Russian Civil War, Stalin led Red Army troops to forcibly take grain from peasants to feed the cities. Anyone who resisted was shot. Stalin was wholly devoted to the vision of a world revolution and had no reservations in using cruel tactics to that end. Millions of Russians died during the conflict. By the early 1920's, Russia was firmly in the grasp of the Communists. In 1922, Stalin was given the power to appoint all party officials. He changed the name from Russia to the *Union of Soviet Socialist Republics* (USSR). Adding to the losses suffered in almost a decade of war, 5 million more Russians starved in 1921-22 as Lenin and Stalin took more food for the cities.

Successor to Lenin

In 1922, Lenin suffered a stroke and his health began to deteriorate. Stalin supervised Lenin's medical care, controlling who had access to him. Lenin, paralyzed and unable to speak, could only watch as Stalin gained power as he treacherously isolated and eliminated

each of his rivals. Lenin left notes with his wife to warn other Communist leaders against allowing Stalin to assume power. After Lenin died in January 1924, Stalin convinced the populace that he was Lenin's chosen successor. He skillfully used back room tactics to build up a following. Ironically, his crudeness, simplicity and lack of eloquence endeared him to the common Russian.

By 1928, Stalin had eliminated all his rivals and was the undisputed leader of the USSR. Stalin turned his attention toward making the Soviet Union an industrial super power. Production improved at the cost of many lives. Peasants forcibly moved to state-run farms and, unable to meet unrealistic quotas, often watched

U.S. National Archives

Soviet Foreign Minister Vyacheslav Molotov adds his signature to the German-Soviet nonaggression pact in Moscow on August 23, 1939. Foreign Minister of Germany Joachim von Ribbentrop stands directly behind Molotov with Josef Stalin on his immediate left. Note the portrait of Vladimir Lenin on the wall.

as the government took all they had raised, leaving them with nothing. In 1933, Communist policy created a great famine, the *Holodomor* (killing by hunger), in the Ukraine. An accurate death toll is difficult to determine, but historians generally agree at least 3 million died during the Holodomor due to Stalin's policies.

Stalin created a secret police, the NKVD, to force his way on people. Between 1929 and 1932, at least 10 million Russians were exiled to Siberia because they opposed Stalin's laws. Some died on the cold plains because housing could not be constructed quickly enough.

Directly responsible for many of the country's problems, Stalin made up enemies to blame. From 1934-37, more than half of the Communist Party membership was executed. Stalin personally signed 230,000 death warrants. No one, friend or foe, was safe from Stalin's cruelty. He imprisoned the wives and children of the men closest to him in order to secure their loyalty. In the late 1930s Stalin purged the military, killing more than 40,000 army and naval officers. The void of leadership left after the purge had powerful consequences. The Soviet Army, devoid of competent leaders, struggled to conquer tiny Finland in 1939.

HITLER INVADES RUSSIA

In August 1939, Russia and Germany secretly signed the Molotov-Ribbentrop Pact in which they pledged nonaggression toward one another. When Germany invaded Poland, Russia stepped in and took over parts of eastern Poland agreed upon in the pact. While Stalin still felt conflict with Germany was inevitable, he believed war before 1943 unlikely.

In early 1941, Stalin expressed concern to Hitler about German forces gathering in Poland. Hitler lied, saying he had no intention of

breaking the nonaggression treaty, but the forces were in Poland for safekeeping out of the range of British bombers. It is no small irony that the paranoid and unstable Stalin, who did not even trust his own family and friends, trusted Hitler.

When the Germans launched *Operation Barbarossa* on June 21, 1941, Stalin initially hesitated, believing it was a mistake. Ashamed that he had allowed Hitler to fool him, Stalin locked himself in a room for a time and got drunk. After regaining his composure, Stalin set about repelling the Nazi invaders. He created a *State Defense Committee* (GKO) consisting of five members, of which he was chairman, to direct the war effort. He left no doubt that it would be he who would run the war.

Stalin used patriotism and fear to entreat the Russian people to fight. Russians embraced the challenge, referring to the struggle as "The Great Patriotic War." On November 7, 1941, the annual parade marking the anniversary of the 1917 Revolution was held in Moscow despite the presence of German forces several miles away. Stalin gave two passionate speeches that helped galvanize the Russian people into fighting the Germans.

The patriotic Russian people sacrificed greatly to support the war effort. Early in the war, they succeeded in moving hundreds of factories eastward where they were reassembled and resumed the production of war materials. By Christmas 1941, more than 1300 factories had been relocated. Following the factories, more than 20 million workers were packed onto freight cars for a trip hundreds or even thousands of miles east. Many died on the journey. In the factories, workers toiled long hours without adequate food and shelter. Some of the factory machines were reassembled and put into production before walls and a roof could be built

---

TRIVIA

Stalin loved to watch foreign films, especially American cowboy flicks. He often watched them late at night and did not eat dinner until after midnight.

Red Army soldiers defend Josef Stalin's namesake city, Stalingrad, in late 1942 or early 1943.

Peasants struggle to survive in Stalingrad. The Russian people suffered greatly from inhumane treatment at the hands of the German Army and from crushing demands placed upon them by Josef Stalin and other Communist leaders.

around them. One steel mill worked 24 hours-a-day in rain and snow. Even as the Germans continued to advance in 1942, Soviet production soared above government quotas.

FATHER OF FEAR

Stalin's orders were followed not just out of patriotism, but out of fear. Russian generals and soldiers, more afraid of Stalin and the Communists than the Germans, would obey bad orders rather than show any hesitancy. No matter how senseless the order, there was at least a chance to survive an attack but none for disobedience. Commissars, dedicated Communist party officials, were assigned to observe military leaders to make certain they did their duty.

For a Russian soldier to become a prisoner of the Germans was a horrible fate. The Germans purposely mistreated Russian prisoners, leaving many to starve or freeze. Stalin labeled soldiers who surrendered as traitors and enemies. Even the soldier's family suffered, as they were denied food rations because of the "traitor." Stalin's NKVD police kept a constant vigil for any grumbling or sign of disagreement. Even civilians who showed the slightest sign of defeatism could be arrested and killed.

Stalin's personal pride was at stake during the battle of Stalingrad in late 1943 when he had pompously renamed the city, formerly Volgograd, after himself. At the cost of an estimated 750,000 Russian lives, the Germans were denied Stalingrad. The battle signified a great shift in momentum. The Russians seized the initiative from the Germans and would hold it until the end of the war.

In the spring of 1945, Stalin purposely set his two leading Marshals, Georgii Zhukov and Ivan Konev, against one another in a race to see who could reach Berlin first. Stalin was obsessive in his desire to reach Berlin before the Western Allies. In doing so, he placed himself in a prime position to extend Communist influence over all of Eastern Europe.

POTSDAM

A conference held in Potsdam, Germany in July 1945 greatly shaped the post-war world in Stalin's favor. Throughout the war, Stalin, Franklin Roosevelt and Winston Churchill were considered the "Big Three." At Potsdam, recently installed American President Harry Truman was attending his first conference. Churchill was distracted by an election back home. He would lose the election and be replaced mid-conference by the new Prime Minister, Clement Attlee.

Stalin had the upper hand from the beginning, already having placed a puppet government in Poland despite a previous agreement that the Poles would be allowed a democratic one. He received his wish to have one-third of the German Navy and to collect war reparations from occupied zones in Germany, Romania, Hungary and Bulgaria.

Many other issues were postponed, giving Stalin time to shore up Communist positions in Eastern Europe that would lead to the erection of what Churchill coined the "Iron Curtain" in a 1946 speech at Fulton, Missouri. The Soviet Union was the main victor in terms of expansion and influence in Europe while Great Britain and France struggled to recover. Germany would remain divided until 1990.

RUSSIA'S WAR LEGACY

Stalin declared war on Japan in early August. During the final weeks of the war, the Russians recaptured Manchuria and gained a foothold in Korea. Stalin helped establish a Communist regime in North Korea that led to the Korean War in 1950 and continuing tensions into the 21st Century.

During the Second World War, no country suffered more loss of life than Russia. About 8 million Russian soldiers and 18 million civilians died in the war. After the war, Stalin was not content to let the nation rest. He continued to persecute anyone he thought might remotely threaten his hold on power. In 1948, he announced a five-year rearmament program. In 1949, the first Russian atomic bomb was detonated. The Cold War was on in earnest.

The fear he instilled in those around him likely led to his premature death. Entering his bedroom after an all-night dinner and movie, Stalin issued strict orders not to be disturbed. His guards thought it unusual when he did not wake at his usual time but were afraid to enter. Many hours later, an aide finally entered the room to find an incoherent Stalin on the floor. He had suffered a cerebral hemorrhage. He died four days later on March 5, 1953.

Stalin was embalmed and preserved in Lenin's mausoleum until 1961. His remains were then buried outside the walls of the Kremlin. It will never be accurately known how many people died as victims of Stalin's repression. Including outright murders, deaths in dreadful camps and victims of famine caused by abusive policies, it is likely that Stalin was responsible for the deaths of at least 15 million people. The true toll is likely much higher.

U.S. National Archives

From left, British Prime Minister Clement Attlee, American President Harry Truman and Soviet leader Josef Stalin pose for a group photo during the Potsdam Conference in 1945.

Review Questions

1. *Josef Stalin was not a native Russian; he was born and raised in* _____.
   a. Latvia
   b. The Ukraine
   c. Moldava
   d. Georgia

2. *As a youth, Stalin was an* _____.
   a. excellent singer
   b. intelligent student
   c. published poet
   d. All of the above

3. *In 1905, Stalin met the prominent Boshevik leader* _____.
   a. Leon Trotsky
   b. Karl Marx
   c. Vladimir Lenin
   d. Vyacheslav Molotov

4. *Stalin led Bolshevik Red Army troops during the* _____.
   a. Russian Civil War
   b. First World War
   c. Sino-Japanese War
   d. Mongolian Incident

5. *It has been estimated that at least 3 million people died of starvation in* _____ *during 1933 due to Stalin's harsh policies.*
   a. Latvia
   b. the Ukraine
   c. Moldava
   d. None of the above

6. *Stalin signed the* _____ *Pact pledging nonaggression with Germany.*
   a. Hitler-Stalin
   b. Nazi-Soviet
   c. Molotov-Ribbentrop
   d. Molotov-Hitler

7. *When Germany attacked Russia on June 21, 1941 Stalin* _____.
   a. gave an inspiring speech
   b. flew to Siberia
   c. toured the front line
   d. got drunk

8. *The Russian people managed to pack up, move and rebuild more than 1300* _____ *vital to the Russian war effort before they could be overrun by the German Army.*

9. _____ *were dedicated Communist party officials who were assigned to observe military leaders and ensure they did their duty.*

10. *At the* _____ *Conference in July 1945, Stalin was able to shore up Communist positions in Eastern Europe.*
    a. Potsdam
    b. Yalta
    c. Moscow
    d. Berlin

11. *In the final weeks of the Second World War, Stalin declared war on* _____.

12. *It is estimated conservatively that Stalin was responsible for the deaths of at least* _____ *people.*
    a. 1 million
    b. 5.5 million
    c. 11.5 million
    d. 15 million

Raoul Wallenberg

Swedish Diplomat
Born: August 14, 1912
Died: Uknown

Swedish Public Domain

Many men became famous during the course of the Second World War. And though all had flaws, many fought with honor and integrity, while others fought only for personal glory at the expense of others. For Adolph Hitler, the war was about much more than conquest or power. His hatred led him to despise anyone who did not meet his warped standard of perfection. Romani (Gypsies), Poles, Russians, prisoners of war, outspoken church leaders and political prisoners were among those ruthlessly killed.

However, it was the Jews who Hitler hated most; they were the ones he desired to exterminate. Hitler believed that Jews were out to destroy his *Aryan* (a specific Caucasian subgroup) race. Before the war ended, more than 6 million Jews were murdered in what is known as the *Holocaust*, a Greek word meaning "sacrifice by fire."

A CAMPAIGN OF HATE

Defeat in the First World War devastated the German people. As their economy collapsed in the 1920's, a movement began to blame Jews. As Nazi influence began to grow, it was common for Jews to face Nazi thugs on the streets. Hitler's message that the German Aryan people were destined for greatness connected with voters. In 1933, Hitler came to power in Germany.

Hitler blamed all the woes of the German people on the Jews. He began to plot how he could rid Germany of all Jews. He dealt shrewdly with Jewish people, methodically isolating them from society in steps.

In 1933, Jews were prohibited from owning land, and their businesses were boycotted. The first concentration camp opened at Dachau, Germany.

In 1934, Jews lost their rights to health insurance and were prohibited from serving in the military.

The Nuremberg laws were passed in 1935, stripping German Jews of citizenship. Marriage and any form of intimacy between Aryans and Jews was forbidden. Many Jews began to seek ways to escape Germany.

More than 30 nations met at a conference in Evian, France in July 1938 to discuss the plight of Jews attempting to escape the Nazi terror. To their discredit and shame, almost every country declined to take in more than a token number of Jews. Australia feared importing a racial problem. The United States refused to fill its immigration quotas. Great Britain refused to expand immigration to Palestine. The Dominican Republic was the lone exception, generously agreeing to accept up to 100,000 Jews.

The situation in Germany grew worse. Jews were forbidden to practice medicine or law. A large red *"J"* was stamped in passports, restricting movement. Jewish children were expelled from public schools. Jews older than 10 years were required to wear a yellow star. During the night of November 9-10, 1938, Jews were the target of a night of destruction, known as *Kristallnacht*, "The Night of Broken Glass."

THE HOLOCAUST

As *Wehrmacht* troops conquered new lands, special *Schutz-Staffel* ("protection squadron") SS death squads followed behind to exterminate

Jews. Early executions were accomplished by taking Jews into the countryside, where they were lined up by the edge of a large pit, forced to strip and then shot. After their bodies fell into the pit, bulldozers would push dirt over the victims, many of whom were wounded but still alive.

This brutal method was not very efficient and predictably caused much mental stress to the troops ordered to murder. Toxic gas became the preferred method of murder. Soviet prisoners of war and mental patients were victims of experiments to perfect gas chambers. Between September 1939 and August 1941, 80,000 German mental patients and 10,000 concentration camp prisoners were gassed.

Large extermination camps were built in Poland. All over occupied Europe, Jews were forced out of their homes and told they were being relocated to recently conquered areas. Packed like cattle in freight cars with the doors nailed shut, victims typically traveled for days without bathrooms, food or water. Some went insane, while others died on the trip.

Upon arrival at the camp, some victims were selected to work as slaves or for terrible medical experiments. The others were led into a building and told they needed to shower after their long trip. Posted signs instructed the victims to leave their clothes neatly so nothing would be lost. Upon entering a room equipped with shower heads, poison gas was pumped in, killing everyone within five minutes. Prisoners would remove the bodies and burn them in large crematoriums.

RAOUL WALLENBERG

One of the truly sad aspects of the Holocaust is that many people, fearing the Nazis, said or did nothing. However, there were exceptions. Dutchman Jaap Penraat managed to help 406 Jews escape to safety. Ger-

Jews wait on the selection ramp at Auschwitz after disembarking from railway freight cars. The boy in the center is wearing the yellow star required by the Nazis. The vast majority of the people pictured were likely murdered by toxic gas within hours of the taking of this photograph.

man citizens secretly sold or gave food to Jewish friends. However, nothing compares to one Famous man who, as a result of his brave and tireless effort, saved more than 100,000 Jews from certain death. That man was Raoul Wallenberg.

While some Famous men such as George Patton or Erich von Manstein seemed to be born for leadership, no one could have imagined what Wallenberg would achieve during the war. Wallenberg belonged to one of the richest families in Sweden. As a young man, he attended the University of Michigan, where he studied to become an architect. Between semesters, he loved to tour America. He traveled from place to place by hitchhiking. Wallenberg said the appeal of hitchhiking "... is the great practice it offers in the art of diplomacy and negotiating." He once was robbed by four men who had picked him up; Wallenberg was unshakable, calling it a great adventure.

Wallenberg spent six months working in Haifa (a city in modern-day Israel) with Holland Bank. During that time, he listened to Jews who had escaped Nazi Germany. Working for a food import business during the war, Wallenberg traveled all over Europe, including Germany, where he witnessed Nazi brutality.

By 1944, despite German efforts to suppress them, reports of the Holocaust became common. Allied leaders determined to do something to stop the bloodshed. The American *War Refugee Board*, formed by President Franklin Roosevelt, approached neutral Sweden because it still maintained reasonably good relations with Germany.

Hitler's plan to exterminate European Jews, callously referred to as the *"Final Solution,"* was very efficient and, by mid-1944, few Jews remained in Europe. The last large pocket of Jews was in Hungary. Despite being Germany's ally, Hungary's ruler, Miklos Horthy, had protected Hungary's 630,000 Jews. On March 19, 1944, Germany occupied Hungary, and the next day Adolph Eichmann, a Reinhard Heydrich disciple, began to round up Jews. Heydrich had devised the "Final Solution." Eichmann brought an eagerness to his work, desiring only to follow orders and please Hitler.

Each day, thousands of Hungarian Jews were sent by rail to Auschwitz-Birkenau, where they were gassed and their bodies cremated. By the time Wallenberg arrived in Budapest, Hungary's capital, 148 trains had already sent 400,000 Jews to Auschwitz' gas chambers. Only 230,000 Jews remained in Hungary.

To protect the remaining Jews, Wallenberg began to issue *Schutz-passes* (protection passes), placing the Jews under the protection of the Swedish government. The passes appeared to be official documents but had no legal basis. As incredible as it may seem, German respect for procedure and paperwork rarely questioned the passes. Wallenberg, using his natural gift of diplomacy, tirelessly bribed and blackmailed Hungarian officials into honoring the Schutz-pass. Wallenberg rented buildings to hide Jews. Outside the buildings, he flew the Swedish flag and put up signs such as "library" to disguise their true purpose. He demanded that the buildings be given diplomatic protection.

Originally authorized to offer only 1500 passes, Wallenberg and his staff created many more. Wallenberg labored persistently to get the passes into the hands of Jews. In one incredible episode, he climbed onto the roof of a deportation train about to depart for Auschwitz.

Wikimedia Commons: Kwz

A gas chamber at the Dachau, Germany camp as it appears to visitors today. Prisoners would be led into the "shower" room and gas released through the "shower heads."

U.S. National Archives

Bones can still be seen in the crematoriums used to dispose of bodies in the Buchenwald concentration camp at Weimar, Germany. This photo was taken after the camp was liberated by the U.S. 3rd Army in 1945.

The squalor of camp life is evidenced by the deplorable conditions of prisoners in the Buchenwald concentration camp.

He handed passes through openings as German and Hungarian troops shot over his head. Wallenberg then ordered all passholders to exit the train and enter waiting transportation. The stunned Nazis did nothing to stop him.

On October 15, 1944, Horthy announced on radio that Hungary would surrender to the Russians. The Hungarian "Red Arrow" Nazis quickly seized power in a coup. Horthy was arrested and Budapest descended into lawlessness. No Jew was safe as Hungarian Red Arrow groups joined German SS troops in hunting down Jews.

Eichmann no longer sent trains into Hungary but instead marched Jews to the border to board trains for Auschwitz. Many died in the freezing sleet and ice as they trudged toward the border. Those who fell behind or collapsed were shot. Wallenberg followed them, giving food and encouragement. He would secretly give passes and then shout at German and Hungarian officers to release his "Swedish" pass-holders.

Knowing that the Russians would soon arrive, Wallenberg arranged a special dinner with Eich-

mann to try to persuade him to stop the killing. Eichmann refused and warned Wallenberg that his diplomatic immunity might not protect him from an "accident." Several days later, a German truck destroyed Wallenberg's car. At the time, he was not inside it. As Eichmann was leaving Hungary shortly before the Red Army arrived, he issued a final order to have 90,000 Jews killed. More than 700 SS and Red Arrow soldiers were assigned to carry out the task. Wallenberg convinced German SS General August Schmidthuber to spare the Jews by warning him, "If you do not stop this now, I can guarantee you will be hanged as a war criminal." Scmidthuber relented, and a massacre was avoided.

Always optimistic, Wallenberg hoped that the Russians would assist him in coordinating food, medicine and housing for the suffering Jews. On January 17, 1945, Wallenberg left Budapest with two Russian officers for a meeting with a Soviet Marshal. He never returned.

There are conflicting stories about what happened to him. It is possible that he was picked up by the NKVD secret police under suspicion of spying for the U.S. The Russians would have found it difficult to believe anyone of Wallenberg's family status would care about

A Russian slave inmate confronts a former Nazi guard who brutally beat prisoners.

INFAMOUS NAZIS AND THEIR FATE

Hans Frank — As a governor of a portion of Poland, Frank murdered many Poles and Jews. He was found guilty at the Nuremberg trials and executed.

Wilhelm Frick — Hitler's Minister of the Interior, he drafted the Nuremberg laws. He was found guilty at the Nuremberg trials and executed.

Reinhard Heydrich — "Himmler's evil genius" turned Germany into a police state. He kept a database of people's dirty secrets that the Nazis used to accuse their enemies. Heydrich created killing squads that followed German troops into conquered areas and murdered thousands of Jews and other civilians. In Czechoslovakia, Heydrich was known as "The Butcher of Prague." Two commandos sent by the exiled Czech government succeeded in assassinating Heydrich in December 1941.

Heinrich Himmler — Along with Hitler, Himmler is most often associated with Nazi brutality. As Chief of the German Police, Himmler used his position of power to murder millions of innocent civilians in an effort to render Germany racially pure. He committed suicide after he was captured and his identity revealed.

Ernst Kaltenbrunner — Heydrich's successor, Kaltenbrunner was placed in charge of the concentration camp system. He took personal interest in the different methods of killing camp inmates. He was found guilty at the Nuremberg trials and executed.

Field Marshal Wilhelm Keitel — He issued orders that were responsible for the mass killings of women and children in German-occupied Poland and Russia. He was found guilty at the Nuremberg trials and executed.

General Alfred Jodl — Hitler's chief of operations, Jodl was accused of violating the rules of war. He was found guilty at the Nuremberg trials and executed.

Joseh Mengele — Known as "The Angel of Death," he performed horrible medical experiments on inmates, including children and pregnant women, in Auschwitz. After the war, he lived 35 years in South America. DNA tests on his remains in 1992 confirmed his identity.

Alfred Rosenberg — A propagandist, Rosenberg was responsible for shaping policies and negative views toward Jews. He was found guilty at the Nuremberg trials and executed.

Jews. Reports emerged that he was in the infamous Lubianka prison. In 1957, the Russians announced he had died of natural causes in 1947. Wallenberg sightings in more than a dozen prisons, hospitals and camps continued until 1980.

For his heroic deeds, Wallenberg left behind thousands of grateful Jews. He was awarded honorary citizenship in Canada, Hungary, the United States and Israel. Nine nations have memorials for Wallenberg; in Israel, at least five streets are named after him.

NAZIS FACE JUSTICE

By the end of the war, few Jews remained in Europe. With defeat a certainty, some Nazis slipped away and began living secret lives in other countries. Many were captured, though some like Hermann Göring and Heinrich Himmler committed suicide rather than face justice for their wicked deeds. A series of war trials was held in Allied countries and in Germany.

The most famous of these trials was held in Nuremberg, Germany. Germany's highest officials were tried for violating the laws of war and for

Office of the U.S. Chief of Counsel for the Prosecution of Axis Criminality.

Nazi leaders sit together during the Nuremberg Trials after the end of the war. Some were found not guilty, but the majority were found guilty and executed. On the far left sits Herman Göring.

crimes against humanity, persecution and extermination. Several were acquitted, but most were found guilty. Those convicted of the most reprehensible acts were executed by hanging. During the next decades, many Nazis who had gone into hiding were hunted down and faced justice.

And what about Adolph Eichmann? Wallenberg's nemesis escaped to Argentina, where he began a new life under a false identity working as a supervisor in an automobile factory. In 1960, Israeli special agents located, kidnapped and smuggled Eichmann out of Argentina. He was taken to Israel, where he was faced a lengthy trial that attracted attention worldwide. Convicted of crimes against humanity and the Jewish people, he was sentenced to death by hanging. Eichmann's execution on May 31,1962 remains the only civil execution in Israel. His body was cremated and his ashes spread in the Mediterranean Sea so that no spot would mark his final resting place.

REVIEW QUESTIONS

1. *During the Second World War, Hitler's Nazi German Government killed many _____.*
   a. gypsies
   b. Russian prisoners of war
   c. Poles
   d. All of the above

2. *During the Second World War Hitler's Nazi German Government also killed many _____.*
   a. outspoken church leaders
   b. political opponents
   c. Jews
   d. All of the above

3. *During the Second World War, more than 6 million Jews were systematically murdered by Nazi Germany in what is known as the _____, a Greek word meaning "sacrifice by fire."*

4. The _____ laws passed in 1935 stripped German Jews of their citizenship.

5. At the 1938 Evian Conference only _____ agreed to take in more than a token number of German Jews.
   a. the United States
   b. Great Britain
   c. the Dominican Republic
   d. Australia

6. German Jews older than 10 years were required to wear _____.
   a. a yellow star
   b. a photo identification
   c. a large red "J"
   d. special caps

7. Early efforts to exterminate Jews consisted of _____ _____ that followed victorious Wehrmacht troops into conquered regions.

8. After extermination camps were constructed in Poland, Jews were brought in packed on _____.
   a. airplanes
   b. trucks
   c. freight railroad cars
   d. All of the above

9. Upon arrival at a death camp, most victims were herded into a room and killed by _____.

10. Swedish diplomat Raoul Wallenberg was responsible for saving the lives of about _____ Jews.
    a. 1000
    b. 10,000
    c. 100,000
    d. 1 million

11. Wallenberg used _____ to save Hungarian Jews.
    a. protection passes
    b. bribes
    c. rented buildings
    d. All of the above

12. Hitler's ominous term for the extermination of the Jews, devised by Reinhard Heydrich, was the _____.

13. Wallenberg's primary Nazi nemesis in Hungary was _____.
    a. Adolph Eichmann
    b. Reinhard Heydrich
    c. Heinrich Himmler
    d. Hermann Göring

14. A number of Nazi leaders faced justice for their participation during the Holocaust at the _____ Trials after the war.
    a. Berlin
    b. Nuremberg
    c. Holocaust
    d. Geneva

Chiang Kai-shek

Leader of Chinese Kuomintang Nationalist Party (KMT)
Born: October 31, 1887
Died: April 5, 1975

A portion of the Burma Road ascends a mountain via a series of switchbacks.

While the best-known battles in the Second World War were fought in Europe or on distant Pacific islands, China and its surrounding countries also were important battlefields during the war. China's ability to continually frustrate Japanese imperial ambitions and tie down many divisions in Asia was a contributing factor to the Allied victory in the Pacific Theater.

China's leader during the Second World War, Chiang Kai-shek, was born in 1887 to a salt merchant in Zhejiang Province. He became involved in politics at an early age, joining the *Kuomintang* (or Nationalist) *Party* (KMT) in 1908. He participated in the overthrow of China's last imperial dynasty in 1911-12.

After the end of the First World War, Kai-shek watched as Germany's colony in Shantung province was given to Japan, instead of being returned to China. A great protest arose, out of which the seeds were planted for the beginning of a two-decade long struggle between Kai-shek's Nationalists and Mao Zedong's Communists.

At first, Kai-shek was willing to work with the Communists. He was named chief-of-staff to the Commander of the Nationalist Army in 1922. The next year, Russian Communist soldiers were brought in to train the Nationalist army. Kai-shek spent time in Moscow attempting to advance the training schedule.

After the fall of the imperial dynasty, China fragmented, with competing warlords controlling large portions of the country. In 1925, Kai-shek was able to defeat five area warlords, securing 10 of China's 38 provinces including the important cities of Shanghai and Nanking. In 1928 Kai-shek successfully drove the Communists out of the KMT and into the mountains of northern China. Kai-shek recaptured Beijing and was named chairman of the State Council. He established his capital at Nanking.

KAI-SHEK AND THE NATIONALISTS

World leaders believed that Kai-shek was establishing peace and stability. The reality was that the KMT was a strange mix of warlords, merchants and others held together by corruption, self-interest and terror. While it boasted a 3 million-man, 300-division army on paper, it was a shoddy organization. Among its corrupt practices, officers typically pocketed pay that was due to starving enlisted men. In reality, China could only field about 30 mediocre divisions.

When the Second World War began with the invasion of Poland in 1939, China had already been at war for years. In 1931 Japan, seeking to expand its influence throughout East Asia, seized Manchuria, defeating a warlord loyal to Kai-shek. In 1937, Japan invaded China after staging an incident at the Marco Polo Bridge. Chinese forces resisted bravely but were ineffective. Kai-shek traded

U.S. Army

While meeting in Maymyo, Burma, Generalissimo and Madame Chiang Kai-shek and American General Joseph Stillwell beam on the day after the successful Doolittle raid, April 19, 1942.

land for time by moving his capital deep inland to Chungking.

Japan made a fateful decision in 1941 when it decided to isolate and cutoff China from the outside world. It proved to be an important factor leading to war with the United States, as President Franklin Roosevelt made Japan's withdrawal from China a condition for lifting sanctions. War with Japan might have otherwise been avoided.

CHINA-BURMA-INDIA (CBI) THEATER

The China-Burma-India (CBI) Theater is often overlooked in discussions about the Second World War. However, it was the scene of much struggle as a number of countries had a stake in fighting for the region. Great Britain wanted Burma held, as it was a buffer to its prized colony of India. The Japanese coveted Burma's abundant natural resources. The Americans needed Burma to keep supplies flowing to China. Kai-shek wanted the Allies to fight the Japanese for him so he could keep his forces intact for a showdown with Mao Zedong.

American public support for China was strong. Kai-shek's wife, Madame Chiang Kai-shek, was very popular with American media and did much to smooth over or hide the defects of the Nationalist Chinese. Even before America officially entered the war, President Franklin Roosevelt approved sending pilots to fight the Japanese in China as members of the American Volunteer Group, or as they were better known, the *Flying Tigers*.

FLYING TIGERS

Led by Colonel Claire Lee Chennault, the daredevil Flying Tigers gave the Japanese all they could handle. Their *Curtiss P-40 Warhawk* fighters, painted with large eyes and shark's teeth, were not as fast as Japanese fighters but were sturdy and deadly in competent hands. What they lacked in speed they

A serviceman standing next to a row of "Flying Tigers" P-40's in China waves at a B-25 bomber flying overhead.

made up for in tactics as Chennault taught the men to attack in groups and disengage before the Japanese could respond.

When the United States officially entered the war, the Flying Tigers formed the nucleus of the U.S. 14th Air Force based in China. It is estimated that they scored a better than 3 to 1 kill ratio against the Japanese.

JOSEPH "VINEGAR JOE" STILLWELL

As the Japanese tightened their grip on the Chinese mainland, only one road, the 681-mile-long Burma Road through the mountains and jungles of Burma, allowed Allied supplies to reach Kai-shek's troops. In early 1942 the Japanese invaded Burma, capturing the Burma Road.

Lieutenant General Joseph "Vinegar Joe" Stillwell commanded American and Chinese forces in Burma. Along with the British under Lieutenant General William J. Slim, Stillwell was forced to make a long retreat to India. Many of the Chinese divisions fought poorly. The 55th Division vanished into the hills of Burma when threatened by the Japanese. Lieutenant General Sun Li-jen, a graduate of the Virginia Military Institute, proved to be the most

TRIVIA

Chiang Kai-shek once stated, "Politics makes man lead a dog's life."

capable Chinese general. Leading the 38th Division, he was aggressive and not defensive like other Chinese leaders. He helped save the 1st Burma Division and the 17th Indian Division at Yenangyuang. Slim and Stillwell completed their retreat into India and immediately began to make plans to recapture the land.

After the Japanese conquered Burma, supplies could only be flown to China on a dangerous route originating in India. The route, known as *"the Hump,"* required pilots to navigate over the Himalaya Mountains, often encountering freak weather conditions or enemy fighters. The ***Curtiss-Wright C-46 Commando***, the Hump workhorse, could carry 4 tons, nearly twice that of a ***C-47 Dakota***, and was affectionately nicknamed *"Ol' Dumbo"* after the Disney elephant. Nearly 600 planes were lost, but more than 650,000 tons of supplies reached China over the Hump before the war ended.

The first effort to take back Burma was led by the colorful eccentric, Orde Wingate. The British officer often wore a sloppy uniform and an old pith helmet. In the field, he strained tea with his socks and regularly quoted the Bible and Greek philosophers. Despite his quirks, he was an effective leader. Known as Chindits, after

Orde Wingate

the savage-looking sculpted lions that guarded Burmese temples, Wingate's 3000 British, Gurkha and Burmese soldiers operated deep behind enemy lines, setting up ambushes and disrupting communications. Wingate did not survive the war: On March 24, 1944 he died while a passenger on a ***North American B-25 Liberator*** that crashed near Imphal, India.

In 1943, Lord Louis Mountbatten was placed in command of the CBI Theater. In October, Stillwell launched an offensive to retake northern Burma. His objective was to push the Japanese out of north Burma, reopen the Burma Road and capture the airfield at Myitkyina so that flying over the Hump would no longer be necessary.

Stillwell's Chinese divisions attacked from India into north Burma while Wingate's Chindit units tied down Japanese in central Burma. Meanwhile, the first American unit to reach the Asian mainland went into action. The 5307th Composite Unit (provisional), better known as *Merrill's Marauders*, was created to operate behind enemy lines much like the Chindits.

Frank Merrill

Led by Brigadier General Frank Merrill, few American units would be asked to endure as much as the Marauders.

After much bitter fighting, the Chinese and the Marauders succeeded in pushing back the Japanese 18th Division. As tough as the Japanese were, the greatest enemy was Burma's climate and topography. Rain was common even in the so-called dry season. Rivers swelled and valleys turned into lakes. Disease, large leeches and a variety of stinging and biting insects constantly tortured the soldiers. During one stretch, 14 soldiers were lost to disease and illness for every combat casualty. On May 17, 1944 the coveted Myitkyina air strip was captured. Fighting for the village of Myitkyina continued until late July. The few remaining Japanese finally withdrew.

JAPAN'S GREATEST LAND DEFEAT

The Japanese launched two offensives in 1944. In central Burma, Japanese General Reyna Mutaguchi launched attacks across the Indian border toward the towns of Imphal and Kohima. Unable to bring enough supplies with them, the Japanese counted on capturing food and supplies from Allied forces. Despite early success, the offensive bogged down. Weak-

The Curtiss-Wright C-46 Commando was a high-altitude transport aircraft. It proved very capable in delivering cargo over the Himalaya Mountains in the CBI Theater during the war. More than 3000 of the aircraft were built, with several still in commercial use in the 21st century.

ened by sickness and hunger, the Japanese were repulsed. With 30,000 men killed and 25,000 sick and wounded, it marked Japan's greatest defeat in a land battle.

In conjunction with the Burma offensives, the Japanese had resumed the offensive in China. Many of Chennault's airfields were captured by the Japanese. Despite occupying more land than ever before, Japan was no closer to defeating the ever-elusive Chinese. The frustrated Japanese reluctantly turned their focus to the American threat in the Pacific.

With the Japanese no longer a threat in Burma, Army engineers eventually connected the Burma Road with one from Ledo, India in January 1945. It was a case of too little, too late. American leaders, dismayed with the poor

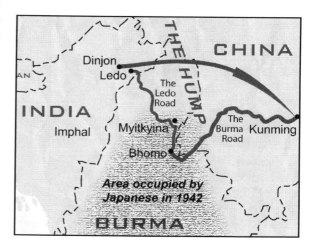

The terrain and climate of the CBI Theater proved treacherous to military efforts as evidenced by these soldiers fording a swift-flowing river that stood between them and Bhamo, Burma.

performance of the Chinese troops, scrapped plans to use China as a large bomber base and gave priority to the island-hopping campaign in the Pacific. Instead of bombing Japan from bases in China, American B-29's would fly out of Saipan, Tinian and Guam in the Mariana Islands. The CBI Theater was irrelevant during the final months of the war.

COMMUNISTS ASSUME POWER

When the war ended, Kai-shek found his government severely weakened and unprepared to reassume Japanese-controlled areas. Kai-shek angered the Chinese people when he requested the Japanese to remain in occupied areas until Kuomintang authority could be established. The Communists, now supported by the Soviet Union, increased their power. In 1949, after mass defections to Mao's cause, Kai-shek and his remaining followers were driven from the Chinese mainland to the island of Formosa (Taiwan).

Kai-shek refused to admit defeat. In 1950, he resumed duties as the President of the Republic of China, claiming all of mainland Chi-

na. During the Cold War period, most western countries recognized Kai-shek's Taiwan as the "Real" China. He supported insurgent efforts on the mainland and even made plans for an invasion in 1962.

Chiang Kai-shek passed away in 1975 from complications suffered from a heart attack and pneumonia. His body was placed in a copper coffin. His wife, Madame Chiang Kai-shek, passed away in 2003. She was buried in a New York cemetery. Today, mainland China and Taiwan continue their tense standoff. It is hoped that one day the political differences will be settled and the Kai-sheks will be buried alongside one another on the mainland.

REVIEW QUESTIONS

1. *During the Second World War, Chiang Kai-shek was the leader of the Chinese _____ party.*
   a. Kuomintang
   b. Communist
   c. Imperial
   d. None of the above

2. For more than 20 years, Chiang Kai-shek fought against _____ Zedong's Communists for control of China.

3. In 1937, Japan invaded China after staging an incident at the _____ Bridge.

4. A 1941 decision by Japan to isolate China ultimately led to _____.
   a. the surrender of China
   b. war against the United States
   c. defeat of the Chinese Communists
   d. intervention by the Soviet Union

5. "CBI" stands for the _____ Theater.

6. Why did Burma play such an important role in the war?
   a. It served as a buffer protecting Great Britain's colony in India.
   b. The Japanese wanted Burma's natural resources.
   c. The United States needed Burma in order to send supplies to China.
   d. All of the above.

7. Colonel Claire Lee Chennault led a group of pilots who fought the Japanese in China, officially called the American Volunteer Group, but were better known as the _____.
   a. Kuomintang Tigers   b. Flying Tigers
   c. Burma Pythons   d. Marauders

8. The American leader of forces in the CBI Theater was _____.
   a. Chester Nimitz
   b. Orde Wingate
   c. Joseph "Vinegar Joe" Stillwell
   d. Douglas MacArthur

9. Chinese troops were generally unreliable because _____.
   a. they were poorly trained and armed
   b. Kai-shek was hesitant to use them
   c. of corrupt and selfish leaders
   d. All of the above

10. After the Japanese captured the Burma Road, supplies could only reach China by cargo planes making a dangerous journey over _____.

11. Orde Wingate was the quirky leader of the _____, operating deep behind enemy lines in Burma.

12. The American 5307th Composite Unit was better known as _____.
    a. the Composite Commandos
    b. Merrill's Marauders
    c. the Burmese Battalion
    d. the Fightin' 5307th

13. The Japanese suffered their greatest land defeat fighting for the village of _____ in 1944.
    a. Myitkyina
    b. Irrawaddy
    c. Rangoon
    d. Mandaly

14. Chiang Kai-shek was driven off the Chinese mainland to the island of _____, known today as Taiwan, by the Communists in 1949.
    a. Borneo
    b. Formosa
    c. Hainan
    d. Luzon

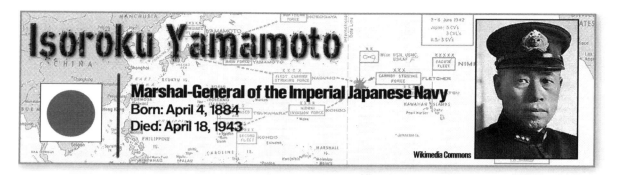

Isoroku Yamamoto

Marshal-General of the Imperial Japanese Navy
Born: April 4, 1884
Died: April 18, 1943

Wikimedia Commons

A young, gifted Japanese naval officer came to the United States in 1919 to study at Harvard University. His charming smile and outgoing personality won many American friends whom he loved to amuse with folk dances and acrobatics such as standing on his head. During one break, he hitchhiked to Mexico. His American friends could scarcely have imagined that he would one day be the architect of one of America's darkest days: Pearl Harbor.

Isoroku Yamamoto was born in 1884, the seventh son in a poor family. His first name is literally "56" — a combination of the numbers *I* (5), *so* (10), and *roku* (6) for his father's age when born. Isoroku could not afford schoolbooks, instead borrowing and carefully copying them. He loved sports and physical activities.

He entered the Japanese Naval Academy at the age of 15 and was onboard the *Nisshin* at the historic Battle of Tsushima in 1904. During the battle, he was knocked unconscious and lost two fingers when a shell hit the ship.

Isoroku, in a practice common for families without heirs, was adopted into the noble Yamamoto family at the age of 30. He rejected marriage offers from several admirals' daughters, and instead married Hiroko, a dairyman's daughter from his home province.

Yamamoto came to the United States for additional education. During his time in America, Yamamoto focused his studies on the American oil industry as it was also a lifeline for Japan. He gained much knowledge about other countries' navies as an admiral's aide on trips through America and Europe.

In 1928, he was made captain of the carrier *Akagi*. He realized before most other officers that aircraft carriers, not battleships, would be the deciding factor in a future naval conflict. The next year he was promoted to Rear Admiral.

PLANNING FOR PEARL HARBOR

Yamamoto was a true patriot, distrustful of the Nazis, and loyal to the Japanese emperor. Though he helped build the *Imperial Japanese Navy* (IJN), he opposed the idea of fighting the United States, stating in 1940 that "Japan cannot beat America."

In January 1941, planning began for war against America. Yamamoto, believing it imperative that the American fleet be destroyed so Japan could have leverage to gain a permanent diplomatic solution with America, Great Britain and the Netherlands, planned an attack on Pearl Harbor. Most Japanese officers

U.S. National Archives

Japanese sailors cheer planes leaving one of the Japanese carriers to attack Pearl Harbor, Hawaii on December 7, 1941.

An aerial photo taken by a Japanese pilot during the Pearl Harbor raid. Note the battleships neatly lined up in "Battleship Row" in the foreground of the photo.

considered the plan too dangerous despite its ultimate approval.

On November 26, the Japanese attack fleet, comprised of six fleet carriers *Akagi, Kaga, Shokaku, Zuikaku, Hiryu* and *Soryu,* two battleships, three cruisers and support ships sailed for Hawaii under strict radio silence. The same day, Secretary of State Cordell Hull rejected the final Japanese diplomatic plan. The Pacific Fleet was issued a "war warning" in anticipation of a Japanese attack. It was expected that the attack would be against the Philippines or somewhere else in the South Pacific, but not against Pearl Harbor.

Japanese leaders believed it was appropriate to officially severe ties before the attack. The Japanese diplomat in Washington D.C. was instructed to deliver a declaration of war to Secretary Hull at 1 p.m. Washington time (7 a.m. Pearl Harbor time), shortly before the raid began. Delays resulted in the message not be-

ing delivered until the attack was under way, heaping insult on the shocked Americans.

Attack on Pearl Harbor

During the hours before the attack, Japanese midget submarines took up positions outside Pearl Harbor and waited for any ships that might try to escape. The destroyer *Ward* sank one sub and another ran aground, its operator being the only Japanese captured that day.

The Japanese fleet took up an attack position 230 miles northwest of Oahu. Carrier support crews roared "Banzai!" as *Mitsubishi A6M "Zero"* fighters, followed by *Nakajima B5N "Kate"* torpedo bombers and *Aichi D3A "Val"* dive bombers, roared off the decks of the carriers. Attack leader Mitsuo Fuchida later said, "I realized my duty as a warrior. Who could be luckier than I?" The planes followed the signal from a Honolulu radio station to their destination. At 7:02 a.m., radar operators detected two

Mitsubishi A6M "Zero"

U.S. Naval Historic Center

The Mitsubishi A6M "Zero" was the best fighter in the Pacific in 1941. While later surpassed by American fighters such as the Grumman F6F Hellcat, the Zero remained in service until the end of the war. The Zero was armed with two 7.7 mm machine guns and two 20 mm cannons and had a maximum speed of 330 mph.

Aichi D3A "Val"

Wikimedia Commons

The Aichi D3A Type 99 "Val" was a two-seat dive bomber capable of carrying a single 550-pound bomb. Vals were responsible for sinking 14 Allied ships, more than any other Axis airplane. On December 7, 1941, Vals attacked both Pearl Harbor and Clark Air Field in the Philippines.

waves of planes approaching Oahu. Reporting their observation to an information center, the lieutenant on duty told them, "Well, don't worry abut it." He thought it was the dozen *Boeing B-17 Flying Fortresses* scheduled to arrive that day.

As Pearl Harbor came into view, Fuchida realized the attack was a total surprise. He radioed the victory signal, *"Tora! Tora! Tora!"* (Tiger! Tiger! Tiger!) to the fleet. As the Japanese planes roared low overhead at 7:55 a.m., many people, enjoying a quiet Sunday morning, took no notice, mistaking them for American planes. As the first bombs and torpedoes began to explode, the realization dawned that Pearl Harbor was under attack.

U.S. Navy

The battleship California settles on the bottom of Pearl Harbor after being hit by Japanese torpedoes and bombs. Smoke pours from the Nevada (LEFT).

Eight battleships were neatly lined up in "Battleship Row." They proved easy targets for the Japanese "Kate" torpedo bombers. Armed with torpedoes specially fitted with wooden fins designed to prevent them from hitting the bottom of the shallow harbor, they began to make their attack runs. The battleship *Oklahoma* was the first hit. The stricken vessel rolled over until only the bottom of the hull was showing, trapping many sailors inside (many were subsequently rescued through holes cut into the hull). The *Nevada* was the only battleship to get under way despite suffering a hit from a torpedo. Harassed by Japanese planes, the captain beached the battleship rather than risk it being sunk and blocking the harbor entrance. The *Utah*, *Pennsylvania*, *Maryland*, *West Virginia* and *Tennessee* were also sunk or heavily damaged.

The *Arizona* was the unluckiest. A great explosion rumbled through the ship, throwing flames 500 feet in the air and knocking dozens of sailors off of nearby ships after a bomb hit her ammunition magazine. The *Arizona* sank so fast she had no time to turn over. The fate of more than 1000 men was sealed in that moment, including Rear Admiral Isaac Kidd, commander of the *Arizona* and the first high-ranking American officer killed in the war.

At nearby Hickam Field, planes parked close together in the middle of the runway to guard against sabotage made for easy targets. As one plane exploded in flames, it would catch its neighbor on fire. The situation was similar at other bases on the island. At Luke Field on Ford Island only one plane managed to get airborne. At Haleiwa, an emergency landing airstrip, two fighters managed to get airborne, accounting for seven of the 29 Japanese planes destroyed that day. The toll of the attack on the Americans was 2403 dead, 1178 wounded, 188 aircraft destroyed, 22 ships damaged or destroyed.

The attack on Pearl Harbor made Yamamoto an overnight celebrity in Japan. Despite the damage caused to the U.S. Pacific Fleet Yamamoto realized that he could only expect to have success against the American fleet for six to 12 months before the economic weight of America would turn the tide.

A recruiting poster appeals to the emotion stirred up in citizens by the attack on Pearl Harbor.

The raid turned out to be a huge strategic mistake. The attack did not cripple the American fleet because all of the battleships, except the *Oklahoma*, *Utah* and *Arizona*, were raised, repaired and placed back on duty. More importantly, the Japanese missed vital targets. Large oil tank farms and repair facilities were left untouched, whose destruction would have pushed the Pacific Fleet back to America's West Coast. Yamamoto was disappointed that the three American carriers were absent from Pearl Harbor at the time of the attack. The carriers would stop Japanese expansion in the upcoming battles in the Coral Sea and at Midway.

Until Pearl Harbor, America had been divided about whether to join the war against the Axis powers. The attack did not demoralize but angered Americans, who resolved to do everything in their power to defeat Germany and Japan. It is no exaggeration to say that despite the apparent success of the raid, Japan lost the war on December 7, 1941.

WAKE ISLAND

Pearl Harbor was not the only location attacked by the Japanese on December 7. An air attack destroyed American bombers in the Philippines. Japanese forces landed in Malaya and Thailand intent on capturing the British colony of Singapore. American forces on Guam, Midway and Wake Islands were also attacked.

Wake Island, a small atoll claimed by the United States in 1899, was uninhabited until 1935. Wake received word of the Pearl Harbor raid shortly before being attacked themselves. Led by Commander Winfield Cunningham, Wake was defended by a dozen *Grumman F4F Wildcats,* 520 marines and army personnel, three 5-inch gun batteries and twelve 3-inch antiaircraft guns.

Thirty-six *Mitsubishi G4M "Betty"* bombers succeeded in destroying seven of the Wildcats on the ground. The Betty pilots believed they

(image caption: ...we here highly resolve that these dead shall not have died in vain... REMEMBER DEC. 7th!)

U.S. Army

had destroyed the Americans, but the damaged runway was quickly repaired and soldiers and civilians prepared to fight. During the next several days, the Japanese continued to bomb the island.

 ## MITSUO FUCHIDA

Isoruko Yamamoto planned the attack on Pearl Harbor, but it was flight commander Mitsuo Fuchida who personally trained the pilots and led the raid. Like Yamamoto, Fuchida became a national hero for his warrior deeds on that fateful day.

During the Battle of Midway, Fuchida broke both ankles while descending a rope from a burning tower onboard the carrier Akagi. His injury was kept secret from the Japanese people. Upon his return to Japan, he was taken to a hospital after dark and ushered through a rear entrance. He later commented that he felt like a prisoner in his own country. He served on the IJN staff for the rest of the war.

Fuchida was present at Hiroshima the day before the atomic bomb was dropped but was called away to Tokyo. After the war, Fuchida took up farming. However, he could not get the painful images of war out of his head. When he visited a friend who was a prisoner of war in the Philippines, Fuchida was amazed to hear him tell of a Christian lady who lovingly cared for the prisoners despite Japanese soldiers having killed her missionary parents. One day in Tokyo, he was given a Christian pamphlet written by a survivor of the Doolittle raid who had become a Christian while a Japanese captive. Fuchida soon purchased a Bible and in 1949 became a Christian.

Fuchida became a minister and traveled and preached the Gospel to audiences around the world. In 1960, he became an American citizen. He wrote a book entitled "No More Pearl Harbors." After his conversion, he said, "I can say today without hesitation that God's grace has been set upon me."

On December 11, the invasion fleet arrived. The fleet included three light cruisers, six destroyers and two transports. The Americans held their fire, luring the Japanese ships closer to shore. When the American 5-inch guns opened fire, they proved very effective. The cruiser *Yubari* limped away after sustaining three hits. The destroyer *Hayate* sank after its ammunition magazine was hit. Captain Henry Elrod, piloting one of the remaining Wildcats, bombed and sank the destroyer *Kisaragi*. Having lost 500 men, the Japanese turned away without attempting to land troops. Only one marine was killed.

Henry Elrod

The Wake defenders expected reinforcements to arrive at any moment. Relief never came. Japanese carrier planes resumed bombing on December 20, and the island's defenses began to deteriorate.

A much larger fleet, including two aircraft carriers, *Soryu* and *Hiryu*, appeared off the coast of Wake on December 23. The transports carried 2000 troops instead of the 450 sent on the first attempt. The Japanese marines landed under the cover of darkness. After an eleven-hour struggle, American resistance ended, but 122 Americans died. The heroic stand at Wake Island, often called "the Alamo of the Pacific," offered a glimpse of hope in the first days of the war for the United States.

DISASTER AT MIDWAY

After Jimmy Doolittle's raid proved that mainland Japan was vulnerable to bombing, Yamamoto sought to extend Japan's defensive perimeter by invading the Pacific island of Midway. Yamamoto also hoped that the invasion would draw out the American fleet for a decisive sea battle.

The Nakajima B5N2 Type 97 "Kate" was a three-seat torpedo bomber with a maximum speed of 235 mph. In addition to sinking a number of battleships at Pearl Harbor, Kates later played a role in sinking the aircraft carriers Yorktown, Hornet and Lexington.

Unknown to him, the Americans intercepted the Midway battle plans. Three American carriers, including two Yamamoto believed had been sunk during the Battle of the Coral Sea, set a trap. The balance of naval power in the Pacific shifted, as the Japanese lost four irreplaceable carriers and hundreds of experienced pilots while sinking just one American carrier.

Though clearly a great strategist, Yamamoto is often criticized for not destroying the American carrier fleet early in the war. He also missed opportunities to destroy Allied merchant ships in the Pacific and Indian Ocean that would have cut off communications to India, Australia and even Hawaii.

In the summer of 1942, Yamamoto used his fleet to support Japanese Army efforts on the island of Guadalcanal. The IJN inflicted heavy losses on the American fleet, but after three Japanese carriers were damaged in the Battle of Santa Cruz, Yamamoto never used them again in close support. The carriers did not go back into action until much later at the Battle of Leyte Gulf.

DEATH OF A NATIONAL HERO

After the Japanese defeat on Guadalcanal, Yamamoto organized a South Pacific inspection trip designed to boost wavering morale. U.S.

Navy Secretary Frank Knox and "Hap" Arnold, Chief of the Army Air Force, informed by intelligence of Yamamoto's movements, worked up a plan to ambush him.

Sixteen *Lockheed P-38 Lightnings* fitted with extra fuel tanks were launched from Henderson Field on Guadalcanal. The P-38's intercepted Yamamoto's two "Betty" bombers on their way to Bougainville, overwhelming six Zero escorts. Yamamoto's damaged plane crashed in a jungle area. His body was recovered and cremated by Japanese troops and then transported back to Japan.

In America, news of Yamamoto's death was suppressed so that the Japanese could not discern that their codes had been broken. It was a month before the Japanese people were told of his death. The announcer who reported the news on Tokyo radio broke down and wept while on air. The Japanese believed Yamamoto became a *kami* (a god) as a result of his heroic death. The grieving nation honored him with only the 12th state funeral in Japanese history; 650,000 mourners filed past his remains. Half of his ashes were interred at a cemetery outside Tokyo and the other half outside his home in Nagaoka.

REVIEW QUESTIONS

1. Isoroku Yamamoto's first name is literal Japanese for _____.
   a. 56
   b. flowing river
   c. 100
   d. green dragon

2. As a young officer, Yamamoto studied for a time in _____.
   a. China
   b. Canada
   c. the United States
   d. Great Britain

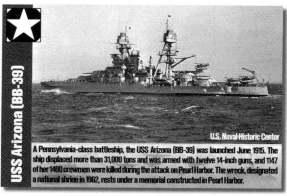

USS Arizona (BB-39)

U.S. Naval Historic Center

A Pennsylvania-class battleship, the USS Arizona (BB-39) was launched June 1915. The ship displaced more than 31,000 tons and was armed with twelve 14-inch guns, and 1147 of her 1400 crewmen were killed during the attack on Pearl Harbor. The wreck, designated a national shrine in 1962, rests under a memorial constructed in Pearl Harbor.

3. Yamamoto _____ the idea of fighting the United States.

4. The goal of the attack on Pearl Harbor was _____.
   a. to invade Hawaii.
   b. to crush the Pacific Fleet.
   c. to neutralize the island for an attack on the West Coast.
   d. to draw America into a long, costly war.

5. Which Imperial Japanese Navy aircraft carrier did not participate in the attack on Pearl Harbor?
   a. Shokaku
   b. Akagi
   c. Zuikaku
   d. Unryu

6. Japanese _____ submarines made an unsuccessful attack on Pearl Harbor.

7. Which Japanese plane did not take part in the attack on Pearl Harbor?
   a. Mitsubishi A6M "Zero" fighters
   b. Nakajima B5N "Kate" torpedo bombers
   c. Mitsubishi B5M "Mabel" bomber
   d. Aichi D3A "Val" dive bombers

8. The flight leader of the Japanese attack on Pearl Harbor was _____.

9. The message transmitted to the Japanese fleet indicating that the Pearl Harbor attack was a total surprise was _____.
   a. Tiger! Tiger! Tiger!
   b. Long live the Emperor!
   c. Banzai!
   d. Dragon! Dragon! Dragon!

10. More than 1000 sailors died onboard the USS _____ when she was hit by a Japanese bomb and exploded.

11. Which vital target did the Japanese miss during their attack on Pearl Harbor?
    a. Oil tanks
    b. American carriers
    c. Repair facilities
    d. All of the above

12. Within hours of the attack on Pearl Harbor, a Japanese attack destroyed bombers at Clark Air Base in the _____ islands.

13. On December 11, 1941, 520 marines and army personnel on _____ Island repelled a formidable Japanese invasion fleet. The Japanese captured the island two weeks later.
    a. Guam
    b. Wake
    c. Singapore
    d. Midway

14. How did Yamamoto die?
    a. *Seppuku* (death by disembowelment)
    b. Shot down while piloting a fighter plane
    c. Drowned when his flagship was sunk
    d. Ambushed by American fighters while traveling on a bomber

Franklin Roosevelt

32nd President of the United States
Commander in chief U.S. armed forces
Born: January 30, 1882
Died: April 12, 1945

Wikimedia Commons

When Germany invaded Poland in 1939, it was not a foregone conclusion that America would join the battle against the Axis powers. When France fell in June 1940, only Great Britain stood between Hitler and total European domination. In that time of uncertainty, American President Franklin Delano Roosevelt began to quietly prepare his country for a war he knew was inevitable. His resolve and foresight helped forge an unlikely alliance and paved the way for post-war peace.

Roosevelt, the son of a wealthy industrialist, was born in 1882. As an only child, he received much attention from both parents. At a young age, he showed a knack for learning quickly and putting what he learned to use. As a youngster, he traveled to Europe with his parents nearly ever summer. He enjoyed birdwatching, photography, stamp collecting, forestry and sailing. A good sailor, he desired to one day command a battleship.

Franklin set it as his goal to become President one day, just like his cousin Theodore Roosevelt. While attending Harvard University, Roosevelt became editor of *The Harvard Crimson*. He took his first step into politics in 1910 when he, a Democrat, won a New York Senate seat that had been held by Republicans for 50 years. Roosevelt loved a good political fight but was willing to go around people when necessary.

During the First World War, Roosevelt served as the Assistant Secretary of the Navy. He fought for a strong, two-ocean navy, able to meet any challenge from the Japanese or the Germans. He devised a plan to mine the English Channel that succeeded in destroying seven U-boats. He also made a visit to the dangerous frontline in France.

His goal of becoming President appeared to be close when he was chosen as the vice-presidential candidate on the 1920 ticket with James Cox. They were defeated soundly by Republican Warren G. Harding. Roosevelt was stricken with polio in August 1921. He refused to accept that his paralysis from the waist down was permanent and worked through the years to try and strengthen his legs. He purchased and upgraded "Warm Springs," a resort in Georgia where he and

Defense Imagery Management Operations Center

Wearing identification tags, members of a Japanese American family await transfer to a "War Relocation Camp." About 110,000 Japanese Americans, the majority American citizens, were relocated against their will during the war. In 1988, the United States government apologized for the shameful treatment of the Japanese Americans.

other polio patients rehabilitated. Roosevelt was careful not to let knowledge of his polio become public. Few Americans knew their President was in a wheelchair.

Roosevelt was elected governor of New York in 1928 despite a poor showing nationally from Democrats. The American economy crashed in 1929, and the Great Depression began. Roosevelt, promising a "New Deal" for Americans, was elected President in a landslide in 1932. He was inaugurated on March 4, 1933, the day before the Nazis were elected to a majority in Germany.

As part of his "New Deal," Roosevelt created agencies such as the *Civilian Conservation Corps* (CCC), the *Works Progress Administration* (WPA) and the *National Youth Administration* (NYA) that put millions of unemployed back to work. He also created a national insurance program known as *Social Security*. Roosevelt's efforts were successful in pulling America out of the Great Depression. However, critics claimed the cost was too high; they believed that Roosevelt had been given too much power.

WAR THREATENS AMERICA

As the economic situation improved in America, the threat of war loomed over Europe and Asia. In 1937, the Japanese invaded America's ally China. In Germany, Jews were being stripped of all their rights. In a 1937 speech, Roosevelt warned Americans that "the peace, the freedom, and the security of ninety percent of the population is being jeopardized by the remaining 10 percent who are threatening a breakdown of all international law and order." The reaction to the speech was negative, reinforcing the position of isolationists. Roosevelt's ability to assist allies was further restricted by neutrality laws passed in the mid 1930's to prevent the use of American ships to supply weapons to any warring nation.

Measured in ground strength, America's army was only the world's 20th largest. Roosevelt petitioned Congress to build up the military, asking for $2 billion for defense in 1939. Many Americans took an "America First" stance, wanting nothing to do with what they viewed as a solely European war. Promising not to send

Women workers prepare nose cones for Douglas A-20 Havoc aircraft at a factory in California. America's concerted industrial effort was a major factor in the Allied victory.
Defense Imagery Management Operations Center

Americans into a "foreign war," Roosevelt became the only President to be re-elected to a third term. Roosevelt sensed war was inevitable, but he believed that if America was attacked he would be released from his promise as it would no longer qualify as a "foreign war."

With the fall of France and the apparently imminent fall of Great Britain, Americans began to worry. Columnist Walter Lippmann summed up the feeling, "The American people now know that if the Allies begin to fail, there will come into being an allegiance of aggressive powers — Nazi Germany, fascist Italy, Soviet Russia and imperialist Japan — which the United States alone is incapable of dealing with." Roosevelt found ways around the *Neutrality Act*, sending hundreds of planes to Great Britain. He also brokered a deal in which 50 aging destroyers were traded for British bases in Bermuda, Newfoundland and the Caribbean.

On March 27, 1941, the *Lend-Lease Law* was signed. The law permitted the President to sell weapons to any ally in need. Roosevelt said "the end of compromise with tyranny" had come. America became the "Arsenal of Democracy" as thousands of tanks, planes and trucks shipped to Great Britain, China and the Soviet Union.

The Atlantic Charter

On August 9, 1941, Roosevelt had his first of many wartime meetings with British Prime Minister Winston Churchill. The two met secretly for the Atlantic Conference in Placentia Bay in Argentia, New Foundland. Roosevelt arrived on the heavy cruiser *Augusta*, while Churchill traveled on battleship *Prince of Wales*. Churchill desperately wanted America to join the war. Roosevelt wanted to help more but could not fully commit at the time.

One result of the meeting was the historic *Atlantic Charter*. The Charter set principles for how the two would wage war and afterwards protect the peace. The Allies would not create

Naval History & Heritage Command

President Franklin Roosevelt and Prime Minister Winston Churchill meet onboard the British battleship Prince of Wales during the Atlantic Conference in 1941.

new territories or territorial changes without consent of the people. Free trade, economic development and, most importantly, self determination for liberated countries were all part of the Charter. On the final day of the conference, a Sunday, sailors from both nations gathered on *Prince of Wales* for a worship service. Hymns were sung as planes roared overhead.

America Goes to War

In October, the destroyer *Kearney* was torpedoed near Iceland while on convoy duty. The 11 men killed were the first American military casualties of the war. Along with the rest of America, Roosevelt was devastated by news of the attack on Pearl Harbor. The day after the attack, Roosevelt addressed the nation, "Yesterday, December 7, 1941 — a date which will live in infamy — the United States of America was suddenly and deliberately attacked by naval and air forces of the Empire of Japan." Roosevelt asked for and was granted a declaration of war by Congress against all Axis powers.

Choosing a course of action against Germany was not easy. Churchill wanted attacks in the Mediterranean Theater in order to knock

Defense Imagery Management Operations Center

President Franklin Roosevelt signs the declaration of war against Japan on December 8, 1941.

Jews and other civilians from the Nazi terror. Roosevelt was instrumental in the creation of the *War Refugee Board* (WRB) in early 1944. It has been estimated that 250,000 Jews were saved through the efforts of the WRB.

Despite declining health, Roosevelt ran for re-election in 1944 and won an unduplicated fourth term. In February 1945, he traveled to Yalta, on the Russian Crimean peninsula, to meet with Churchill and Josef Stalin. It was to be his last international journey.

Upon his return to the United States, Roosevelt began preparations for the first meeting of the United Nations in May. On April 12, while working at his desk, Roosevelt complained of a sharp pain in his neck just before collapsing unconscious. He died several hours later. He was mourned by all Americans and buried on his family estate at Hyde Park. Harry Truman became president. The war in Europe ended less than a month later.

ARSENAL OF DEMOCRACY

An army cannot win a war with men alone. A nation that can acquire raw materials and manufacture them into useful weapons, tools and ev-

out Italy and eventually attack Germany through the Balkans. Roosevelt's military advisors, led by George Marshall, preferred a head-on attack through northwestern Europe. Roosevelt successfully pushed for *Operation Torch*, an invasion of Africa. The move proved a wise choice because in hindsight America was not properly prepared in 1942 to invade Europe.

With the Germans and Italians reeling in Africa, Roosevelt met with Churchill in Casablanca, Algiers in January 1943. Though the Russians were demanding a second front in Europe, the Allies decided against an invasion of France in 1943. They instead opted for invasions of Sicily and Italy. Churchill and Roosevelt reached a critical decision when they decided to accept nothing less than unconditional surrender from Axis powers.

Roosevelt, along with other Allied leaders, was criticized for not doing more to protect

AMERICAN MILITARY PRODUCTION	
American weapons produced during the war	
Aircraft	324,750
Tanks	88,410
Aircraft Carriers	22
Escort Carriers	141
Battleships	8
Cruisers	48
Destroyers	349
Escort ships	420
Submarines	203
Source: Campaigns of World War II Day by Day, Bishop & McNab	

eryday necessities will have a decided advantage. Roosevelt's skillfulness in tapping the American ability to vastly outproduce her enemies might well have been the decisive factor in winning the war.

Roosevelt had the foresight in 1939 to set in motion an *Industrial Mobilization Plan* (IMP) to jumpstart production. In 1940, American industry only produced 331 tanks, but just four years later 29,497 were produced. By 1943, America was producing twice as many weapons as all her enemies combined.

Once weapons have been built and armies trained, logistics becomes all important. The ability to move men and supplies, and keep them supplied, is vital to the success of any military mission. One of the great accomplishments of the war, and of the Industrial Age, was the construction of Liberty Ships. Roosevelt described Liberty ships as "a bridge across the Atlantic." The cargo ships constructed in American shipyards kept Allied troops supplied in all theaters. Another American innovation was the Higgins Boat, a flat-bottomed vessel inspired by boats used in swamps and marshes. More than 20,000 Higgins boats built by Andrew Higgins of Louisiana were used to land troops on enemy-held shores.

War ration books belonging to the Black family of South Carolina.

Civilians on the home front made many sacrifices to support the war effort. Food was rationed and scrap metal drives common. Everyday items such as sugar and gasoline became scarce. Victory gardens were planted in yards and public parks to reduce pressure on the food supply. More than 8 million women found jobs, most of which had been held by men who joined the military.

Hollywood stars encouraged Americans to buy $135 billion in War bonds. Even cartoon characters contributed to the war effort, as Jerry Mouse (Tom & Jerry) and Bugs Bunny courageously battled and defeated stylized versions of Hitler and the Axis forces. Each Disney cartoon during the war started with a headshot of Mickey Mouse, Donald Duck or Goofy wearing a Navy or Army cap.

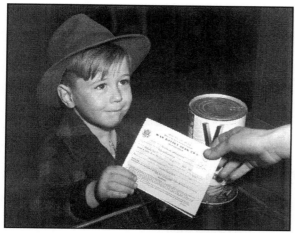

Defense Imagery Management Operations Center

A young boy exchanges stamps from his family's War Ration Book for goods. Many everyday items such as sugar and gasoline were rationed during the Second World War.

REVIEW QUESTIONS

1. Franklin Roosevelt's cousin _____ was the 26th President of the United States.

2. Franklin Roosevelt served as _____ during the First World War.
   a. President of the United States
   b. Captain of the battleship Texas
   c. Secretary of War
   d. Assistant Secretary of the Navy

3. In 1921, Franklin Roosevelt was stricken with _____, paralyzing him from the waist down.

4. Which program was NOT part of President Roosevelt's "New Deal"?
   a. Civilian Conservation Corps
   b. War Refugee Board
   c. Works Progress Administration
   d. National Youth Administration

5. The passage of _____ laws hindered President Roosevelt's ability to aid allied nations before America entered the Second World War.

6. Citizens who wished to keep America out of the war were known as _____.

7. The signing of the _____ Law in 1941 allowed America to freely supply allied nations with weapons.
   a. American Arms
   b. Lend-Lease
   c. Allied Aid
   d. Weapon Freedom

8. In August 1941, Roosevelt had his first of many wartime meetings with British Prime Minister Winston Churchill. Taking place in Placentia Bay in Argentia, New Foundland, the main accomplishment of the meeting was the _____.
   a. agreement to sell destroyers to Great Britain
   b. American entry into the war
   c. Atlantic Charter
   d. planning of Operation Overlord

9. Urged by President Roosevelt's famous "Day of infamy" speech, the United States entered the Second World War on _____.
   a. September 1, 1939
   b. June 20, 1940
   c. December 8, 1941
   d. June 4, 1944

10. In 1944, Roosevelt became the only person to win a _____ term as President of the United States.
    a. third
    b. fourth
    c. fifth
    d. sixth

11. In 1940, America only produced 331 tanks. In 1944, more than _____ were built.
    a. 900
    b. 9000
    c. 19,000
    d. 29,000

Hideki Tojo

General, Imperial Japanese Army
Prime Minister of Japan
Born: December 30, 1884
Died: December 23, 1948

Wikimedia Commons

The course of Japanese history changed dramatically one day in 1853 when several sleek black ships led by American Commodore Matthew Perry entered Edo (Tokyo) Bay. Until that fateful day, Japan had virtually isolated itself from world. The Americans' demand for a trade relationship forced Japan into the modern age. The alternative was to submit to colonial occupation like other Asian nations. Japan embraced the challenge and embarked on a great campaign to educate and industrialize its nation.

Japan's future leader, Hideki Tojo, was born in Tokyo on December 30, 1884. The grandson of a samurai, Tojo was a skinny, short-sighted and average student who was opinionated, stubborn and loved to pick fights. Believing strongly in the power of the will, he turned to hard work to make it through military prep school.

While Tojo was still in school in 1904-05, Japan was fighting Russia for control of Korea. At the Battle of Tsushima, Admiral Togo Heihachir defeated the Russian Baltic Fleet, proving that Japan truly belonged among the military and industrial world elite.

In 1919, Tojo served in Switzerland and Germany as a military attaché. He admired how the German people endured hardship after the First World War. In 1922, while crossing the United States on his way back home from Europe, Tojo judged Americans to be lacking a spiritual strength and dedicated only to material pursuits. Tojo was given his first command in 1928.

JAPAN AND CHINA

The Great Depression caused great hardships for the Japanese. With famine and hunger widespread, the Japanese began to look to Asia for resources. In 1931, Japan launched an attack on China, conquering Manchuria, which they renamed *Manchukuo* (Land of the Manchus) and made an independent state under Japanese protection.

In 1935, Tojo was promoted to Major General and sent to Manchuria as head of military forces. He established a secret police similar to Germany's. In 1936, Japan took a big step toward becoming a member of the Axis by signing the Anti-Comintern pact with Nazi Germany in which each side agreed not to negotiate with the Soviet Union.

Japan launched an offensive in 1937 intended to conquer all of China. Tojo led a successful thrust deep into China securing the whole of Inner Mongolia. The sheer size of the country proved problematic as Chinese Nationalist leader Chiang Kai-Shek ceded most of the

The Japanese heavy cruiser Haguro participated in the Battle of the Java Sea, helping sink the British cruiser Exeter and Dutch cruiser De Ruyter. The Haguro was one of four Myoko-class cruisers, the most heavily armed cruisers in the world when launched in the 1920's.

U.S. Navy

Hideki Tojo and his cabinet pose for a photograph after their first meeting in 1941.

coastal lands while sheltering his government deep in China's interior.

While the Japanese people believed the emperor, Hirohito, was divine, he had little influence over the Imperial Japanese Army. A typical Japanese general was loyal to the Emperor, but more specifically to the Army. Under Japanese Army leadership, the Chinese occupation was often brutal. In a society that valued warriors over all else, compassion was seen as a weakness. In the 1937 Rape of Nanking, an estimated 40,000 Chinese were slaughtered as men

were used for bayonet practice or buried alive and women mutilated and violated.

Many Japanese resented Western exploitation of East Asia. Tojo became a leading supporter of the Japanese concept of a *Greater East Asia Co-Prosperity Sphere* in which it was believed that Japan was destined to assume her rightful place as ruler of all East Asia. The Japanese defended their expansion as an act of self-defense against Western influence and Communism. Tojo truly believed that all the people of Asia would prosper under Japanese control.

Prime Minister

Westerners remember Tojo as a bloodthirsty samurai. Vilified in the same vein as Hitler and Mussolini, Tojo's bald head, mustache and distinctive spectacles were lampooned in many cartoons. In reality, he was merely the representative leader of the military circle in charge of Japan. Because Japanese decision making required consensus, all important decisions were determined in military circles.

The Japanese revered him because he embodied their ideals of hard work, loyalty and dedication to country. He would ride out on horseback each morning to oversee war efforts.

As France and Great Britain struggled against Germany in the early stages of the war, their East Asian colonies opened to easy conquest. In July 1941, the Japanese took over French Indochina. Appalled by Japan's brash action, trade embargoes were announced by the United States, Great Britain and Holland. On August 1, the United States halted all oil shipments to Japan.

For a nation with no natural oil resources, the embargo all but ensured a war between Japan and the United States. Tojo understood that Japan could not conquer the United States

HMS Prince of Wales

The Prince of Wales was a 43,000-ton Royal Navy battleship launched in 1939. Though sunk less than three years after launch, the Prince of Wales played a pivotal role in the hunt for the German battleship Bismarck and transported British Prime Minister Winston Churchill to the Atlantic Charter meeting.

but thought that quick, decisive action would demoralize Americans and result in a favorable treaty. Named prime minister of Japan on October 17, 1941, one of Tojo's first decisions was to approve Admiral Isoroku Yamamoto's plan to attack Pearl Harbor.

SINGAPORE

In sync with the attack on Pearl Harbor, Japan moved aggressively to grab British and Dutch colonies in southeast Asia. Lt. General Tomoyuki "Tiger of Malaya" Yamashita, commanding the 25th Army, launched an offensive to capture Singapore. The Japanese occupied Thailand and began to work their

Tomoyuki Yamashita

way down the Malayan peninsula toward Singapore. A task force, *Force Z*, led by the British battleship *Prince of Wales* and battlecruiser *Repulse* steamed north to intercept and destroy the invasion force. With no protective air cover to interfere, Imperial Japanese Navy (IJN) bombers swarmed the battlewagons. Both ships were hit numerous times and sunk. Only four Japanese planes were lost in the attack. The loss, along with news of the capture of Hong King on Christmas Day, shocked the people of Great Britain.

Dutch East Indies 1942

SUMATRA
BORNEO
• Palembang
Battle of **JAVA SEA**
Sunda Strait
Battle of the Java Sea
SUNDA STRAIT
JAVA
INDIAN OCEAN

The Houston (CA-30) was a Northampton-class heavy cruiser. The ship was a favorite of President Franklin Roosevelt, carrying him on a 14,000-mile journey in 1934. The 368 of her 1061 crew who survived her sinking during the Battle of the Java Sea spent the rest of the war in Japanese POW camps.

Singapore was a fortress and the jewel of Great Britain's East Asian possessions. A mix of Commonwealth forces, including British, Indian and Australian troops, could not stop the Japanese advance. Under the cover of heavy artillery fire, thousands of Japanese landed on the shores of Singapore on February 8, 1942. A week later, Singapore surrendered. The entire campaign took only 70 days, less than the 100 predicted by Yamashita.

JAVA SEA

The day before Singapore surrendered, 700 Japanese paratroopers landed in the Dutch East Indies. Citizens of Palembang on Sumatra worked to destroy oil fields, storage tanks and refineries even as a Japanese division came ashore. The island was soon subdued, but it was months before the Japanese were able to get the precious oil flowing once again. Only the island of Java remained under Dutch control.

The Allies decided to make a concerted effort to deny Java to the Japanese. Dutch

EMPEROR HIROHITO

Japanese Emperor Hirohito, head of the Shinto religion and believed to be the 124th in an unbroken line of emperors dating back more than 2000 years, was born in 1901. Per custom, he was taken from his parents at the age of 10 weeks and subsequently raised by custodians and tutors. At age

12, he alarmed teachers when he disputed whether he truly was a descendant of the sun goddess. He was taught that the Japanese people needed to believe he was divine and not to involve himself in the affairs of the world.

He enjoyed the study of science and collecting biological specimens, publishing several scholarly articles. He also enjoyed poetry and western sports, such as tennis. The young crown prince left the restrictive confines of Japan to visit Great Britain in 1921. The freedom he experienced in England led him to describe the trip as the happiest time of his life.

A shy, quiet man, he never forcefully spoke out against his advisers during the war despite having doubts. The easy, early days of war concerned him: "The fruits of war are tumbling into our mouths almost too quickly." When much of the Royal Palace was destroyed by fire after an Allied bombing raid, Hirohito expressed relief to finally share in Japanese suffering.

Hirohito was overwhelmed by grief upon hearing news of the destruction of Hiroshima. Meeting in a cramped room inside an air raid shelter, Hirohito asked the Japanese government to surrender: "I cannot bear to see my innocent people suffer any longer. Ending the war is the only way to restore world peace and to relieve the nation from the dreadful distress with which it is burdened." On August 15, 1945, Hirohito announced the Japanese surrender on radio. For most of the crestfallen Japanese, it was the first time they had heard his voice. Douglas MacArthur, meeting Hirohito after the war, was impressed, calling him "the First Gentleman of Japan in his own right."

Rear Admiral Karel Doorman led a coalition of American, British, Dutch and Australian ships to intercept the Japanese invasion fleet. The task force was comprised of the heavy cruisers *USS Houston* and *HMS Exeter*, Dutch light cruisers *De Ruyter* and *Java*, Australian light cruiser *Perth* and nine destroyers (three British, two Dutch and four American). Led by Admiral Takeo Takagi, the Japanese invasion force included the heavy cruisers *Nachi* and *Haguro*, light cruisers *Naka* and *Jintsu* and 14 destroyers.

The two forces first engaged on February 27, 1942. The *Exeter* was heavily damaged and destroyers *Kortenser* and *Electra* sunk while the Japanese ships suffered little damage. After dark, the Japanese cruisers moved in on Doorman's fleet. Deadly Long-Lance torpedoes hit the *Java* and *De Ruyter* almost simultaneously. Doorman, along with many Dutch sailors, went down with the doomed ships.

The next evening, attempting to escape through the Sunda Strait, the *Houston* and *Perth* stumbled across Japanese transports unloading near Batavia (Jakarta). Surrounded by overwhelming forces, the *Perth* sank after being hit by four torpedoes. The *Houston*, known as "The Galloping Ghost of the Java Coast" after numerous rumors of her having been sunk continued the struggle alone before succumbing to numerous hits. The *Exeter* and her two destroyer escorts were found and sunk later that day by four Japanese cruisers. Having lost 10 warships without sinking any Japanese, the few remaining Allied ships retreated to Australia. On March 9, the Dutch surrendered the East Indies to Japan.

THE LONG JOURNEY TO DEFEAT

Having won a vast empire in a short period of time, Tojo turned his attention to securing Japan's new possessions. The Japanese found it difficult to exploit the natural resources they had long coveted. With so many men serving in the armed forces, it was difficult to find technical expertise. The great expanses of the Pacific Ocean made it difficult to transport resources to Japan, and as the Japanese never adopted the convoy system, American submarines routinely mauled cargo ships.

Though Tojo and other leaders may have had the best of intentions, natives of Japanese-occupied lands soon realized their "liberators" were actually tyrants. The rapidity of the conquests caught the victors with a shortage of able administrators. Those put in charge were ignorant of native customs and traditions and forced Japanese ways on the people while removing all Western influences. Treatment at the 300 Japanese prisoner-of-war camps varied greatly; some prisoners were treated relatively well, while famine and cruelty was the norm at others.

During the war Tojo juggled a number of high posts including War Minister, Foreign Minister, Home Minister, Minister of Education and Minister of Commerce and Industry. He also took on the role of Munitions Minister in an effort to end bickering between the Army and Navy. When Japan was defeated at the critical Battle of Midway, Tojo covered it up by saying, "Japan is prepared to fight for a hundred years until victory is won and our enemies crushed."

Food became scarce in 1943, as imports dwindled and farm workers were pulled for military service and war production. A lack of fertilizer and bad weather further hindered matters. Many weapons broke down before ever seeing combat because Army officers with no specialized knowledge were put in charge of factories and skilled technicians were drafted into the army.

TRIVIA

The American destroyer *Stewart* was captured by the Japanese at Tjilatjap in the Dutch East Indies. The Japanese refitted the destroyer as *Patrol Boat No. 102*. She was the only American surface ship seized and used in active service by Axis forces during the war.

In 1944, as losses began to mount, a small group of elder statesmen began to seek a way to negotiate an end to the war. Their first goal was to remove Tojo. The men quietly began to win cabinet members to their side. Realizing he no longer had any support, and at the request of the emperor, Tojo stepped down as Prime Minister on July 18, 1944. He continued to wield influence through his Army commanders.

Many Japanese, including the emperor, wanted out of the war. However, the Allies' insistence on unconditional surrender made the Japanese fear that surrender would mean the end of the emperor. As the IJN had essentially ceased to exist, the Army prepared to defend the Japanese home islands, teaching women and children to fight with sharpened bamboo sticks.

In August 1945, atomic bombs leveled Hiroshima and Nagasaki. While the Japanese cabinet argued over how to respond, Emperor Hirohito asserted himself, ordering that the Allied demand for unconditional surrender be met. His quick action made certain that factions that might seek to overthrow him did not have time to do so.

Dispirited by defeat, Tojo prepared to commit suicide. He convinced a doctor to mark the spot on his chest where his heart was so he would not miss. On September 11, 1945, as American troops broke into his home, he shot himself. Despite his preparations, the attempt failed as an American doctor saved him.

Tojo was charged with crimes against peace and humanity as he had done nothing to order the military to observe international conventions for the treatment of prisoners

Grumman TBM Avengers and Curtiss SBC2 Helldivers from the carrier Essex drop bombs on Hokadate, Japan in July 1945. Future American President George H. Bush was an Avenger pilot onboard the carrier San Jacinto during the war.

and occupied peoples. Tojo knew of atrocities, but in keeping with Japanese military tradition believed officers should be given wide discretion in every situation. His testimony was contradicted by his orders to make sure every prisoner worked, even if ill-nourished or sick. Sixteen Japanese generals were given life imprisonment at the Tokyo war crime trials. Tojo, along with General Yamashita, Masaharu Homma and Iwani Matsui, were given the death sentence.

Tojo was executed by hanging in 1948. The greatest fear of the Japanese never happened — while American General Douglas MacArthur led the effort to rebuild Japan's government, emperor Hirohito was spared. He continued to serve in a mostly ceremonial capacity as emperor until his death in 1989.

REVIEW QUESTIONS

1. *Japan proved it could compete as a world power after it defeated _____ in 1904-05.*
   a. Great Britain
   b. China
   c. Russia
   d. the Philippines

2. *In a bid to gain access to more natural resources, Japan invaded Manchuria, a region of _____ in 1931.*

3. *Hideki Tojo was a strong supporter of the _____.*
   a. Greater East Asia Co-Prosperity Sphere
   b. Imperial Empire Expansion Plan
   c. isolation policy of Japan
   d. Japan-China Mutual Benefit Program

4. In late 1941, Lt. General Tomoyuki "Tiger of Malaya" Yamashita successfully led Japanese troops on an expedition to capture the British stronghold of _____.

5. The British battleship Prince of Wales and battlecruiser Repulse were sunk by _____.
   a. the battleship Yamato
   b. Japanese planes
   c. Long-Lance torpedoes
   d. none of the above

6. The Japanese invaded the Dutch East Indies to gain much-needed _____ supplies.

7. An Allied task force of American, British, Dutch and Australian ships that attempted to stop the Japanese invasion of the Dutch East Indies was led by Dutch Admiral _____.
   a. Lodewjik van Bylandt
   b. Conrad Emil Lambert Helfrich
   c. Jan Wilem de Winter
   d. Karel Doorman

8. The cruisere USS Houston and HMAS Perth were sunk during the Battle of the _____ _____.

9. Which post did Hideki Tojo NOT hold during the Second World War?
   a. Munitions Minister
   b. Emperor
   c. Foreign Minister
   d. Minister of Education

10. Why did the Japanese find it difficult to exploit their newfound empire?
    a. Military demands created a lack of capable manpower.
    b. The Japanese tried to force their customs and traditions on the occupied people.
    c. The vast size of the empire made the transportation of goods difficult.
    d. All of the above.

11. The greatest barrier to Japanese surrender was the belief that they would lose _____.
    a. the emperor
    b. personal rights
    c. religious freedom
    d. their independence

12. How did Tojo ultimately die?
    a. He successfully committed suicide rather than surrender
    b. He died of an unknown cause shortly after the war ended
    c. He was convicted of war crimes and executed
    d. He died in a firefight rather than surrender

13. After the cities of Hiroshima and Nagasaki were destroyed by atomic bombs, _____ asked the Japanese government to surrender.
    a. Hideki Tojo
    b. Isoroku Yamamoto
    c. Emperor Hirohito
    d. Tomoyuki Yamashita

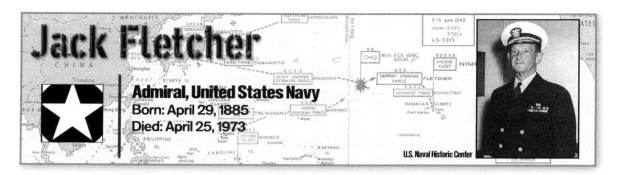

Jack Fletcher

Admiral, United States Navy
Born: April 29, 1885
Died: April 25, 1973

By early 1945, the Imperial Japanese Navy (IJN) was practically non-existent and the United States Navy (USN) ruled the Pacific. The situation was a dramatic reversal from just three years before when the IJN was on the offensive. During the early days of the war, the USN needed commanders who could make bold attacks while avoiding unnecessary risks. During that time of uncertainty, a number of strong leaders emerged, including Chester Nimitz, William Halsey, Raymond Spruance and Frank Jack Fletcher.

Fletcher was born April 29, 1885 in Marshalltown, Iowa. The military was important to Fletcher's family. His father was a Civil War veteran who had fought for the Union, and his uncle was Admiral Frank Friday Fletcher.

Fletcher, nicknamed "Flap Jack," exuded confidence but was down to earth. He carried a positive outlook and was known for his hearty laugh. He preferred to look at the big picture while allowing his subordinates to work out details.

Following in his uncle's footsteps, Fletcher attended the Naval Academy at Annapolis, graduating in 1906. He was given his first command, the destroyer *Dale* in the Pacific, in 1910.

In 1914, while Fletcher's uncle led the occupation of Veracruz, Mexico, young Fletcher whisked 350 civilians to safety while under fire onboard the mail ship *SS Esperanza*. During the First World War he participated in convoy duty in the North Atlantic as captain of the destroyer *Benham*. He was given his first command of a battleship, the *New Mexico*, in 1936.

Fletcher was onboard the heavy cruiser *Astoria* assisting the carrier *Lexington* in delivering planes to Midway when the Japanese struck Pearl Harbor. He was ordered to take the carrier *Saratoga* to relieve the defenders on Wake Island. He was one day from the island when told to wait for the *Lexington*. The Japanese captured the island the next day.

THE BATTLE OF THE CORAL SEA

The early days of the Pacific campaign were a tense time for the Navy. Outnumbered by Japanese carriers, Fletcher and his fellow officers could not afford any major losses. American tactics focused on disrupting the Japanese advance. In May 1942, *MAGIC* (Allied intelligence) intercepted and decrypted Japanese plans for an attack on Port Moresby in New

The carrier Lexington (CV-2) as seen from Yorktown early on May 8, 1942 during the Battle of the Coral Sea. "Lady Lex" was struck by two torpedoes and three bombs from Japanese aircraft that started uncontrollable fires. The ship was abandoned and scuttled.

The light carrier Shoho burns during the Battle of the Coral Sea. The Shoho (meaning "auspicious phoenix") was the first Japanese carrier sunk during the war.

Guinea. The Allies viewed the defense of Port Moresby as a necessity to prevent a Japanese invasion of Australia.

Fletcher moved his carrier task force, including the *Lexington* and *Yorktown*, into the Coral Sea north of Australia. The Battle of the Coral Sea was the first naval battle in history in which surface participants did not see one another; all the fighting was done with planes.

The Japanese invasion force was supported by three carriers: *Shoho, Shokaku* and *Zuikaku*. Fletcher's planes found and sank the *Shoho* and damaged the *Shokaku*. Commander R. E. Dixon of the *Lexington* reported "Scratch one flattop!" as the *Shoho* sank. Japanese planes sank the tanker *Neosho* and destroyer *Sims*. The *Lexington* was hit several times but kept sailing. The Japanese invasion fleet turned back. Shortly after the battle, a leak in an aviation fuel line caused a great explosion deep inside the *Lexington*. The "Lady Lex" had to be abandoned and scuttled.

Despite losing more ships, the Battle of the Coral Sea is considered the first American victory in the Pacific, as it stopped the Japanese from capturing Port Moresby. Perhaps more significantly, the two damaged Japanese carriers were unavailable for the Battle of Midway one month later. *Shokaku*

was undergoing repairs while *Zuikaku* required time to replace pilots lost during the Battle of the Coral Sea.

THE BATTLE OF MIDWAY

The Doolittle raid on Japan in April 1942 caused little physical damage but shook Japanese confidence. As American carriers could only approach Japan from the east, Isoroku Yamamoto determined to prevent future bombing raids on the Japanese home isles by capturing the island of Midway.

Yamamoto's plan was complex, counting on the element of surprise to capture the island and lure in the USN for a decisive battle. An attack on the Alaskan Aleutian islands intended to divert American ships was timed to coincide with the invasion of Midway. Unknown to Yamamoto, MAGIC had already alerted Chester Nimitz that an attack on Midway was imminent. It was the Japanese who would be surprised. The attack on the Aleutians would be unopposed, with Nimitz concentrating his naval

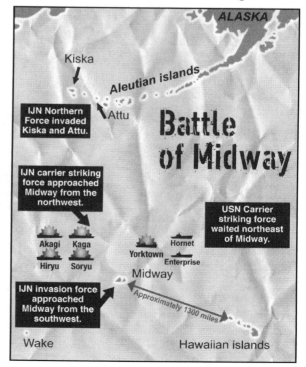

forces around Midway. Admiral Nimitz reinforced Midway with Marines, *Grumman F4F Wildcat* and *F2A Brewster Buffalo* fighters and *Boeing B-17 Flying Fortress* bombers.

More than 200 IJN ships and submarines were involved in Yamamoto's plan. Four carriers — *Akagi*, *Kaga*, *Hiryu* and *Soryu* — led the air attack on Midway. The fleet carrier *Junyo* and light carrier *Ryujo*, heading up the diversion fleet, supported 6000 troops landed on the Aleutian islands of Attu and Kiska.

The USN had only two undamaged carriers, the *Hornet* and *Enterprise*. The *Yorktown*, damaged during the *Battle of the Coral Sea*, was expected to require 90 days to repair. She was declared battle-ready after just 48 hours of hasty repairs at Pearl Harbor. Fletcher took the *Yorktown* to rendezvous with Raymond Spruance, already with the other carriers. On June 2, Fletcher took command of the combined fleet.

Japanese Admiral Chuichi Nagumo's carrier battle group approached Midway from the north-

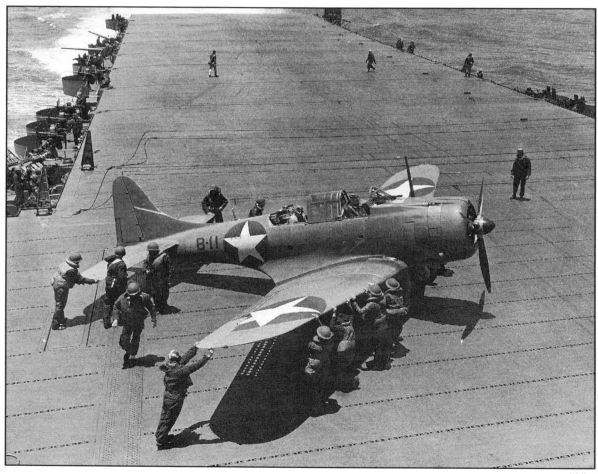

U.S. Navy

The Douglas SBD Dauntless was a two-seat dive bomber capable of carrying more than 2000 pounds of bombs. Though its maximum speed was a sluggish 245 mph, no other Allied aircraft sank more Japanese ships during the war.

west while the invasion force approached from the southwest. Before dawn on June 4, a strike force of 36 *Nakajima B5N Kate* torpedo bombers, 36 *Aichi D3A Val* dive bombers and 36 *Mitsubishi A6M Zero* fighters headed toward Midway. The attack was intended to destroy any aircraft that might be on the island. While the attack did damage the base, it ultimately failed as, alerted by radar, all American airplanes were off the ground at the time of the attack.

Nagumo ordered his reserve bombers, loaded with torpedoes in case American ships were sighted, to be rearmed with bombs for a second strike against Midway. While the rearming was in process, Nagumo received a report about the American fleet. More time was lost as he tried to determine the composition of the fleet. The need to recover planes returning from the strike on Midway added to the confusion.

American *Douglas TBD Devastator* torpedo bombers were already en route to attack the Japanese carrier group sighted in the early morning by a *Consolidated PBY Catalina* patrol bomber. The American attack was launched in stages, greatly impairing its effectiveness. One squadron of Devastators never located the Japanese carriers. The slow, unescorted bombers that did find the carriers were easy targets for Japanese Zeros. No Japanese ships were hit, and only six of the 41 Devastators survived the attack. However, the carriers were forced to take evasive action, frustrating efforts to reload and launch their planes. The Devastator's greatest contribution was to pull the Japanese Zeros down out of their prime attack position.

At 10:28 a.m., 37 *Douglas SBD Dauntless* dive bombers from the *Yorktown* screamed down on the vulnerable carriers, dropping their bombs onto decks covered with loaded planes, fuel lines, bombs and torpedoes. Japanese fighters watched helplessly as they were unable to climb quickly enough to counter the threat. The *Akagi* was hit by three bombs. Four

The Japanese aircraft carrier Hiryu burns after being hit by four bombs from Dauntless dive bombers. The forward flight deck collapsed after planes in the hangar directly underneath caught on fire and exploded. The Hiryu sank a few hours after this photo was taken.

bombs hit the *Kaga*, killing her captain and many officers. The *Soryu* was hit three times. On each carrier, one explosion followed another as planes and munitions ignited. Each ship soon sank or had to be scuttled. In what was perhaps the most decisive five minutes of the war in the Pacific, three irreplaceable Japanese carriers were destroyed.

The *Yorktown* was attacked mid-afternoon by planes from the remaining Japanese carrier, the *Hiryu*. Hit by three bombs and two torpedoes, the carrier refused to sink and was taken in tow. A little more than two hours later, dive bombers from the *Enterprise* and *Yorktown* found the

Hiryu racing away from Midway. Four bomb hits turned the carrier into an inferno. The Japanese scuttled the ship early the next morning.

Early on the morning of June 5, Yamamoto ordered a general retreat but waited two days in a futile attempt to bait the Americans into an engagement with his battleships and cruisers. On June 6, carrier planes located and sank the heavy cruiser *Mikuma* and heavily damaged the *Mogami*. While under tow, the Japanese submarine *I-168* approached unnoticed and fired four torpedoes. One hit and sank the destroyer *Hammann*, while two others finished off the *Yorktown*.

After the battle, Japanese troops, living in miserable conditions, held the strategically unimportant islands of Attu and Kiska until American forces finally evicted them in May 1943.

Like El Alamein in the Mediterranean Theater and Stalingrad on the Eastern Front, the Battle of Midway was the turning point in the Pacific. In losing four of their six large fleet carriers, 332 aircraft and most of their experienced pilots, the Japanese lost their naval advantage. For the moment, it created a balance that would soon turn in favor of the United States as a result of its massive ship-building program. Japan would complete only a dozen carriers before the war's end while the United States would launch 23 *Essex-class* fleet carriers in addition to more than 100 smaller escort carriers.

U.S. Naval Historic Center

The doomed heavy cruiser Quincy, burning and beginning to sink, is illuminated by Japanese searchlights during the Battle of Savo Island off Guadalcanal in the early hours of August 9, 1942. The Quincy was one of four USN heavy cruisers sunk in the battle.

CRITICISM AT GUADALCANAL

Despite success in the Battle of the Coral Sea and at Midway, Fletcher has never had the public acclaim that Nimitz, Halsey and other admirals experienced. Much of this is due to his actions during a critical point in the Guadalcanal campaign.

On August 8, 1942, one day after the first Marines stepped ashore on Guadalcanal, Allied reconnaissance planes spotted Japanese ships far to the north near Bougainville. The size and direction of the task force was uncertain. About the same time, Fletcher began a planned withdrawal of his carriers away from Guadalcanal.

The ensuing Battle of Savo Island was one of the darkest moments of the war for the USN. As transport ships unloaded men and supplies onto Guadalcanal, American and Australian ships formed three protective screens nearby. During the early morning hours of August 9, Japanese Vice Admiral Gunichi Mikawa led seven cruisers — five heavy, two light — toward Guadalcanal. Japanese float planes spotted the

Douglas TBD Devastator

U.S. Navy

The Douglas TBD Devastator was the world's most advanced torpedo bomber when it first flew in 1937 but was outdated by the time the United States entered the war. After a poor showing at the Battle of Midway, the Devastators were immediately replaced with Grumman TBF Avengers.

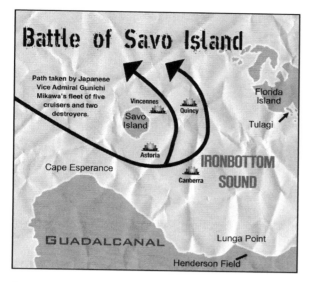

Battle of Savo Island

Path taken by Japanese Vice Admiral Gunichi Mikawa's fleet of five cruisers and two destroyers.

Vincennes
Quincy
Savo Island
Astoria
Cape Esperance
Canberra
Florida Island
Tulagi
IRONBOTTOM SOUND
GUADALCANAL
Lunga Point
Henderson Field

first group and silently approached their unsuspecting prey.

At 1:38 a.m., the Japanese guns opened fire while their deadly Long-Lance torpedoes streaked through the water. The Australian heavy cruiser *Canberra* was hit first and quickly knocked out of action. A torpedo ripped a huge hole in the heavy cruiser *Chicago*, forcing her to retire from the battle.

Several miles away, the second Allied group, obscured by rain squalls, could hear the raging battle but was slow to prepare for combat. Japanese searchlights located the second group and surged forward to attack. The Japanese ships formed two columns on either side of the Americans. They made quick work of the heavy cruisers *Quincy*, *Vincennes* and *Astoria*; all three were soon on the seabed of Ironbottom Sound, the location of the many ships sunk during the Guadalcanal campaign. In 30 minutes, the Japanese had managed to destroy four heavy cruisers with only moderate damage to three of their cruisers. The engagement was the worst naval defeat of the war for the USN.

Despite the heavy losses, the Japanese failed to reach the vulnerable transports. Mika-

wa, fearing an air attack as dawn approached, turned his cruisers toward home. If the Japanese had succeeded in destroying the transports, it is quite possible that the developing American invasion would have been easily repelled or even abandoned.

In light of the circumstances, it can be argued that Fletcher was appropriately cautious. Fletcher did not receive the news of the Japanese movements until after dark, hours after the force had first been sighted. Second, launching an air attack on a moonless night against a foe whose exact location was unknown involved extreme risk. Third, Nimitz had previously ordered his commanders to only take calculated risks, as it would be months before any new carriers would join the fleet. Finally, Fletcher was not made aware of the battle until after sunrise, thus missing an opportunity to attack the retreating Japanese ships.

Criticism from the *Battle of Savo Island* took its toll on Fletcher's career. In 1944, he was moved to the North Pacific, an area of little significance, in which he had only a handful of ships larger than destroyers. He raided and harassed Japanese positions on the Kuril islands north of Japan. In September 1945, Fletcher was the U.S. representative to accept the surrender of Japanese forces in northern Japan.

After the war, Fletcher served in Washington until his retirement in 1947. He was decorated by the U.S. Army for "...expertly solving the many problems involved in combined Army-Navy air operation." His service was also recognized by Great Britain and Canada. Noticeably missing is any recognition by Australia, the beneficiary of Fletcher's victory in the Coral Sea. Fletcher spent his retirement on a farm in Maryland. He passed away in 1973 and was buried in Arlington National Cemetery.

REVIEW QUESTIONS

1. During the early days of the war in the Pacific, what was the U.S. Navy strategy?
   a. Go on the offensive.
   b. Seek out the Japanese battleships.
   c. Disrupt the Japanese advance while avoiding unnecessary risks.
   d. Defend Hawaii until more ships arrived.

2. Allied intelligence in the Pacific was code-named _____.

3. What was different about the Battle of the Coral Sea?
   a. It was the last battleship engagement in history.
   b. It was the first battle in which surface participants did not see one another.
   c. It was the first-ever naval battle involving the Australian Navy.
   d. None of the above.

4. Despite losing three ships, including the carrier Lexington, the Battle of the Coral Sea is considered an Allied victory because it prevented the invasion of _____.

5. Who planned the invasion of Midway in 1942?
   a. Emperor Hirohito
   b. Hideki Tojo
   c. Isoroku Yamamoto
   d. Chuichi Nagumo

6. A June 1942 diversionary attack on the _____ Islands proved fruitless due to Allied intelligence learning that the real attack was against Midway.

U.S. Naval Historic Center

Under terms of the 1922 Washington Naval Treaty, the Japanese converted the hull of a battlecruiser into the fleet carrier Akagi (Japanese for "Red Castle"). The Akagi participated in the raids on Pearl Harbor and Darwin, Australia before being scuttled during the Battle of Midway.

7. How many of the four Japanese carriers at Midway were sunk?
   a. One
   b. Two
   c. Three
   d. Four

8. Which U.S. Navy carrier was sunk during the Battle of Midway?
   a. Yorktown
   b. Hornet
   c. Enterprise
   d. All survived

9. The Battle of Midway was the _____ point in the Pacific campaign.

10. The Battle of _____ Island during the Guadalcanal campaign was the worst naval defeat of the war for the U.S. Navy.

11. The area where many ships were sunk during the Guadalcanal campaign was christened _____.
    a. Davy Jones Sea
    b. Ironbottom Sound
    c. Guadalcanal Graveyard
    d. Battleship Bottom

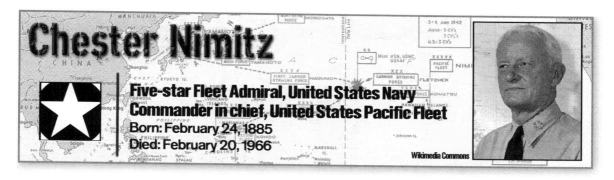

Chester Nimitz

Five-star Fleet Admiral, United States Navy
Commander in chief, United States Pacific Fleet
Born: February 24, 1885
Died: February 20, 1966

Wikimedia Commons

As his plane approached Hawaii on Christmas Day 1941, Chester Nimitz, the new *Commander in Chief Pacific* (CinCPac), asked the pilot to circle over Pearl Harbor. The devastation left behind by the Japanese raid was still evident. From his plane, the outline of Nimitz' former flagship, the battleship *Arizona*, could clearly be seen in the blue water. Entombed in the ill-fated ship were more than 1000 sailors. Nimitz would lead the United States Navy (USN) out of the dark days of Pearl Harbor and on to final victory over Japan.

Naval History & Heritage Command

A photo of Chester Nimitz as a young officer.

Nimitz was born and raised in the German-American community of Fredericksburg, Texas in 1885. His father passed away before he was born. Nimitz was close to his grandfather and during high school worked in the family hotel.

Nimitz entered the Naval Academy in 1901 and graduated four years later. During that time, he developed relationships with many of the officers he would work with during the Pacific campaign. Nimitz took command of the destroyer *Decatur* at the young age of 22.

During the First World War, Nimitz served on submarines. He gained a reputation as a diesel engine expert and campaigned to have submarine gas engines replaced with diesel. After the war, Nimitz was responsible for building a submarine base at Pearl Harbor.

In 1933, Nimitz took command of the heavy cruiser *Augusta*. He took the ship on a tour of Asia, visiting many locales that would be critical battlegrounds in the coming war. During the spring of 1938, he was promoted to Rear Admiral, taking over command of Battleship Division One, including the ill-fated *Arizona*. When the Japanese attacked Pearl Harbor, Nimitz was the Head of the Bureau of Navigation, in charge of staffing all the new ships coming online during the large pre-war buildup.

Nimitz enjoyed long afternoon hikes and entertaining listeners with stories. A powerful swimmer, he once saved a man from drowning. He worked hard at keeping the peace between battleship and carrier officers despite recognizing early that carriers would be the key to winning the war in the Pacific. He tried to avoid de-

U.S. Marine Corps

U.S. Marines take cover during the invasion of Saipan in the Mariana Islands in June 1944.

moting his subordinates, instead moving them where they could better serve.

In his early days as CinCPac, Nimitz was frustrated that he could not go on the offensive until the fleet was built up to a sufficient strength. He thought it likely he would be fired in his first six months. Nimitz was pleased when the Japanese advance toward Australia was turned back at the Battle of the Coral Sea. Still, there was concern as the loss of the carrier *Lexington* left the USN with only three operational carriers, less than half of the number of the Japanese. Several weeks after the battle, the tables would turn on the Japanese.

THE MIDWAY TRAP

The success of the Battle of Midway can be directly attributed to Nimitz. Once code breakers made Nimitz aware of the Japanese plans, he set a trap. He reinforced Midway with Marines and aircraft in order to repel any invasion attempt. He concentrated all three of his carriers north of the island in anticipation of the Japanese fleet approaching from the northwest.

Though 1500 miles from Midway, Nimitz remained at Hawaii during the battle. Being on shore allowed Nimitz the freedom to radio in-

structions without fear of the Japanese tracing his location. Admiral Isoroku Yamamoto, onboard the battleship *Yamato*, was forced to observe strict radio silence lest American aviators determine his location and attack. The Japanese lost four precious carriers during the battle. Thanks to the courage of the Navy's fighting men and inspired leadership from Nimitz and other officers, the battle changed the course of the war in the Pacific Theater.

USN STRUGGLES AT GUADALCANAL

The Guadalcanal naval campaign in the summer and fall of 1942 proved costly for the U.S. Navy. However, despite heavy losses, the Japanese rarely achieved their objectives. Nimitz mourned the loss of many good sailors but realized that wresting Guadalcanal from the Japanese would stop their advance and prevent the isolation of Australia.

The first and costliest battle, the Battle of Savo Island, took place in the early hours of August 9. Less than 48 hours after the first Marines stepped on Guadalcanal, a Japanese battle group moved in to attack vulnerable transport ships unloading men and supplies.

Defense Imagery Management Operations Center

U.S. Marines turn a captured gun against the Japanese during the struggle for Saipan.

Admiral Chester Nimitz speaks at a high-level meeting with President Roosevelt, General Douglas MacArthur and Admiral William Leahy during a visit by Roosevelt to Hawaii.

The Japanese engaged American heavy cruisers protecting the transports, heavily damaging the *Chicago* and sinking the *Vincennes, Astoria, Quincy, Canberra* (Australian) and two destroyers. While the battle was a disaster, the Japanese failed to find and sink the transports.

During the Battle of the Eastern Solomons, Japanese forces damaged Admiral Jack Fletcher's carrier *Enterprise* and battleship *North Carolina*. U.S. forces sank the light carrier *Ryujo* and prevented the Japanese from landing reinforcements on Guadalcanal.

On September 15, Japanese sub *I-19* sank the carrier *Wasp*, leaving the *Hornet* as the only operational carrier in the South Pacific. One of the torpedoes intended for the *Wasp* struck the *North Carolina*, forcing her to retire to Pearl Harbor. Despite the loss of a valuable carrier, Americans successfully landed more than 4000 reinforcements and critical supplies.

During the Battle of Cape Esperance, USN ships surprised a Japanese force intent on bombarding Henderson Field, sinking the heavy cruiser *Furutaka* and a destroyer. Planes from Guadalcanal located and sank two more destroyers the next day. The heavy cruiser *Boise* was damaged and the destroyer *Duncan* sunk. The battle did not prevent the battleships *Kongo* and *Haruna* from shelling Henderson Field several days later.

Nimitz was forced to admit that the Japanese controlled the sea around Guadalcanal but believed the situation could be reversed. On October 18, Nimitz replaced Robert Ghormley with William "Bull" Halsey. His appointment marked a turning point in the Guadalcanal campaign.

Defense Imagery Management Operations Center

Two American soldiers plant the first American flag on Guam minutes after U.S. Marines and Army troops began to retake the island on July 20, 1944. The Japanese originally occupied the American protectorate on December 10, 1941.

During the Battle of the Santa Cruz Islands, Halsey's carrier planes located and heavily damaged the Japanese carriers *Shokaku* and *Zuiho*. The carrier *Enterprise* was damaged and the *Hornet* sunk, much to the satisfaction of the Japanese who remembered the Hornet's role in the Doolittle raid. Despite the loss of yet another carrier, American forces downed more than 100 Japanese planes, forcing the Japanese to withdraw their carriers from the region. It would be 20 months before carriers would again battle one other.

The Naval Battle of Guadalcanal was a multi-day battle in mid-November. On the night of the 13th, Hiroaki Abe led two battleships, a light cruiser and 11 destroyers, on a mission to bombard Henderson Field. They were intercepted by the heavy cruisers *San Francisco* and *Portland*, light cruisers *Helena*, *Juneau* and *Atlanta*, and eight destroyers. The ships, intermingled in

> ### TRIVIA
> As a young boy, Nimitz enjoyed visits to his Uncle Otto's ranch where a mowing machine was used to flush out rattlesnakes. Nimitz and the other boys would kill the snakes and collect their rattles.

the darkness, waged a savage battle at close range. The destroyer *Fletcher* came within 10 yards of the *Hiei*, raking the battleship's superstructure with her five-inch guns. Despite spoiling the Japanese mission, the USN got the worst of the battle. The *Atlanta*, *Juneau* and four destroyers joined a growing list of ships sitting on the bottom of the sea in Ironbottom Sound. The next morning, American planes located and finished off the crippled *Hiei*.

Yamamoto was upset with the loss of a battleship but determined once more to strike Henderson Field. A cruiser force succeeded in bombarding the field in the early morning of the 14th but caused little damage. After dawn, American planes found the retiring ships, sinking the *Kinugasa* and seven of 11 transports bringing in reinforcements.

On the night of the 14th, the battleship *Kirishima*, escorted by heavy cruisers *Atago* and *Takao*, and 11 other ships sailed into Ironbottom Sound. They were met by the battleships *Washington* and *South Dakota*. The *South Dakota* suffered a major electrical malfunction and was peppered by fire from the *Kirishima*. Unnoticed, the *Washington* moved in and opened fire, hitting the *Kirishima* multiple times and causing heavy damage. The Japanese lost three destroyers and scuttled the *Kirishima*. The remaining four transports were run aground on Guadalcanal and destroyed.

The battle convinced the Japanese that the fight for Guadalcanal was not sustainable. After this battle, the Japanese began to consider the best way to withdraw their troops.

CENTRAL PACIFIC DRIVE

After Guadalcanal, Nimitz was given the task of moving westward across the Pacific while

★ CHARLES LOCKWOOD

While officers such as Chester Nimitz and Douglas MacArthur were making headlines, Admiral Charles Lockwood and his men in the "silent service" were systematically depriving Japan of war supplies.

The Japanese failed to realize the impact their subs could have on Allied shipping, instead sending their subs on long missions to lob a few shells on a target or ferrying supplies to isolated troops. American submarines occasionally ferried troops and picked up downed aviators, but their main focus was the disruption of Japanese shipping.

Early submarine patrols proved unproductive due to defective torpedoes. Complaints by sailors were ignored until Lockwood was made head of the Asiatic command in 1942. Lockwood tested the torpedoes, discovered the defects and prompted improvements that made them effective weapons.

Though a disciplinarian, Lockwood was concerned about the well-being of his men. Nicknamed "Uncle Charlie" by his men, Lockwood often personally met submarines returning from assignments. Between tours, Lockwood rewarded the men with fancy hotels and luxuries including ice cream and fresh vegetables.

U.S. subs proved remarkably effective, accounting for the sinking of 1113 ships, or 55% of Japanese shipping, during the war. Fifty-two submarines, about one-sixth of the fleet, were lost during the Pacific campaign. Lockwood guarded the success of the "secret service" lest the Japanese fully appreciate the threat.

Lockwood wrote a number of books on naval history after the war. When he died in 1967, he was buried at Golden Gate Cemetery next to Admirals Chester Nimitz, Raymond Spruance, Richard Kelly and their wives in accordance with a deal made while they were alive.

Nimitz revived a custom that each new captain had an audience with him before assuming command in his fleet. This was no small task as the fleet grew by the hundreds.

While fighting to secure Guam, Tinian and Saipan in the Mariana Islands, the Japanese, led by Admiral Jisaburo Ozawa, dispatched a large force of nine carriers, 430 combat planes, five battleships (including the super battleships *Yamato* and *Musashi*), 13 cruisers and 28 destroyers to attempt to force a decisive battle. Though an imposing force, Ozawa's pilots were poorly trained and had no combat experience. In addition, the Americans had succeeded in destroying most of the land-based aircraft in the Marianas that Ozawa was counting on for assistance.

Task Force 58, under Vice Admiral Marc Mitscher, countered with 15 carriers and dozens of other ships. Ozawa launched the first strike on the morning of June 19. The strike was picked up by American radar, and Navy Grumman *F6F Hellcat* fighters rose to intercept. Several attacks were launched that day, but few Japanese planes found their way to the U.S. fleet. The battleship *South Dakota* was hit once while the carrier *Bunker Hill* was slightly damaged. On the first day, only 130 of 373

Marc Mitscher

Japanese planes returned. Believing most of his "missing" planes had landed on airstrips in the Marianas, Ozawa remained in the area.

Late on the second day, the Japanese fleet was sighted. Mitscher made the difficult decision to launch a strike, knowing it would be difficult to recover his planes after dark. The U.S. planes sunk the carrier *Hiyo* and downed another 65 Japanese planes. Mitscher made another risky decision to light up his carriers for the returning planes. Despite this assistance, many ran out of fuel and were forced to ditch in the ocean. Fortunately, no Japanese submarines were in the

Douglas MacArthur would clear New Guinea and capture Rabaul. Nimitz had to plan attacks about eight months in advance to get a budget approved and men and materials organized.

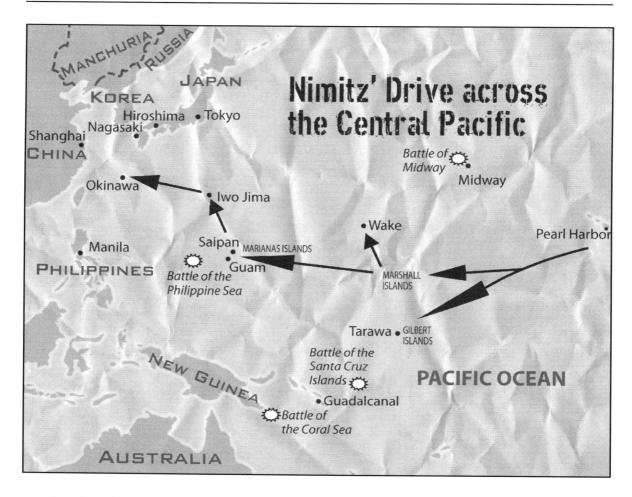

area to take advantage of the illuminated ships. American subs located the Japanese fleet, sinking the carriers *Shokaku* and *Taiho.*

The long-anticipated decisive battle had gone against the Japanese as they lost three carriers and all but 35 of their 430 combat planes. As a result, the Japanese Naval Air group basically ceased to exist. The U.S. lost 130 planes. Officially known as the of the Battle of the Philippine Sea, Americans remember the encounter as *"The Great Marianas Turkey Shoot."*

The capture of Guam in July 1944 lifted American morale as it was the first U.S.

protectorate to be liberated. The capture of Saipan was particularly damaging to the Japanese as it cut off communications to their remaining South Pacific islands and was close enough for their mainland to be reached by the new *Boeing B-29 Superfortress* bombers.

Planned Invasion of Japanese Mainland

Nimitz endured an anxious period of time during the Battle of Leyte Gulf in October 1944 when Halsey moved to intercept Japanese carriers, leaving a small group of destroyers and escort carriers unprotected

By mid-1945, Saipan was serving as a huge base for B-29 Superfortress bomber raids on the Japanese mainland. In this photo, dozens of B-29's can be seen lined up on Isley Field.

against a powerful Japanese task force. Their survival was, he wrote, "...nothing short of special dispensation from the Lord Almighty." The path to Japan was cleared as a result of the battle. The loss of three battleships and four carriers in addition to access to oil from the Dutch East Indies meant the IJN was powerless to stop the American advance. In December 1944, Nimitz gained five-star rank when he was promoted to Fleet Admiral.

As early as the fall of 1944, the Army began preparing plans for an invasion of the Japanese home islands. Nimitz would be in charge of the amphibious landings of Kyushu (*Operation Olympic*) and the Tokyo plain (*Operation Coronet*) with MacArthur taking over once ashore. Nimitz believed that bombing and blockade by submarine would end the war before invasion was necessary. Ultimately, it was the dropping of atomic bombs on Hiroshima and Nagasaki that convinced the Japanese to accept unconditional surrender. When Nimitz was first informed of the advanced state of the atomic program in February 1945, he was awed at the destructive potential. While Nimitz had reservations about the bomb, he agreed that it was necessary to prevent further bloodshed.

After the war ended, Nimitz replaced Ernest King as *Chief of Naval Operations* (CNO). It was a bittersweet job as he began dismantling the wartime navy he had helped to build. During his two-year tenure, he oversaw atomic testing at Bikini Atoll and laid the groundwork for the first nuclear submarines. After stepping down as CNO, Nimitz stayed active giving speeches, working with the United Nations and building goodwill with the Japanese. Nimitz passed away on February 20, 1966. Though he had requested a quiet funeral, hundreds of people turned out to line the processional route to Golden Gate National Cemetery. As the procession reached the gravesite, 70 Navy planes flew over and a 19-gun salute was fired.

The Japanese battleship Kongo and carrier Chiyoda attempt to evade attacks by American carrier aircraft during the Battle of the Philippine Sea on June 20, 1944. The Kongo was sunk by an American submarine in November 1944.

REVIEW QUESTIONS

1. What ill-fated ship did Chester Nimitz command several years before America entered the Second World War?
   a. The battleship *Arizona*
   b. The carrier *Lexington*
   c. The heavy cruiser *Augusta*
   d. The escort destroyer *Samuel B. Roberts*

2. Shortly after the attack on Pearl Harbor, Nimitz was promoted to Commander in Chief _____, or CinCPac for short.

3. Nimitz planned a trap that led to the destruction of four Japanese carriers at the Battle of _____.

4. Despite heavy losses, in the summer of 1942 the U.S. Navy played a crucial role in denying the island of _____ to the Japanese.

5. The turning point of the Guadalcanal campaign was Nimitz' appointment of _____ to replace Robert Ghormley.
   a. Frank "Flap Jack" Fletcher
   b. Marc Mitscher
   c. William "Bull" Halsey
   d. Ernest King

6. The Battle of the _____ Islands was the last battle between carriers until 20 months later in June 1944.
   a. New Georgia
   b. Solomon
   c. Philippine
   d. Santa Cruz

7. The Japanese battleship Hiei and American ships Atlanta, Juneau and four destroyers were all sunk during the Naval Battle of _____.

8. Nimitz planned invasions of Guam, Tinian and Saipan in the _____ Islands.

9. Admiral Marc Mitscher led a carrier task force that destroyed almost 400 Japanese planes in what Americans remember as _____.
   a. the Battle of Tarawa
   b. the Great Marianas Turkey Shoot
   c. the Tinian Sitting Duck Hunt
   d. the Marianas Massacre

10. The first American protectorate to be liberated was _____.
    a. Wake
    b. Guam
    c. the Philippines
    d. Midway

11. During the fall of 1944, Nimitz began planning Operation Olympic, the first invasion of mainland _____.

12. American submarines in the Pacific focused the majority of their attention on _____.
    a. sinking Imperial Japanese Navy ships
    b. sinking Japanese merchant ships
    c. rescuing downed airmen
    d. delivering supplies on secret missions.

13. Working quietly behind the scenes, Charles Lockwood's submarines were known as the "_____ _____."

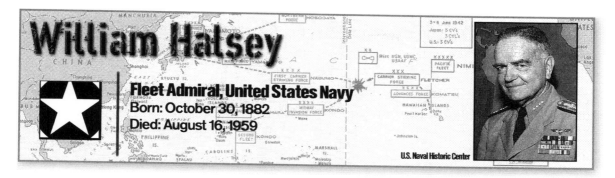

William Halsey

Fleet Admiral, United States Navy
Born: October 30, 1882
Died: August 16, 1959

The key to winning the Pacific Theater was control of the seas. Outposts on the many islands dotting the vast Pacific could only be held if they could be kept in supply. Aircraft carriers proved to be the decisive weapon in controlling the vast reaches of the Pacific Ocean. Admiral William "Bull" Halsey, Jr. proved to be one of the most daring and colorful aircraft carrier commanders of the Second World War.

Halsey was born in 1882 in New Jersey. His father, a U.S. Navy (USN) officer, was at sea during his birth. Halsey loved to play sports, especially football, while growing up. One of his football teams had the unusual name of the *Little Potatoes*. Desiring to follow his father in attending the Naval Academy, Halsey only secured an appointment after his mother arranged a private meeting with President William McKinley.

Soldiers of the U.S. 25th Infantry Division struggle through the jungle along the Zieta Trail on New Georgia, largest of the Solomon Islands, in August 1943.

While at the Naval Academy, Halsey played on the football team. After his graduation in 1904, Halsey's first assignment was on an early battleship, the *Missouri*. In 1909, Halsey circled the globe as part of the year-long *Great White Fleet* world tour. The tour was the idea of President Theodore Roosevelt, who wished to showcase America's growing power to the world. Painted gleaming white, the fleet visited ports around the world. Halsey was assigned to the battleship *Kansas*.

Halsey was given command of the destroyer *Lamson* in 1910. Throughout the next 20 years, he would serve almost exclusively on destroyers. During the First World War, he escorted convoys but saw little combat.

In 1934, Halsey was given command of the carrier *Saratoga*. To prepare for the new challenge, Halsey underwent a rigorous flight training with men half his age in order to learn the details of flight operations. It was in his role as carrier commander that Halsey would help lead the United States to victory over Japan.

AMERICA STRIKES BACK

Halsey's bold, aggressive spirit and habit of saying exactly what he thought endeared him to the press and the American people. Though his frankness occasionally got him into trouble, he had a charming personality that won him many friends and the respect of the men who served under him. His instinct, which usually proved correct, was an important part of his decision-making process.

At the time of the Japanese attack on Pearl Harbor, Halsey was onboard his flagship, the carrier *Enterprise*, returning from delivering aircraft to Wake Island. Halsey gave American morale a boost when he led the carrier task force that made the first successful raids against Japanese bases in the Marshall and Gilbert Islands in early 1942. He was in command of the carrier *Hornet* during the Doolittle Raid on Japan in April 1942.

Shortly before the Battle of Midway, Halsey contracted a serious skin condition, dermatitis. Admiral Chester Nimitz sent Halsey straight to the hospital, but not before asking Halsey who should take his place in the upcoming battle. Halsey recommended Raymond Spruance. Well known as a cruiser commander, Spruance would prove to be one of America's most-gifted com-

U.S. National Archives

40mm guns defend the Hornet (CV-12) against Japanese aerial attacks as the carrier's planes raid Tokyo in early 1945. The Essex-class carrier was named in honor of the USS Hornet (CV-8) lost in the Battle of the Santa Cruz Islands in October 1942.

manders during the war. Missing the Battle of Midway was Halsey's greatest disappointment during the war.

NEW GEORGIA

Halsey replaced Robert Ghormley as *Commander of the South Pacific* (ComSoPac) after the USN suffered several defeats during the Guadalcanal campaign. The announcement of his appointment delighted American sailors. In his first battle as ComSoPac, the Battle of Santa Cruz Island, Halsey ordered, "Attack. Repeat. Attack." Despite the loss of several ships during the campaign, his aggressive tactics hampered Japanese efforts to reinforce Guadalcanal.

With Guadalcanal secured, in 1943 Halsey coordinated with Douglas MacArthur to capture New Georgia. The invasion, expected to last days, not weeks, began on July 6, 1943 when the Army's 43rd Division landed several miles from the Munda airstrip. As the Japanese had done on Guadalcanal, it was now the Americans' turn to fight through the jungle. The airfield was captured on August 5 but not before many American casualties. Halsey decided to bypass Kolombangara, instead isolating the island by capturing small islands to the north.

In early October, Halsey led a major raid on Formosa (modern-day Taiwan) in preparation for the invasion of the Philippines. During the three-day attack, nearly 600 Japanese planes and three dozen freighters were destroyed. The heavy cruisers *Chicago* and *Canberra* (an American ship named after the Australian city) were damaged.

BATTLE OF LEYTE GULF

The Battle of Leyte Gulf was the last and greatest surface naval battle in terms of area covered and tonnage of ships. The Japanese knew that the loss of the Philippines would cut off oil resources in the Dutch East Indies. The weakened but still dangerous Imperial Japanese Navy (IJN) initiated a desperate attempt, *Operation Sho-go* (Victory), to destroy the American invasion force.

Sho-go required close coordination between four battle groups: three composed of surface ships and one with carriers. As the Japanese were unable to properly train replacement pilots, the carriers had few planes. The carrier group under Admiral Jisaburo Ozawa would be sacrificed, drawing away Halsey's powerful *Task Force 38* and allowing the other three groups to converge on the vulnerable invasion fleet.

The battle commenced on October 23, 1944 when the American submarines *Darter* and *Dace* sank the heavy cruisers *Atago* and *Maya*. The subs alerted USN forces that the Japanese fleets were heading toward the Philippines. Halsey was optimistic that he would finally have his chance to wipe out the IJN. Due to the complexity of the battle, it is typically broken into four smaller actions.

BATTLE OF THE SIBUYAN SEA

On October 24, Halsey's *Task Force 38* scout planes discovered the main (Center Force) Japanese group in the Sibuyan Sea. Five large strikes against the group were

Defense Imagery Management Operations Center

Ships of Task Group 38 enter the anchorage of Ulithi in December 1944 after strikes against the Japanese in the Philippines. The ships shown here are the Langley, Ticonderoga, Washington, North Carolina, South Dakota, Santa Fe, Biloxi, Mobile and Oakland.

LEYTE GULF ORDER OF BATTLE

Task Force 38
Commanded by William Halsey, Jr.
Fleet Carriers: *Wasp, Hornet, Hancock, Intrepid, Lexington, Essex, Enterprise, Franklin*
Light Carriers: *Monterey, Cowpens, Independence, Princeton, Langley, San Jacinto, Belleau Wood*
Battleships: *New Jersey, Iowa, Massachusetts, South Dakota, Washington, Alabama*
Heavy Cruisers: *Chester, Pensacola, Salt Lake City, Boston, Wichita, New Orleans*
Light Cruisers: *San Diego, Biloxi, Oakland, Vincennes, Miami, Santa Fe, Birmingham, Mobile, Reno*
48 destroyers

Japanese Northern Force
Commanded by Admiral Ozawa
Fleet carriers: *Zuikaku, Ise, Hyuga*
Light carriers: *Zuiho, Chitose, Chiyoda*
Light Cruisers: *Oyoda, Tama, Isuzu*
8 destroyers

Japanese Center Force
Commanded by Admiral Takeo Kurita
Battleships: *Yamato, Musashi, Nagato, Kongo, Haruna, Yamashiro, Fuso*
Heavy Cruisers: *Takao, Chokai, Myoko, Haguro, Kumano, Atago, Maya, Tone, Chikuma, Suzuya*
Light Cruisers: *Noshiro, Yahagi*
15 destroyers

Taffy 3
Commanded by Clifton Sprague
Escort Carriers: *Fanshaw Bay, St. Lo, White Plains, Kalinin Bay, Kitkun Bay, Gambier Bay*
Destroyers: *Hoel, Heerman, Johnston*
Destroyer Escorts: *Dennis, John C. Butler, Raymond, Samuel B. Roberts*

Battle of Surigao Strait
Seventh Fleet Support Force
Commander Admiral Jesse Oldendorf
Battleships: *West Virginia, Maryland, Mississippi, Tennessee, California, Pennsylvania*
Heavy Cruisers: *Louisville, Portland, Minneapolis, Shropshire* (Australian)
Light Cruisers: *Denver, Columbia, Phoenix, Boise*
28 destroyers
39 PT torpedo boats

Japanese Southern Force
Commander Shoji Nishimura
Battleships: *Yamashiro, Fuso*
Heavy Cruiser: *Mogami*
4 destroyers

ordered throughout the day. The battleship *Musashi*, attacked by 200 airplanes, finally sank after being hit by 17 torpedoes and 19 bombs. The Japanese ships turned back in the face of resistance. American losses were 18 planes.

The Japanese carrier group was finally discovered during the late afternoon. Halsey, believing that the Center Force no longer threatened the invasion fleet, headed north to battle the carriers, just as the Japanese had planned. He made a fateful decision to take his entire fleet, including its six battleships, leaving the San Bernardino Strait unprotected. Due to confusion in communications, Nimitz and Thomas Kinkaid, commander of the Seventh Fleet, believed Halsey had left his surface ships to guard the northern approach to the invasion fleet. The oversight would prove costly.

BATTLE OF SURIGAO STRAIT

The *Seventh Fleet Support Force* led by Admiral Jesse Oldendorf decimated Admiral Shoji Nishimura's Southern Force in history's final engagement between battleships. Nishimura led his two battleships, the *Yamashiro* and *Fuso*, the heavy cruiser *Mogami* and four destroyers northward through the Surigao Strait directly into a trap set by Oldendorf.

The two forces made contact in the early hours of the morning of the 25th. Dozens of PT boats and destroyers aligned along the side of the strait harassed the Japanese ships with torpedoes. At the north end of the strait, Oldendorf aligned six older battleships, all but the *Mississippi* survivors of the attack on Pearl Harbor. A combination of torpedoes and withering fire from the American battleships sank the two Japanese battleships. The lone survivor of Nishimura's group was a destroyer, the *Shigure*.

BATTLE OF SAMAR

Halsey underestimated the damage caused to the Center Force. After dark on the 24th, the group once again turned east and slipped through the unguarded San Bernardino Strait. Shortly after dawn, the Japanese located *Taffy 3*, the northernmost of three groups supporting the invasion, and opened fire at 7:01 a.m.

Taffy 3 was composed of six escort carriers, three destroyers and four small destroyer escorts. Greatly outnumbered and outgunned, the destroyers *Hoel*, *Heerman* and *Johnston* valiantly charged the Japanese battleships, launching torpedoes and releasing smokescreens while the escort carriers attempted to escape. The *Johnston* was heavily damaged while hitting the heavy cruiser *Kumano* with three torpedoes. The *Hoel* managed to damage the battleship *Kongo* before sinking. The super battleship *Yamato*, followed by the *Nagato*, was forced out of the battle while evading torpedoes from the *Heerman*. The *Heerman* miraculously survived the encounter.

A providential rain squall partially protected the retreating carriers though Japanese ships managed to heavily damage the carriers *Gambier Bay*, *White Plains* and *St. Lo*. A determined attack by the tiny 2000-ton destroyer escort *Raymond* forced the heavy cruiser *Tone* away from the *Gambier Bay*. The destroyer escort *Samuel B. Roberts* managed to fire 608 five-inch shells before being sunk.

The aggressiveness of the destroyers and the arrival of planes from *Taffy 1* and *Taffy 2* convinced Kurita that the USN fleet carriers must be nearby. Fearing his fleet would soon be overwhelmed, he ordered a retreat, missing the opportunity to destroy the invasion fleet. The *Gambier Bay* and *St. Lo* eventu-

ally sank, the *St. Lo* after being struck by a Kamikaze. The Japanese lost three cruisers. Nimitz commended the bravery and sacrifice of the men of Taffy 3 by saying, "The history of the United States Navy records no more glorious two hours of resolution, sacrifice, and success."

BATTLE OF CAPE ENGANO

On the morning of October 25, as the Japanese Center Force closed in on Taffy 3, Halsey and Task Force 38 launched air strikes against the Japanese carrier force to the north. The Japanese managed to launch only one ineffective strike against Halsey's ships.

American pilots swarmed over the helpless carriers, sinking the fleet carrier *Zuikaku* (the

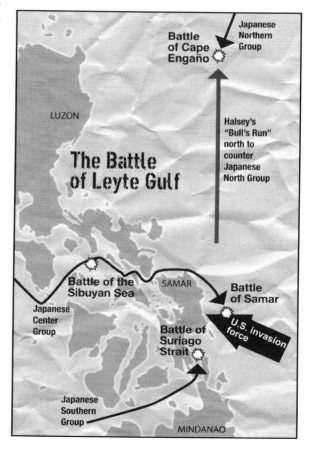

The Battle of Leyte Gulf

Sailors onboard the Zuikaku salute as the Japanese flag is lowered during the Battle of Cape Engaño on October 24, 1944. Shortly after this photo was taken, the ship rolled over and sank. The Zuikaku was the last surviving carrier from the attack on Pearl Harbor.

last survivor of the Pearl Harbor raid), three light carriers and two destroyers. Halsey, sensing that the destruction of the fleet was at hand, detached his battleships and cruisers to finish off the fleeing Japanese.

Halsey had received a number of vague messages about the plight of Taffy 3 throughout the morning. At the time, he believed that the combination of Oldendorf's battleships and the Taffy planes could repel the remnants of the Center Force. At 11 a.m. Halsey received a message from Nimitz that read, "WHERE IS RPT WHERE IS TASK FORCE THIRTY-FOUR RR THE WORLD WONDERS." Halsey was infuriated, believing Nimitz was mocking him. "The paper rattled in my hands. I snatched off my cap, threw it on the deck, and shouted something I am ashamed to remember," he said. What Halsey did not know was that the phrase after the double consonant was padding, nonsense words added to transmissions in order to confuse the Japanese. Nimitz intended it merely as a question.

 ## KAMIKAZES

Late in the war, Japan took a desperate step, Kamikaze suicide attacks, in an attempt to thwart Allied progress. Because of a lack of trained pilots, mechanical breakdowns and lack of fuel for training, conventional air tactics proved futile. *Kamikaze* meant "Divine wind" in memory of the strong winds, credited to the god Amaterasu, that destroyed the invading fleets of Kublai Khan in 1281.

Droves of young men volunteered for Kamikaze suicide attacks. Kamikaze pilots were regarded as heroes. Elaborate ceremonies for departing pilots included the reading of a death poem and prayers for the family. The pilots were given medals, Japanese flags, a special headband (*hachimaki*) with the rising sun and a *sennibari*, a belt sewn together by 1000 women who each sewed one stitch.

First used in the Philippines in late 1944, Kamikaze pilots had a much larger role at Okinawa. The goal of Operation *Ten Go* (Heavenly Operation) was to send *Kikusui* (floating chrysanthemums) waves of Army and Navy planes at American ships as human-guided bombs.

The first Kikusui was launched on April 6 when 335 Kamikazes headed for the American fleet off Okinawa. The pilots had been instructed to target large ships, preferably carriers, but many could not resist attacking vulnerable destroyers guarding the edges of the fleet. While only 33 Kamikazes succeeded in hitting American ships, the results were deadly. Six ships were sunk and seven others damaged severely enough to knock them out of the war.

Two days later, several Kamikazes managed to damage the carriers *Enterprise* and *Essex*. The battleship *Tennessee* was hit the next day. British carriers, protected by 3-inch armor decks (American carriers had wooden decks), fared better against the attacks. One Kamikaze only managed to dent the deck of a British carrier.

During the Okinawa campaign, there were a total of 1465 Kamikaze attacks: 120 ships were hit and 29 sunk, killing more than 3000 Allied sailors.

Though he lamented giving up the opportunity to destroy the remnants of the Northern Force, Halsey ordered the fleet back south at full speed. By the time he arrived, the Center Force had already escaped back through the San Bernardino Strait. Halsey never admitted in his lifetime that the Northern Force was a decoy. The great battle cost the lives of about 2800 Americans and 10,500 Japanese. Halsey's determined charge up and down the Pacific has gone down in history as "Bull's Run."

TYPHOON

In mid-December, Halsey's Task Force 38 moved into position to launch strikes against airfields on Luzon in support of MacArthur's invasion of the island of Mindoro. Through a combination of inadequate information about a tropical disturbance and Halsey's desire to fulfill his mission, Task Force 38 walked into the middle of a typhoon.

According to Halsey, the storm tossed the battleship *New Jersey* "as if she were a

U.S. Navy

The carrier Bunker Hill burns after being hit by two Kamikaze pilots off the coast of Kyushu within a span of just 30 seconds on May 11, 1945. The Bunker Hill and Franklin were the only Essex-class carriers not to see active service after the war.

U.S. National Archives

Admiral Bill Halsey greets Fleet Admiral Chester Nimitz onboard the battleship South Dakota in Tokyo Bay, Japan on August 29, 1945.

canoe." On Halsey's destroyers, a fraction of the size of a battleship, the typhoon was a struggle between life and death. Three destroyers were swamped and sunk by the angry waves, with the loss of more than 800 men. Onboard the carriers nearly 200 aircraft were damaged or swept overboard. An inquiry into the tragedy found Halsey responsible but commended him for trying to fulfill mission requirements.

THE WAR ENDS

During the latter months of the war, Halsey led his carriers on raids up and down the coast of Japan. When Halsey received news of the Japanese surrender he ordered a "Well Done" flag hoisted and sounded his ship's horn for a full minute. He was still wary of individual Japanese who might ignore the surrender, ordering his pilots to "Investigate and shoot down all snoopers — not vindictively, but in a friendly sort of way."

Halsey's flagship, the battleship *Missouri*, was the sight of the Japanese surrender on

Battleship Yamato

Sister battleships Yamato and Musashi were the heaviest battleships ever launched. Nine 18-inch guns could lob 3200-pound shells more than 25 miles. The Yamato never had the chance to engage U.S. warships in surface combat. She was sunk by USN carrier aircraft while making a one-way suicidal voyage to shore up the defense of Okinawa in April 1945.

Wikimedia Commons

September 2, 1945. Halsey stood behind Nimitz as he signed the documents. Halsey retired two months later.

During the years after the war, he served on a corporate board and led fundraising efforts to convert the carrier *Enterprise* into a museum. The effort fell short, and the *Enterprise* was scrapped. In 1959, while vacationing, he was found dead in his room. Halsey was given a state funeral that included two 19-gun salutes and jet fighters roaring overhead as he was laid to rest in Arlington National Cemetery.

REVIEW QUESTIONS

1. *Which weapons were the most important in winning the war in the Pacific Theater?*
   a. Tanks
   b. Battleships
   c. Flamethrowers
   d. Carriers

2. *As a young officer, William "Bull" Halsey, Jr. participated in President Theodore Roosevelt's Great _____ Fleet world tour.*

3. *Halsey exhibited which characteristic as a commander?*
   a. A bold, aggressive spirit.
   b. Charming personality.
   c. Frankness that sometimes got him into trouble.
   d. All of the above.

4. *Halsey gave American morale a boost in 1942 with successful raids against Japanese bases in the _____ Islands.*
   a. Solomon
   b. Marshall and Gilbert
   c. Wake and Midway
   d. All of the above

5. *Halsey was in command of the carrier Hornet during the _____ raid on Japan.*

6. *Where was Halsey during the critical Battle of Midway?*
   a. At a conference in San Francisco with high-level USN commanders.
   b. In the hospital with a skin disease.
   c. Onboard the carrier Yorktown.
   d. Onboard the carrier Hornet.

7. *In 1943, after helping turn around the Guadalcanal campaign, Halsey assisted General Douglas MacArthur in capturing _____.*
   a. New Georgia   b. New Guinea
   c. Formosa   d. All of the above

8. *Operation _____ (Sho-go), a desperate attempt by the IJN to stop the American invasion of the Philippines, is better known as the Battle of Leyte Gulf.*

9. The Battle of Leyte Gulf is typically viewed as _____ separate actions or battles.

10. The intended purpose of the Japanese Carrier Group during the Battle of Leyte Gulf was _____.
    a. to seek and destroy Task Force 38
    b. to seek and destroy the American invasion force
    c. to lure away Task Force 38 so other groups could attack the invasion force
    d. to intimidate the Americans into abandoning the invasion

11. Two Japanese battleships, the Yamashiro and Fuso, were sunk in the Battle of _____ _____ by American battleships that survived the attack on Pearl Harbor.
    a. Surigao Strait   b. Samar
    c. Wake Island   d. Cape Engaño

12. During the Battle of Samar, U.S. Navy _____ bravely charged Japanese battleships and cruisers in order to protect Taffy 3, the northernmost of three groups supporting the invasion of the Philippines.

13. What was the historical significance of the Battle of Leyte Gulf?
    a. It was the last major surface naval battle.
    b. It was the greatest surface naval battle in terms of area covered and tonnage of ships.
    c. The Battle of Surigao Strait was the last time battleships fought one another.
    d. All of the above.

14. The Japanese surrender was signed aboard Halsey's flagship, the _____, in Tokyo Bay.
    a. Enterprise
    b. Missouri
    c. Hornet
    d. New Jersey

15. More than 3000 Allied sailors were killed by Japanese Kamikaze suicide attacks. What does the term Kamikaze mean in Japanese?
    a. Divine wind
    b. Revenge
    c. Wilting flower
    d. Death from above

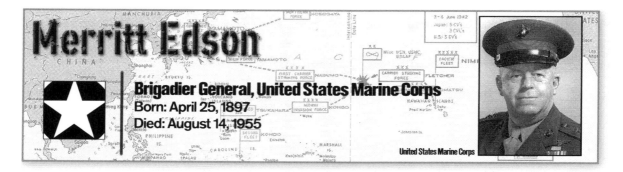

Merritt Edson

Brigadier General, United States Marine Corps
Born: April 25, 1897
Died: August 14, 1955

United States Marine Corps

By early 1942, the Japanese controlled most of the islands dotting the western Pacific. America would have to defeat the Japanese one island at a time. The U.S. Marines would be the primary means of rooting out the Japanese from their fortress islands.

Merritt "Red Mike" Edson was representative of many Marine officers who worked under unimaginable conditions to lead their men against a determined foe. Edson was born and raised in Vermont. He served a short time with the First Vermont National Guard Regiment before joining the Marine Corps Reserve in 1917. Edson sailed to France with the 11th Marines but did not see combat during the First World War.

In 1922, Edson earned his gold wings as a Naval aviator. He was forced to give up flying status in 1927 due to physical reasons. During the next two years, he led specially trained Marines in a number of engagements against bandits in Nicaragua. Sporting a distinctive red beard, he gained the nickname *"Red Mike."* Shortly before the Second World War began Edson spent time observing Japanese military operations as an operations officer in China.

Edson gained a reputation for training men in excellent marksmanship. He was not the stereotypical Marine, often coming across as shy and not quick to show his emotions. His dedicated brand of leadership earned fervent loyalty from the men under his command.

STRUGGLE FOR GUADALCANAL

In mid-1942, the Japanese began to construct an airfield on Guadalcanal in the Solo-

mon Islands. Allied planners, realizing that a Japanese presence on the island would threaten supply convoys between America and Australia, promptly planned to seize the airfield before it could be finished.

Guadalcanal (code name *"Cactus"*), like many South Pacific Islands, was sparsely populated and beautiful to behold from a distance. Soldiers who lived and fought on the island thought it anything but beautiful. The steamy jungle island was covered with swamps and lagoons inhabited by crocodiles, leaches, scorpions and mosquitoes. Plants and animals rotting in the warm sun created a stench. It was on this remote island that men lived, fought and died during a bitter six-month campaign.

On August 7, 1942, Edson and his Marines landed on Tulagi, a tiny island north of Guadalcanal. American soldiers quickly learned that the Japanese fought to the death, believing that to surrender would bring eternal dishonor on themselves and their families. While some Japanese swam to nearby Flori-

Lockheed P-38 Lightning

U.S. Air Force

The Lockheed P-38 Lightning was a twin-engine fighter that was also used for dive bombing, ground attacks and reconnaissance missions. The P-38's long range made it invaluable in the vast Pacific Theater. Sixteen Lightnings flew a long-range mission from Guadalcanal to destroy a plane carrying Japanese Admiral Isoroku Yamamoto in April 1943.

da Island, more than 700 of the 800 defenders were killed and only a handful taken prisoner.

The landing on Guadalcanal, *Operation Watchtower*, was unopposed. The Marines captured the almost-completed airfield the next day. Most of the Japanese on the island were workers who fled into the jungle, leaving behind all their food and equipment. This proved providential, as the threat of Japanese warships chased off the American transports before they could be unloaded.

Using Japanese tools and supplies, Navy SeaBees worked feverishly to complete the airstrip, named Henderson Field after a Marine aviator killed during the Battle of Midway. On August 20, welcomed by cheering Marines, the first *Douglas SBD Dauntless* and *Grumman F4F Wildcats* of the *Cactus Air Force* arrived. Despite the primitive runway, limited repair facilities and poor living conditions, the Cactus Air Force fought well and was instrumental in the success of the campaign.

The Japanese succeeded in landing 1000 troops under Colonel Kiyono Ichiki near Henderson Field. Planning an attack on the night of August 20, Ichiki was so confident that he wrote in his diary, "21 August. Enjoyment of fruits of victory." However, the Japanese had greatly underestimated the number of Marines on the island. After losing more than 800 men in a nightlong battle, Ichiki realized that he had also underestimated the resolve of the Marines.

Both sides rushed to deliver more troops to the island. The Americans sent reinforcements

U.S. National Archives

U.S. Marines cross the Matanikau River on the island of Guadalcanal in September 1942.

during the day when the Cactus Air Force could provide cover, while the Tokyo Express delivered Japanese troops at night in order to avoid the American planes.

By mid-September, the *Tokyo Express* had swelled Major General Kiyotake Kawaguchi's force to more than 6000. Kawaguchi's plan to attack Henderson Field from three sides might well have been successful. However, the unforgiving jungle hindered efforts to get in position. General Alexander Vandegrift, commander of Marine forces, anticipated an attack over a ridge from the south and placed Lieutenant Colonel Edson and his 1st Marine Raider Battalion at that point.

The Battle of Bloody Ridge began at about 9 p.m. on September 12. Edson exposed himself to enemy fire as he moved quickly between positions, encouraging and correcting

TRIVIA

Of the many items left behind by the Japanese on Guadalcanal, perhaps none was as cherished as a shed housing an ice-making machine. Marines placed a sign above the door christening it the *"Tojo Ice Factory."*

soldiers. Edson's men slowly retreated back up the ridge. The Japanese drew within 1000 yards of the airstrip, but as dawn arrived the attack faltered. Eight-hundred Marines succeeded in holding off repeated assaults from more than 2500 Japanese. The attacks from the east and west were also repelled. For his courage and leadership under fire, Edson received the Medal of Honor.

The Japanese refused to give up. During the next month, 13,500 fresh troops landed on the island. They brought with them 150mm guns capable of bombing Henderson Field from the other side of the Matanikau River. On the night of October 13, the battleships *Haruna* and *Kongo* bombarded Henderson Field destroying many planes.

October 23 marked the beginning of the last major Japanese offensive. Lieutenant General Harukitchi Hyakutake moved up the coast with tanks and artillery while the Sendai Division attacked from the south. The tank attack across the Matanikau sand bar was stopped by Marine anti-tank guns. The Sendai Division, delayed by a difficult jungle trek, did not attack until the 24th. Attacking after dark in a downpour, the Japanese achieved several breakthroughs before stalling due to horrendous losses.

At the end of October, a number of highly effective *Lockheed P-38 Lightning* fighters reinforced the overstretched Cactus Air Force. Convinced that the tide of battle had turned in their favor, Edson, now leading the 5th Marines, began to move west and seek out the Japanese. In early November, the Tokyo Express brought in the Hiroshima Division. At the same time, William "Bull" Halsey aggressively moved in his carrier group. During a three-day engagement, naval ships and planes from the Cactus Air Force and carrier *Enterprise* found and sank seven of 11 Japanese transports and the battleships *Hiei* and *Kirishima*. The remaining transports were run aground on Guadalcanal,

where they were destroyed, effectively ending the Tokyo Express.

Edson and the other Marines were relieved by Army units in December. In February 1943, with their ability to fight rapidly declining, the Japanese evacuated their remaining troops from Guadalcanal.

TARAWA

After Guadalcanal, Edson was promoted to Chief of Staff of the 2nd Marine Division. In his new position, he prepared an estimate for the amphibious attack on Tarawa Atoll that proved very accurate.

An aerial view of Betio Island in the Tarawa Atoll taken in September 1943. U.S. Marines invaded the island on November 20, 1943 and wrested control from the Japanese defenders. The stripe on the island is an airstrip. The whitish areas surrounding the island are coral reefs just below sea level.

The primary target was the island of Betio. At just 291 acres and barely large enough to hold an airstrip, the island bristled with coastal defense guns, artillery and machine guns manned by 2600 experienced troops. The troops were protected in pillboxes covered by sand and logs that were resistant to bombardment.

After an intense aerial and naval bombardment, Marines boarded Higgins boats and Amtracs and headed for shore. Boat bottoms caught on the coral reef shelf surrounding Betio, forcing Marines to wade through neck-high water over uneven coral while under fire. Many never made it to shore; some were shot, while others stepped into craters in the reef created by bombs and were never seen again. Of the Marines who made it to the beach, some huddled behind a sea wall while others bravely began to set about destroying the Japanese defenses.

The situation began to improve on the second day of the assault. The tide was higher, allowing the Higgins boats to reach the shore. Several tanks landed successfully and began to clear out pillboxes. The determined Marines moved slowly forward. To neutralize Japanese positions, the Marines developed a "corkscrew and blowtorch" method. Grenades or explosives were thrown through slits in the coconut log pillboxes. After the resulting explosion flushed out the Japanese, a flamethrower would be unleashed on them.

On the second night, hundreds of screaming Japanese charged the Marine lines. One company counted more than 300 Japanese bodies around their position the next morning. The first Navy *Grumman F6F Hellcat* landed on Betio's airstrip on the third day. A few stragglers were killed in the following days, but only 17 of Betio's fanatical defenders surrendered.

Allied leaders reflected on the hard lessons learned at Tarawa. More Amtracs were built and equipped with thicker armor and weapons. More research went into studying tides and water depth. New headquarters ships coordinated naval fire support. In a similar attack on Kwajalein in the Marshall Islands three months later, only 334 Americans were killed, compared to 1056 at Tarawa.

Edson was the Assistant Commander of the 2nd Marine Division during the invasions of Saipan and Tinian before being named Chief of Staff, Fleet Marine Pacific in 1944. Late in the war, Edson was asked by a younger officer when he would rotate home. Edson answered, "When the war's over; when the job's done."

Iwo Jima

The most costly fight was still to come. The target was Iwo Jima, an eight square-mile pork-chop-shaped volcanic island just 660 miles from Japan. Capturing the island with its airfields would allow American fighters to escort *Boeing B-29 Superfortresses* from Saipan to Japan and serve as an emergency landing site for damaged planes.

U.S. National Archives

Heavy Japanese fire pins U.S. Marines on the invasion beach during early moments of the invasion of Iwo Jima. The black cinders made digging foxholes impracticable.

U.S. National Archives

Destroyed Amtracs and other Marine vehicles litter the black sand beach of Iwo Jima. Mount Suribachi looms in the background.

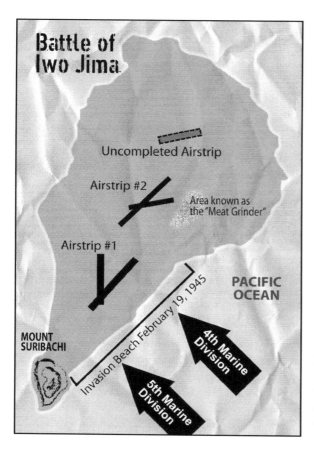

The 23,000 Japanese troops stationed on the island awaited an American attack. General Tadamichi Kuribayashi honeycombed the island with a network of tunnels and caves. As one U.S. officer said, "The Japanese were not on Iwo Jima, they were in it." An extensive 72-day bombing campaign preceding the invasion had little effect, as the soft volcanic ash absorbed the impact.

The first Marines on shore on February 19, 1945 were met with silence, as Kuribayashi ordered his men to hold their fire. As men and supplies piled up on the beach, the Japanese opened fire. Marines struggled to climb the steep cinder dunes. Digging a foxhole was futile as the sides kept falling in. The Americans suffered 2500 casualties on the first day. Overlooking the island was an extinct volcano, Mount Suribachi. Marines moving from one fortification to another worked their way up the volcano, succeeding in planting an American flag on the peak three days after the initial landing.

As the grueling fight for Suribachi wound down, the right flank of the attack was locked in a struggle so fierce the Marines named the area the *Meat Grinder*. On one day alone, the 4th Division lost 792 men while gaining only 200 yards.

The weight of the American attack could only be delayed, not stopped. Aided by eight American Sherman *"Zippo"* flamethrower tanks, the Marines pushed the Japanese back into a smaller area. In early March, the first B-29 made an emergency stop on the island.

The island was secured by late March: 6821 Marines were killed and 19,217 wounded while only 1083 Japanese surrendered during the battle and in the following days, months and years up until 1951. It was the only Pacific land battle in which American losses were greater than Japanese. By the end of the war, 2400 damaged planes landed on Iwo Jima, saving thousands of lives.

OKINAWA

Marines were part of the Tenth Army that invaded Okinawa. Led by Army General Simon Bolivar Buckner, Jr., the invasion force was backed by an immense 1600-ship armada that included 40 carriers. The invasion of Okinawa was the largest amphibious invasion in the Pacific Theater. The landings began April 1, 1945.

An elongated, twisting island that resembled a snake or dragon, the Japanese chose to defend only the two ends of Okinawa, allowing the Americans to walk ashore and capture the airfields in the center of the island. Veteran Marines were both ecstatic and extremely leery during the first five quiet days. Their suspicions proved well-founded as the Japanese bitterly contested the rest of the island.

Though fewer Japanese were defending the northern part of the island, they waged gueril-

U.S. National Archives

A Marine targets a Japanese sniper with his tommy-gun in an effort to take Wana Ridge on the island of Okinawa.

PELELIU

U.S. Marine Corps

A Chance Vought F4U Corsair aircraft pulls away after attacking a Japanese position on Mount Umurbrogol with napalm bombs.

In 1944, the Japanese changed their strategy for defending islands. Abandoning beach defense and fruitless Banzai charges, they began to build fortified bunkers and caves inland that required much effort to clear. One battle of this type that has been largely overlooked was the Battle of Peleliu in the Papau Islands. Located at the far western end of Chester Nimitz' Central Pacific drive, the capture of Peleliu would help cut off Japanese communications to the South Pacific.

The small island of Peleliu was dominated by Mount Umurbrogol. Led by Lieutenant General Sadae Inoue, 11,000 troops hid inside 500 caves dug into the mountain. Initial Marine losses were heavy during the September 15, 1944 landing, but the attackers were soon moving inland. In a rare Japanese tank charge, 13 light tanks roared across an airfield before several Sherman tanks and machine gunfire stopped them.

The 1st Marines were tasked with clearing Umurbrogol. The fight for the mountain was a yard-by-yard struggle that lasted a month. More than 8000 Americans were injured and almost 2000 killed while more than 10,000 Japanese died in the battle. Though overshadowed by the sheer number of casualties at Iwo Jima, many Marines claimed that the battle for tiny Peleliu was the most bitter struggle in the Pacific campaign.

la-style warfare in the dense forests in the island's interior. The struggle for the southern tip of the island would last more than two months. The veteran Japanese 62nd Division under the leadership of Lieutenant General Mitsuru Ushijima contested the ridges that rippled through the southern extremity of Okinawa. The Marines gave pleasant names to the ridges, such as *Chocolate Drop* and *Strawberry Hill*, that were at odds with the death and suffering that took place fighting for them.

Ushijima's troops blunted many frontal attacks while Kamikaze planes harassed the American fleet. However, the end result was never in doubt. Buckner did not live to see victory, as he was killed by an enemy shell on June 18. Several days later, Ushijima committed suicide as the last pockets of Japanese resistance were eliminated.

The dropping of the atomic bombs in August negated the need for an invasion of the Japanese homelands. For Edson, the Marines and everyone else, the war was finished. Edson retired in 1947 at the age of 50. He served as the first Commissioner of the Vermont State Police. In 1955, Edson took his own life. He was buried at Arlington National Cemetery. In 1958, the Navy named a destroyer *Edson* (DD-946) in his honor.

REVIEW QUESTIONS

1. The task of taking Pacific islands from the Japanese was primarily undertaken by the _____.
   a. U.S. Marines
   b. U.S. Army
   c. U.S. Navy
   d. British Army

2. An _____ being constructed by the Japanese on the island of Guadalcanal threatened to cut supplies to Australia.

3. What was NOT true about the island of Guadalcanal?
   a. Dotted with swamps and lagoons.
   b. Home to unfriendly natives.
   c. Inhabited by crocodiles, leaches, scorpions and mosquitoes.
   d. Covered with hot, steamy, dense jungles.

4. The U.S. invasion of Guadalcanal was known as Operation _____.
   a. Palm Tree
   b. Watchtower
   c. Solomon's Mine
   d. Kiwi

5. The airfield on Guadalcanal finished by Navy SeaBees became the home of the _____ Air Force.
   a. Cactus
   b. Solomons
   c. 15th
   d. Henderson

6. The _____ Express was a series of Japanese convoys bringing troops and supplies to Guadalcanal.
   a. Yamamoto
   b. Guadalcanal
   c. Rabaul
   d. Tokyo

7. Lieutenant Colonel Mike Edson's Marines successfully repelled Major General Kiyotake Kawaguchi's Japanese troops during the Battle of _____ _____.

8. One-thousand fifty-six Marines died taking the tiny but heavily defended island of _____ in the Tarawa Atoll.

9. Lessons learned at Tarawa and applied in future amphibious invasions included _____.
   a. Amtracs equipped with thicker armor and weapons
   b. more research into tides and water depths
   c. headquarters ships to coordinate Naval bombardments
   d. All of the above

10. _____ Japanese troops awaited U.S. Marines on the island of Iwo Jima.
    a. 10,000
    b. 13,000
    c. 23,000
    d. 33,000

11. The capture of Iwo Jima was of strategic importance because it _____.
    a. was Japan's largest island base
    b. was a major Japanese naval base
    c. could be used to support the strategic bombing of the Japanese mainland
    d. was a training site for Kamikaze pilots

12. The invasion of the Japanese island of _____ was the largest amphibious assault in the Pacific Theater during the war.

13. The battle for the island of _____ was especially difficult because of the extensive Japanese defenses built into Mount Umurbrogol.
    a. Peleliu
    b. Formosa
    c. Saipan
    d. Iwo Jima

14. The only island battle in which American losses were greater than Japanese was on _____.
    a. Okinawa
    b. Wake
    c. Tarawa
    d. Iwo Jima

15. Which high-ranking American general was killed during the Battle of Okinawa?
    a. Douglas MacArthur
    b. Simon Bolivar Buckner, Jr.
    c. Alexander Vandegrift
    d. Edson Merritt

Douglas MacArthur

Supreme Commander Southwest Pacific
Supreme Commander Allied Powers
Born: January 26, 1880
Died: April 5, 1964

U.S. National Archives

The Second World War brought many great leaders to the world's attention. Among American military leaders, no one had a larger profile than Douglas MacArthur. Brilliant and pompous, dedicated and self-serving, revered and reviled, every American of his day either loved or hated him. Though his political ambitions fell short in America, he wielded great power in two other countries: first as Field Marshal of the Philippines and later as *Supreme Commander Allied Powers* (SCAP) over Japan.

Born in an army barracks in Little Rock, Arkansas in 1880, MacArthur appeared destined for military glory. His father, Arthur MacArthur, a career soldier who had earned a Medal of Honor during the Civil War, moved his family between military posts in the Old West. MacArthur claimed he learned to ride and shoot before learning to read. His lifelong relationship with the Philippines began when his father was named governor of the archipelago in 1900.

A hard-working student, MacArthur graduated first in his 1903 West Point class. After graduation, he was assigned to the Philippines, the first of five tours in the region. He rose quickly through the ranks in the years leading up to the First World War. During the war, MacArthur was decorated for bravery nine times. He was promoted to brigadier general in 1918 and given command of the 42nd Rainbow Division. MacArthur was the youngest general in the Army and the only to serve in both world wars in that role.

After the war, MacArthur held a number of high-profile positions. In 1919, he was named the Superintendent of West Point. As president of the U.S. Olympic Committee, he prepared and led the American delegation to the 1928 Olympic games in Amsterdam. In 1930, he became the youngest person at the time to serve as Army Chief of Staff.

In 1935, Filipino President Manuel Quezon asked his longtime friend, MacArthur, to supervise the creation of a Philippine Army. First serv-

U.S. National Archives

Then Brigadier General Douglas MacArthur sits in a chair in St. Benoit Chateau, France several weeks before the end of the First World War in 1918.

ing as a military advisor, the grateful Filipinos conferred the title of Field Marshal on MacArthur in 1936.

FALL OF THE PHILIPPINES

MacArthur retired in 1941 only to return to active service when President Franklin Roosevelt placed him in command of U.S. forces in the Far East. MacArthur had 125,000 American and Filipino soldiers under his command, though 100,000 were ill-trained and armed reserve troops.

On December 8, 1941, the Japanese attacked Clark Field, destroying most of MacArthur's aircraft on the ground. Two days later, Japanese troops led by General Masaharu Homma began landing on Luzon. *War Plan Orange* was initiated in which Manila was declared an open city, and MacArthur withdrew his forces into the Bataan Peninsula.

MacArthur spent most of his time on Corregidor, an island fortified in 1914 to pro-

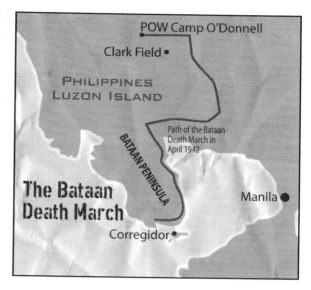

The Bataan Death March — map showing POW Camp O'Donnell, Clark Field, Philippines Luzon Island, Bataan Peninsula, Path of the Bataan Death March in April 1942, Manila, Corregidor.

tect Manila from sea attack. A labyrinth of concrete-reinforced tunnels was cut deep into the island; Corregidor had its own power plant, 21 fresh water wells and large 12-inch coastal guns.

The Battle of Bataan began January 7, 1942. American morale was high, but a lack of food and ammunition led to sickness and inevitable defeat. Roosevelt ordered MacArthur to slip through the Japanese blockade and make his way to Australia. On March 12, he, his family and several key officers boarded four PT boats and left the Philippines.

Though even the safety of Australia was in doubt and he had almost no forces, MacArthur told the press that he had come to Australia to organize "the American offensive against Japan. ... I came through and I shall return."

On April 9, General Edward King surrendered 78,000 men on Bataan. Though the Japanese promised proper treatment for the prisoners, at least 6000, and likely many more, died on the way to prisoner of war camps in what became known as the Bataan Death March. The Japanese forced Filipino and American troops to walk for days without food

Surrendering U.S. troops are escorted out of the island fortress of Corregidor in May 1942.

American and Filipino troops carry litters during the Bataan Death March in April 1942.

or water in the intense tropical heat with death the inevitable result. Stragglers were shot or stabbed with bayonets. After the war, General Homma was convicted of war crimes in connection with Bataan and executed.

On May 6, after weeks of constant bombardment, General Jonathan Wainwright surrendered Corregidor to the Japanese. He also officially surrendered the entire Philippines lest the men, nurses and civilians on Corregidor be slaughtered.

THE OFFENSIVE BEGINS

MacArthur was named *Supreme Commander, Southwest Pacific* (SWPA) area. The Joint Chief of staffs approved a two-pronged attack. MacArthur was ordered to clear New Guinea and drive to the north while Chester Nimitz drove across the central Pacific.

On July 22, 1942, the Japanese landed 16,000 men at Buna on the north coast of Papua, New Guinea. They planned to hike the Kokoda Trail over the 13,000-foot Owen Stanley mountain range and capture Port Moresby. Australian and American troops thwarted the attack, pushing the Japanese back to Buna, where they suffered their first major land defeat.

MacArthur had many troubling character traits. He was vain, arrogant and craved publicity. However, he did learn from his mistakes. The cost for Buna was high, three times the casualty rate of Guadalcanal. MacArthur promised no more Bunas. In future attacks, he isolated strong Japanese positions, surrounding them and leaving them to wither. He used General George Kenney's Fifth Air Force to pin down the weak Japanese air forces in the Southwest Pacific. With the assistance of Admiral Daniel Barbey's VII (Seventh) Amphibious Force, MacArthur staged 56 amphibious landings during the war.

The Japanese soon realized they were facing a great strategist as MacArthur moved troops fluidly, always striking where least expected. In February 1944, MacArthur struck quickly and captured the Admiralty Islands, further encircling the powerful base of Rabaul and isolating Japanese troops in New Guinea. In April, a major amphibious landing was made at Hollandia. A 580-mile jump past other Japanese positions, Americans had little trouble capturing Hollandia's air bases and other facilities. Only 159

American troops exit Higgins boats during the invasion of Wadke Island in Dutch New Guinea.

Americans died, while 7000 Japanese took to the jungle. Other small islands captured north of New Guinea included Biak and Noemfoor.

On July 26, MacArthur met with President Roosevelt and Nimitz at Pearl Harbor. He persuaded the two men to make the next step to recapture the Philippines. Four days later, troops landed on the western end of New Guinea at Sansapor, officially ending the New Guinea campaign. As would be the case on many Pacific islands, pockets of Japanese troops remained in hiding until the end of the war.

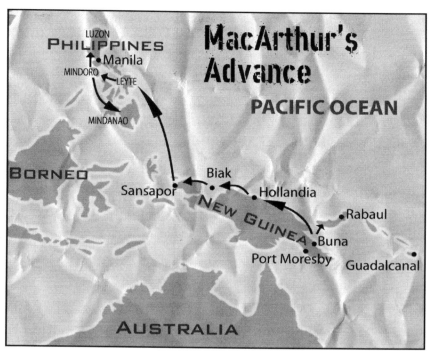

MACARTHUR RETURNS

In the fall of 1944, MacArthur finally realized his ambition to return to the Philippines. The planned invasion of Mindanao, the second-largest island of the Philippine archipelago, was scrapped after Admiral William Halsey alerted MacArthur that the Central Philippines was undefended. Centrally located, Leyte would be the first island retaken. Airfields established there would support the invasion of the surrounding islands.

A great armada that included 18 carriers, 17 escort carriers, 12 battleships, 28 cruisers, 150 destroyers and hundreds of support vessels supported the Leyte invasion forces.

TRIVIA

In 1943, MacArthur oversaw the largest parachute drop in the Pacific campaign. The Fifth Air Force dropped 1700 paratroopers on Nadzab, New Guinea as MacArthur watched from a B-17 overhead. The Japanese were surprised by the assault and offered no resistance.

On October 20, 1944, MacArthur, along with a large contingent of journalists documenting his every move, stepped off a transport into knee-deep water and splashed ashore at Leyte Gulf. He broadcast a message to the Filipino people that began, "People of the Philippines, I have returned. By the grace of Almighty God, our forces stand again on Philippine soil."

Halsey's claim of Japanese weakness turned out to be false; they were holding back in anticipation of the invasion. Heavy rains postponed the construction of airfields. The U.S. Sixth Army, under General Walter Krueger, advanced slowly. In a three-week struggle for Breakneck Ridge, both sides poured in reinforcements before the Americans finally broke the stalemate. Organized resistance on Leyte ceased in late December.

In early January 1945, an American invasion force headed toward Lingayen Gulf on Luzon, largest of the Philippine islands. The fleet was plagued by *Kamikazes*. The battleships *New Mexico* and *California* were both hit. The light carrier *Columbia* had a bomb blow up deep inside, knocking out her steering. Twelve ships in all were heavily damaged and one minesweeper sunk. The attacks left few Japanese planes to counter the actual invasion.

The invasion of Luzon began on January 9, 1945. Troops advanced south from Lingayen Gulf across Luzon's central plain. MacArthur became impatient when the advance on Manila was slowed because supplies could not be brought up rapidly. Clark Field was recaptured on January 30. General Tomoyuki Yamashita defended San Jose with 150 dug-in tanks just long enough to evacuate his forces to the northern mountains. Yamashita and 50,000 of his men would hold out in the mountains until *V-J Day*. Five-hundred Americans prisoners of war from the Bataan campaign celebrated their liberation at a nearby camp.

The equivalent of 10 divisions converged on Manila, with the first units entering on February 3. They immediately headed for Santo Tomás University, converted into a prison camp in 1942, to free 3700 Allied civilians; 24,000 Japanese, mostly naval troops under General Sanji Iwabuchi, defended the city. Iwabuchi had ordered water, electrical and military facilities destroyed. Much of the city burned and an estimated 100,000 citizens were killed as the month-long fight moved from street to street.

On February 16, paratroopers landed on Corregidor, paving the way for amphibious troops. The exterior of the island fortress was quickly captured while thousands of Japanese remained in tunnels. American troops began to seal the exits. Ten days later, a huge explosion rocked the island as the Japanese, buried alive, detonated their ammunition in an act of suicide. MacArthur borrowed four PT boats from the Navy so he could return to the island the same way he had left.

JAPANESE SURRENDER

MacArthur was making plans for the invasion of Japan when the atomic bombs were dropped in August. He served as the master of ceremonies at Japan's official surrender on September 2, 1945. Wainwright, having endured four unpleasant years in captivity, stood behind him as he signed the surrender documents.

MacArthur wielded almost unlimited power over the 83 million Japanese when he was appointed *Supreme Commander of the Allied Powers* (SCAP) by President Harry Truman. Overseeing the Japanese occupation until 1951, MacArthur shaped the future of Japan by rewriting their constitution, setting a foundation for industrial development and transforming the country from one based on cult-worship of the Emperor into a republic.

U.S. National Archives

MacArthur signs surrender documents onboard the battleship Missouri on September 2, 1945. Standing behind him is General Jonathan Wainwright.

U.S. National Archives

The battleship Pennsylvania leads a line of U.S. Navy ships into Lingayen Gulf preceding the landing on the Philippine island of Luzon in January 1945.

CONFLICT IN KOREA

Called by his country to help in the Korean War, MacArthur became the first commander of United Nations forces. He was credited with a great victory at Inchon that led to the recapture of Seoul. MacArthur's military career ended in 1951 over a dispute with President Harry Truman about the possible use of atomic weapons. Truman wanted a limited war, not a bigger one; MacArthur wanted all possible resources made available to win the war. When MacArthur arrived in Washington shortly after his dismissal, he gave a memorable speech in the House of Representatives and was the recipient of a ticker-tape parade in New York attended by an estimated 7.5 million people.

MacArthur accumulated more than 100 awards, commemorative medals and unofficial decorations. He made one final, emotional visit to the Philippines in 1961. MacArthur passed away in 1964. His state funeral was watched on television by millions. He was buried in the rotunda of the old Norfolk, Virginia courthouse that is now known as the MacArthur Memorial.

REVIEW QUESTIONS

1. Douglas MacArthur was the only American to serve as a _____ in both world wars.

2. Which high-profile position did MacArthur not hold?
   a. President of the U.S. Olympic Committee
   b. Superintendent of West Point
   c. Governor of California
   d. Field Marshal of the Philippines

3. When the Japanese invaded the Philippines in 1941 MacArthur coordinated war efforts from _____, an island fortress.

4. _____ ordered MacArthur to escape from the Philippines to Australia.
   a. Admiral Chester Nimitz
   b. President Franklin Roosevelt
   c. President Harry Truman
   d. General George Marshall

5. After American and Filipino forces on the Philippines surrendered, they were subjected to the brutal Bataan _____ March in which many died on the way to prisoner of war camps.

6. MacArthur's first offensive was to remove the Japanese from the island of _____.
   a. Luzon   b. Guadalcanal
   c. Borneo   d. New Guinea

7. In April 1944, MacArthur's forces jumped more than 580 miles of Japanese positions to capture _____.
   a. Hollandia   b. Leyte
   c. Sansapor   d. Mindanao

8. *The first Philippine island to be recaptured by Allied forces was _____ in December 1944.*
   a. Mindanao   b. Leyte
   c. Luzon   d. Samar

9. *The bitter battle for control of the Philippine capital city of Manila resulted in the deaths of 100,000 _____.*
   a. Japanese   b. Americans
   c. Filipinos   d. Prisoners of war

10. *Where was MacArthur at the end of the war?*
    a. Remained in the Philippines
    b. Accepted Japanese surrender onboard the battleship Missouri
    c. Moving into the Japanese emperor's palace
    d. Retired and back home in the States.

Landing Ship, Tank

U.S. National Archives

The Landing Ship, Tank (LST) was the primary means of getting heavy weapons and supplies onto invasion beaches. Here, soldiers work feverishly to unload two LSTs on a Leyte Island beach.

11. *Appointed Supreme Commander of the Allied Powers (SCAP) in 1945, MacArthur wielded almost unlimited power over the country of _____ until 1951.*

12. *MacArthur's career ended after a disagreement with President _____ over handling of the war in Korea.*

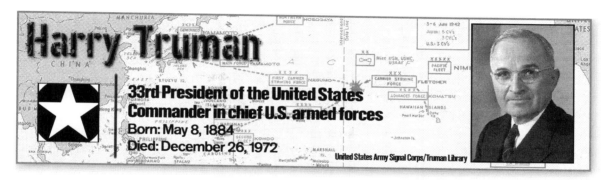

Harry Truman

33rd President of the United States
Commander in chief U.S. armed forces
Born: May 8, 1884
Died: December 26, 1972

United States Army Signal Corps/Truman Library

On April 12, 1945 President Franklin Roosevelt suffered a stroke and died several hours later. With his passing, a mourning nation looked to the relatively unknown vice president who would replace him, Harry S. Truman. Truman took the oath of office just hours after Roosevelt's passing. The war was winding down in Europe, but Truman would be faced with many critical decisions during his first few months in office that would shape the world in coming decades. Among these were the decision to use the atomic bomb and the post-war makeup of Europe.

Truman was born in Lamar, Missouri on May 4, 1884. He grew up in the town of Independence near Kansas City. He received no education beyond high school but was an avid reader as his parents made books a priority for the family. He loved to read about history and the classics. He read through the Bible twice by the time he was 12.

Truman joined the Missouri National Guard in 1905 after he was turned down by West Point because of poor vision. During the First World War, Truman was captain of an artillery unit in France. His unit supported Colonel George Patton's advance during the Meuse-Argonne offensive.

ENTRY INTO POLITICS

After the war, Truman owned a haberdashery (men's clothing store) in Kansas City for several years. He spent eight years as judge of Jackson County, an administrative position in which he helped build up Kansas City.

TRIVIA

Due to his poor vision, Truman received his first pair of eyeglasses at age six. He said the glasses opened up the world for him.

In 1934, he was elected senator for the state of Missouri. Arriving in Washington broke, he was forced to take out a loan to pay for furnishings for his family's apartment. Truman earned a reputation in Washington for being hard working and honest. During the early days of the Second World War, Truman headed the *Special Committee to Investigate the National Defense Program*. He saved taxpayers money by uncovering waste and corruption.

In 1944, Truman was nominated to run as Vice President on a ticket with President Roosevelt. Roosevelt and Truman won. Truman's time as Vice President was brief, as Roosevelt's failing health led to his death. Less than three months after taking office Truman found himself as the leader of America. About an hour after taking the oath of office, Truman was informed about a spectacular new weapon being developed that had the potential to end the war quickly — the atomic bomb.

THE MANHATTAN PROJECT

Hungarian-born physicist Leo Szilard, convinced German scientists were working to create an atomic bomb, raised the alarm in 1938. Though much of what scientists knew at the time about atomic energy was still theoretical, Szilard succeeded in persuading Albert Einstein to warn President Roosevelt about the potential danger. Roosevelt established a committee that became the nucleus of the *Manhattan Project*, so named because the original offices were located in Manhattan, New York.

Alarm over the German atomic program increased when the Germans captured Belgium's uranium deposits in the Congo and Norway's "heavy water" facility at Vermork. Many scientists believed that heavy water would be essential to operation of a nuclear reactor. It was not known until much later that German scientists had made many wrong assumptions. Despite their optimism and efforts until the end of the war, Germany never came close to producing a bomb.

In America, scientists pursued the theory of using graphite instead of heavy water to control atomic reactions. Enrico Fermi and other scientists constructed a 500-ton pile of graphite bricks on a squash court at the University of Chicago. On December 2, 1942, using long control rods inserted into the pile, the scientists achieved the first controlled release of energy from the atomic nucleus.

Having proved that atomic power was feasible, Colonel Leslie Groves, an Army engineer who had supervised the construction of the Pentagon, was placed in charge of the project. Groves did not understand the scientific side of the project, so he hired Dr. J. Robert Oppenheimer to recruit and lead the scientists. A boys' preparatory school at Los Alamos, New Mexico was converted into the site for the project. Oppenheimer used his charm and persuasion to assemble a brilliant and prestigious group of scientists to work on the project.

Despite a tight cloak of secrecy, rumors about the project abounded. Oppenheimer actually encouraged a rumor that they were building electric rockets to serve as a cover story. The Manhattan Project eventually involved

U.S. Department of Energy

The military leader of the Manhattan Project, Leslie Groves, talks with the scientific leader, Professor J. Robert Oppenheimer.

"Fat Man" Atomic Bomb

The "Fat Man" atomic bomb was detonated over Nagasaki on August 9, 1945. The rotund weapon with a plutonium core was delivered by the B-29 "Bockscar." The bomb dropped on Hiroshima was known as "Little Boy."

U.S. Department of Defense

U.S. National Archives

Paul Tibbets, captain of the B-29 Superfortress Enola Gay, waves before takeoff on the mission to drop the first atomic bomb on Hiroshima.

4000 civilians and 2000 military personnel at Los Alamos, in addition to tens of thousands of others who worked at secretive factories in Oak Ridge, Tennessee and Hanford, Washington processing plutonium.

After the war in Europe ended, work on the atomic bomb continued. On Monday, July 16, 1945 the first atomic bomb was successfully tested at Alamogordo Bombing Range. Eager scientists watching 10 miles from the detonation were awed by the bright light and terrible sound. Truman, at the Potsdam conference in Germany, received a cryptic message confirming success, "Operated on this morning. Diagnosis not yet complete but results seem satisfactory and already exceed expectations." Truman hinted to Stalin that America had developed a new powerful weapon. Stalin was not surprised; due to espionage, he had known about the Manhattan Project even before Truman became President.

At the conclusion of the meeting, the leaders issued the Potsdam Declaration calling on Japan to surrender unconditionally. The declaration promised that Japan would not be destroyed as a people or nation, but ominously promised "utter destruction" if she chose to continue to fight.

On July 26, the heavy cruiser *Indianapolis* delivered the core of the "Little Boy" bomb to Tinian Harbor in the Marianas Islands. The *Indianapolis* was sunk four days later by a Japanese

sub. Amazingly, it was several days before anyone realized the cruiser was missing. Only 315 of her 1196 men were rescued after spending 85 hours in the ocean. Few men died during the attack; clumped together in small groups clinging to debris, most died in the water as a result of shark attacks or losing their mind and drowning. The *Indianapolis* holds two historical distinctions in that she was the last major American warship sunk in the war and the greatest single loss of men in U.S. Navy history.

Some historians say that Truman agonized over whether to unleash the dreadful and powerful new weapon. Truman said he viewed the bomb as a military weapon and claimed to have no doubts about using it. Once the decision was made, he said he "went to bed and slept soundly."

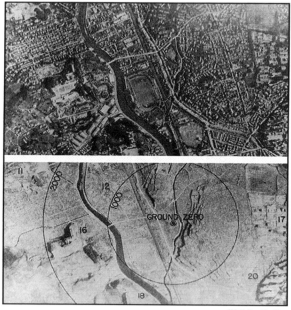

A before and after photo of Nagasaki illustrates the magnitude of devastation caused by a single atomic bomb.

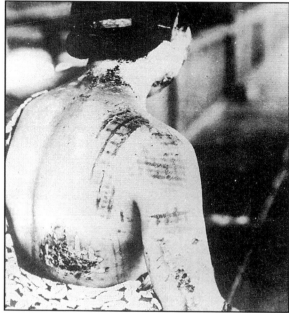

An atomic bomb survivor exhibits severe radiation burns that penetrated through her kimono.

In the early morning of August 6, 1945, Captain Paul Tibbets headed his B-29 *"Enola Gay"* (his mother's name) down the runway at Tinian. The city of Hiroshima was targeted because it was one of few remaining intact Japanese cities. It had military facilities and no prisoner of war camps. The bomb was delivered at 8:15 a.m. local time. As Tibbets and his crew fled the area at top speed, they saw a blinding light and the telltale mushroom cloud.

The bomb detonated at a height of 1900 feet above ground. Victims nearest the blast may have been the most fortunate because they were instantly vaporized and felt nothing. Upwards of 80,000 people were killed instantly. Farther from the blast, badly injured survivors were unable to help themselves or one another. The blast caused painful burns that led to many more agonizing deaths during the ensuing days and weeks. There was no one to help the victims; more than 90% of the doctors and nurses in Hiroshima had been killed, and those who survived were badly injured themselves.

JAPAN REACTS TO THE BOMBS

Traveling home from the Potsdam Conference onboard the cruiser *Augusta*, Truman received the news of the successful bombing of Hiroshima while eating lunch with servicemen. Truman excitedly announced the success to the crew. News of the bombing brought relief to many Americans, convincing them that the war would soon end. It also gave them reason to pause and ponder what such a powerful and terrible weapon could mean for the future.

Scientists at Los Alamos cheered wildly when they received the news of Hiroshima while shocked Japanese leaders deliberated about how to respond. Perhaps the Americans had only the one bomb? On August 9, a second

U.S. National Archives

Harry Truman announces the Japanese surrender from the Oval Office in the White House in Washington D.C.

bomb, "Fat Man," was dropped on Nagasaki; 40,000 Japanese were killed instantly, while another 30,000 died of their wounds in the following days. Years and decades later, survivors continued to suffer side effects and premature deaths as a result of radiation.

After the second bomb was dropped, Truman ordered that a third bomb be delayed to give the Japanese time to ponder their plight. Emperor Hirohito convinced his government that the war must end. On August 14, after several days of nervous waiting, the Japanese surrendered. The official treaty was signed onboard the battleship *Missouri* on September 2. The Second World War was over.

POSTWAR

After the war, Truman struggled to transition the American economy to peacetime. Having sensed the dark side of Stalin while at Potsdam, Truman took a hardline stance against Communism. In response to pressure on Greece and Turkey from the Soviet Union, Truman set forth the principle of helping free

peoples to resist Communism in what came to be known as the *Truman Doctrine*. Truman embraced the *Marshall Plan*, which sought to give aid to rebuild Europe, as another way to contain Communism.

In 1948, Truman was elected to a second term in an upset victory over Thomas Dewey. Truman issued several executive orders that provided support for the blossoming civil rights movement. In 1951, he made the difficult and extremely unpopular decision to remove Douglas MacArthur from command in Korea. Truman wanted to limit the spread of the war, while MacArthur wished to pursue it aggressively.

The sacking of MacArthur and two years of legislative stalemate led to Truman reaching a low in popularity. He canceled his reelection campaign rather than risk an embarrassing defeat. Truman lived out his final years in Independence, Missouri. He established a presidential library and published memoirs about his years in office. Truman died in 1972 from complications from pneumonia. Declining the option of a state funeral, he was buried in his library in Independence in a private ceremony.

REVIEW QUESTIONS

1. *Harry Truman's career in national politics began in 1934 when he was elected as a senator from the state of* _____.
   a. Missouri
   b. Kansas
   c. Illinois
   d. Iowa

2. *How long did Truman serve as Vice President before he became President?*
   a. Three weeks
   b. Three months
   c. Three years
   d. Truman was never Vice President

Boeing B-29 Superfortress

U.S. Air Force

The B-29 Superfortress was one of the most advanced weapons to come out of the war. The pressurized bombers could deliver 20,000 pounds of bombs at a range of more than 2600 miles. B-29's were instrumental in systematically leveling many Japanese cities.

3. Scientist Albert _____ was instrumental in convincing President Franklin Roosevelt to pursue the development of atomic weapons.

4. Scientist _____ successfully led the effort to achieve the first controlled release of energy from the atomic nucleus in experiments at the University of Chicago.
   a. Albert Einstein
   b. J. Robert Oppenheimer
   c. Leo Szilard
   d. Enrico Fermi

5. The Manhattan Project's military leader was _____.

6. The Manhattan Project's scientific leader was _____.

7. The main research site for the Manhattan Project was _____.
   a. Manhattan Island
   b. Los Alamos, New Mexico
   c. Washington, D.C.
   d. Oak Ridge, Tennessee

8. Truman learned of the success of the first atomic bomb test while attending the _____ Conference.
   a. Yalta
   b. Tehran
   c. Quebec
   d. Potsdam

9. The heavy cruiser _____ was the last major American warship sunk in the war and the greatest single loss of men in U.S. Navy history.

10. The first atomic bomb was dropped on the Japanese city of _____ on August 6, 1945, instantly killing upwards of 80,000 people.
    a. Hiroshima
    b. Nagasaki
    c. Tokyo
    d. Osaka

11. The second atomic bomb was dropped on the Japanese city of _____ on August 9, 1945, instantly killing upwards of 40,000 people.
    a. Hiroshima
    b. Nagasaki
    c. Tokyo
    d. Osaka

12. The Truman _____, set forth by President Truman, established the principle of helping free peoples to resist Communism.

13. President Truman saw his popularity decline after removing General _____ from command in 1951.
    a. Dwight Eisenhower
    b. Omar Bradley
    c. George Patton
    d. Douglas MacArthur

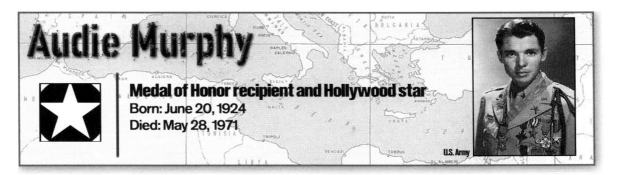

For every Famous man who shaped the events of the Second World War while in the public eye, there were thousands who served in obscurity. These men did not fight for political agendas but for their families and countries. One of the more remarkable stories is of a young Texan, Audie Murphy, who became the most-decorated soldier in the history of the United States Army.

Murphy was born on June 20, 1925 on a farm near Kingston, Texas. The son of poor Irish-American sharecroppers, Murphy was the sixth of 12 children. He was slight-of-build and often fought other kids to prove his toughness. With his father gone for long periods of time, Murphy dropped out of school after the fifth grade to help support his family. He later credited his incredible shooting skills to having been forced to hunt small game to feed his family. "If I missed, we didn't eat." he said. He was at his mother's side when she passed away. Only 15 at the time of her death, Murphy took care of his family until he enlisted, when he placed three younger siblings, whom he reclaimed after the war, in an orphanage.

Murphy wanted to enlist after Pearl Harbor but was still too young. He lied in an attempt to join the Marine Corps. He was turned down by the Marines and the Navy because he was too small. He was finally accepted into the Army infantry on his 18th birthday. At the time, he was 5 feet, 5 inches tall and weighed 110 pounds.

After passing out during his first drill at Camp Wolters, Texas, Murphy gained the nickname of "Baby." His commanding officer tried to transfer him out of the infantry to become a cook where things weren't so rough, but Murphy refused to leave. Murphy wanted to fight.

Farm Security Administration

The Medal of Honor is the highest honor awarded by the United States. The award is given to members of the armed forces who show great courage and sacrifice while risking their life in action against the enemy. Since 1941 more than half the awards have been given after the death of the recipient, most dying during the action that earned them the medal.

Sicily and Italy

In January 1943, Murphy embarked on a ship for North Africa. He endured several months of training before taking part in *Operation Husky*, the invasion of Sicily. Murphy was assigned to the 3rd Infantry Division under General George Patton. Members of the 3rd Division would see more than 500 days of combat and earn an incredible 46 Medals of Honor during the war. When not in a hospital, Murphy would be in almost continuous combat for the next two years.

A pre-invasion storm buffeted the small landing craft, making Murphy and the other soldiers sick. In his first combat shortly after landing, in which Murphy killed two Italian officers on horseback, he showed no hesitancy to fight. A

Susan Highsmith

The author and his son pose beside a statue of Audie Murphy at the Audie L. Murphy Hunt County Veteran's Exhibit in Greenville, Texas. Murphy holds a German MG-42 machine gun like the one he used to clear a ridge full of Germans shortly after the death of his buddy, Lattie Tipton.

serious case of malaria sidelined him for a week shortly before the end of the campaign.

The attack on the Italian mainland was expected to be easy after the Italians surrendered. Little did Allied troops know that German soldiers under the leadership of Field Marshal Albert Kesselring would make them pay for every yard. Murphy landed at Salerno. He was promoted to Sergeant after fighting his way out of a German ambush. Murphy and the 3rd Division fought through the tough Italian winter against stubborn German defenses.

One day, Murphy watched his best friend Lattie Tipton take out a machine gun nest, killing five Germans in the process. Murphy thought Tipton was the bravest man he knew. As the Italian campaign continued, Murphy could not help but notice that one-by-one his friends were suffering grave injuries or being killed. Of the 232 men in his company, he would be one of only two not to be killed or sent home before the end of the war.

Murphy fell sick once again shortly before the landing at Anzio. He arrived with a boatload of replacements several days after the first troops stepped ashore. During the four-month long struggle to break out of the fragile beachhead, Murphy led a number of raids to reconnoiter and disrupt the Germans. Still a young-looking 19, as Platoon Sergeant, Murphy was in charge of four squads comprising 40 men (when full strength). Murphy won a Bronze Star for denying the Germans the chance to recover a slightly damaged tank. Once again, Murphy fell ill with a high fever and was sent to a field hospital. Murphy spent time in Rome before he took part in his fourth amphibious assault, *Operation Dragoon,* the invasion of Southern France.

FRANCE

Though he had seen enough war in Sicily and Italy for a lifetime, Murphy's greatest accomplishments were still to come. During five months of fighting in France, Murphy would be wounded three times, promoted to officer on the battlefield and win numerous medals and honors.

On August 15, 1944, Murphy landed in southern France with the first wave while an Allied rocket barrage screamed overhead. Shortly after landing, he and Tipton were clearing a machine gun nest when a German soldier held up a white rag signaling surrender. Murphy recognized it as a ruse, but Tipton, ignoring his warning, stood up and was promptly shot and killed. Half-crazed, Audie picked up a German machine gun and charged up the hill, shooting and hurling grenades. His actions eliminated several machine gun nests and cleared an entire ridge of Germans. For his actions that day, he was awarded the Distinguished Service Cross. After his return to America, Murphy gave the award to Tipton's daughter, who was only 9 years old when her father left for the war.

German General Friedrich Wiese began to retreat his 19th Army during what U.S. soldiers called the "Champagne Campaign." During this time, a mortar shell once landed several feet from Murphy. The blast killed the two men standing next to him, but merely knocked out Murphy and left him with a few splinters. Another time, out of concern, Murphy followed two colonels and a captain who insisted on scouting the frontline. Murphy saved their lives by wiping out a machine gun crew that pinned down the officers.

On October 14, Murphy was commissioned as a Second Lieutenant. Twelve days later, he was hit in the side and buttocks by a sniper. He managed to kill the sniper before going to the hospital, where he eventually had five pounds of dead flesh removed. Murphy was discharged from the hospital on December 28.

Under fire near Holtzwihr, France on January 26, 1945 and with his unit down to 19, Murphy sent his men back and faced a German advance alone. After running out of rifle ammunition, Murphy climbed onboard a burning M10 tank destroyer and continued fighting with the tank's .50 caliber machine gun. Calling down artillery on top of his position and shooting at anything that moved, Murphy held off an estimated 250 Germans (killing at least 35) for an hour. A break in the clouds allowed Allied air support to attack, driving back the Germans. Though injured in his leg, he returned to his men and organized a counterattack. The M10 exploded shortly after Murphy dismounted. For his actions, Audie Murphy was awarded America's highest award for bravery, the Medal of Honor.

Several days later, shortly after capturing six Germans, Murphy noticed a large number of German tanks and men approaching. Grabbing the captured Germans' helmets, Murphy and his men waved at the passing tanks and infantrymen. He and his men were fortunate not to be recognized.

Murphy was awarded the Distinguished Service Cross and Silver Star March 5, 1945. Having come to the attention of high-level officers who wanted to protect Murphy for publicity purposes, he was promoted to staff as a liaison officer. Murphy was not really cut out for staff work. His primary responsibility was to drive around in a Jeep making contact with individual units to keep headquarters informed. Never shaking his habit of seeking out danger, Murphy found a way to sneak up to the front and lead his old Company B across the Siegfried Line.

Murphy returned to America in June 1945, receiving a hero's welcome along with a number of generals in Houston. He appeared on the cover of *LIFE* magazine on July 16, 1945. For his wartime service, Murphy was awarded 33 medals from the United States, five from France and one from Belgium. It is estimated that Mur-

U.S. National Archives

Allies march through the Siegfried Line, Germany's last major defensive fortification on the Western Front.

Courtesy of Mary Black

Boyd Cecil Yount, ABOVE, of South Carolina was one of the many Americans who died while fighting the German Wehrmacht in France. The author's grandfather, Kenneth Highsmith, LEFT, served in the U.S. Navy as a postal clerk. The vast majority of enlisted men did not fill combat roles but served in support roles such as mechanics, cooks, logistics and training.

phy killed about 240 Germans. He claimed that he tracked many more who he could have killed but did not, as he judged them to be of no immediate threat.

HOLLYWOOD CALLS

With the war finished, Murphy faced the daunting prospect of returning to civilian life as a 20-year-old war hero. While many veterans attended school or returned to pre-war jobs, Murphy was at a loss. Actor James Cagney saw the *LIFE* magazine article on Murphy and figured the young man had star potential. Cagney brought him out to Hollywood and put him on the payroll to begin studying acting. Though acting did not thrill him, Murphy admitted, "I came to Hollywood because I had no place to go."

Murphy found a niche in Hollywood, appearing in 44 movies, most of which were low-budget westerns. Murphy became known as the "King of the B-westerns." In the 1950's, Murphy starred as himself in "To Hell and Back." The movie was based on his autobiography written with the help of his friend and ghostwriter David McClure. The U.S. Army backed the movie in the hopes that it would bolster recruiting. General Walter Bedell Smith volunteered the entire 44th Infantry Division to be used in filming the movie at Fort Lewis in Washington state. The movie was a great success.

POST TRAUMATIC STRESS SYNDROME

Though he claimed to carry a weary indifference with him throughout the war, the horrors of combat had a lasting effect on Murphy. Like many other veterans, Murphy suffered from *Post Traumatic Stress Syndrome*. Little was known about the illness at the time. Victims experience restlessness, nightmares, are quick to anger and are apathetic about civilian affairs.

Tortured by nightmares about the war, Murphy slept with a loaded pistol under his pillow. McClure claimed that much of Murphy's autobiography was made up because it obviously pained Murphy to share his war experiences. Murphy gambled just for the thrill, not caring if he won or lost. Though married twice, he struggled to have healthy relationships with women. He also went through a dark period of addiction to sleep medicine in the 1960's.

Murphy was killed in a plane wreck in West Virginia on May 28, 1971. Though he had requested a simply ceremony, he was buried in Arlington National Cemetery with full military honors. His grave is one of the most visited (second only to President John F. Kennedy) at Arlington. To the day he died, Murphy insisted that the real heroes were the 291,000 Americans who died in combat and did not return.

A soldier mourns the loss of his friends on a small atoll in the Pacific Ocean in 1944. More than 400,000 Americans perished (291,000 in combat) in the Second World War.

REVIEW QUESTIONS

1. Audie Murphy was the most highly _____ American soldier of the war.

2. Audie Murphy was turned down by the _____.

  a. Navy
  b. Marines
  c. Both a and b
  d. Audie was not turned down by any service branch

3. Which amphibious assault was Audie Murphy NOT part of?

  a. Northern France
  b. Sicily
  c. Mainland Italy
  d. Southern France

4. While in France, Murphy was wounded _____ times.

  a. one
  b. two
  c. three
  d. four

5. For single-handedly holding off 250 Germans for an hour near Holtzwihr, France, Murphy was awarded the _____.

  a. Distinguished Service Cross
  b. Medal of Honor
  c. Silver Star
  d. Purple Heart

6. Murphy helped lead his Company B across the German _____ Line.

  a. Deustchland
  b. Barbarossa
  c. Hindenberg
  d. Siegfried

7. After returning from the war, Murphy became a _____ star.

8. Like many veterans returning from the war, Murphy suffered from Post Traumatic _____ Syndrome.

9. About how many Americans died in combat during the Second World War?

  a. 191,000
  b. 291,000
  c. 491,000
  d. 891,000

Famous Women

While the names of the Famous men of the Second World War will be remembered for generations to come, it would be a shame not to recognize the countless women who served without recognition, toiling and sacrificing to help their country's war effort.

American women served in a number of roles. Millions of men left civilian jobs to enlist in the military just as President Roosevelt's "Arsenal of Democracy" was expanding production. Women filled the employment gap, undertaking many traditionally male-only jobs.

Women performed not only standard assembly line work, but sweated in foundries, drove tractors, served as volunteer firemen, operated huge hydraulic presses and labored in dingy mines. Women tested ordnance, machine guns, antiaircraft guns and other weapons before they were sent to the troops. One recent high school graduate found herself operating a 15-ton crane. Women also performed delicate chores such as assembling navigation equipment in clean rooms. There were only 36 women shipbuilders in 1939, but 23,000 worked the shipyards just four years later.

The repetitive nature of most jobs was a big challenge for the women, who often worked more than the standard 48-hour work week. In addition to long hours, women often managed a household alone as many men were overseas. Even "normal" housewives struggled as rationing forced them to improvise.

Margaret Bourke-White was the first woman photographer to fly on a combat mission. Hired by *LIFE* magazine in 1936,

Bourke-White documented both combat and the experiences of women serving in the military. She was one of the first journalists to cover the liberation of Nazi death camps, about which she wrote a book, *Dear Fatherland, Rest Quietly*.

AMERICAN WOMEN IN THE MILITARY

Almost all the nurses who served in the *Army Nurse Corps* (ANC) were commissioned officers. Nurses tended to be women in their late 20s or early 30s. Many of their patients, who they called "their boys," were in their teens or early 20s.

Nurses were more likely to face combat situations than other military women. Army nurses first saw action in the Philippines. They shared the hardships of the men they served. Sixty-six nurses in the island fortress of Corregidor were captured by the Japanese and spent the remainder of the war in a prisoner-of-war camp. They were generally well treated but underfed and overcrowded with 500

Po-2 Biplane

The Polikarpov PO-2 was the most-produced biplane in history. The unspectacular, but sturdy and reliable, plane served as a trainer, in reconnaissance and as an inexpensive bomber. Russian women flew PO-2 on night bombing missions to disrupt the Germans.

American factory workers attend to every detail in constructing an airplane.

A lathe operator machines parts for airplanes at the Consolidated Aircraft Corporation plant in Fort Worth, Texas.

women and just three showers and five toilets. The nurses were freed on February 3, 1945, almost three years later.

Learning from the experience of Corregidor, Army nurses were given field training that included 20-mile hikes with 30-pound backpacks. Nurses learned to quickly set up and take down mobile hospitals. Serving close to the front lines, nurses were sometimes killed in the line of duty. Army flight nurses frequently accompanied patients on transport planes.

Navy Nurse Corps (NNC) nurses typically were not exposed to combat situations, as they served on hospital ships. Navy nurses, having spent years learning their trade, trained male Navy medics. By the end of 1942, Army nurses were allowed to marry, while the Navy did not allow its nurses to marry until 1944. Female physicians found much resistance to their willingness to serve and less than 100 were commissioned.

First Lady Eleanor Roosevelt was instrumental in the creation of the *Women's Army Corps* (WAC). WAC was an auxiliary serving mainly in clerical or technical tasks. Douglas MacArthur called the Corps members his best soldiers. Dwight Eisenhower, impressed with their competence, could not get as many women assigned as he wished.

Women serving in the Navy were known as *Women Accepted for Voluntary Service* (WAVES). Like nurses, WAVES were required to have a college degree or some work experience.

George Marshall hoped to build the WAC to a strength of 500,000, but it never exceeded 100,000. Many women were willing to serve but were not able to because of domestic commitments. High educational standards further limited the pool of candidates. Older women and minorities were often rejected due to discriminatory practices. Finally, women in the mili-

For your country's sake today—

For your own sake tomorrow

GO TO THE NEAREST RECRUITING STATION
OF THE ARMED SERVICE OF YOUR CHOICE

Defense Imagery Management Operations Center

A recruiting poster urging women to join the United States armed forces.

tary suffered from bad publicity as many people thought serving in the military encouraged women to live inappropriate lifestyles; however, this belief proved incorrect.

More than 25,000 women applied for the opportunity to join the *Women Airforce Service Pilots* (WASP). The 1102 women who were accepted and completed training at a remote base in Sweetwater, Texas performed several important duties. The WASP freed men for combat duty by flying airplanes from factories to air bases, towed gunnery targets for troops and performed test flights on repaired aircraft. WASP pilots ferried every kind of plane, including advanced fighters and large bombers. Thirty-eight WASP pilots died in the line of duty due to accidents or malfunctions.

GREAT BRITAIN

British women who flew airplanes were part of the *Air Transport Auxiliary* (ATA). Several American women pilots served in the ATA where, unlike in America, they faced additional dangers including German planes, barrage balloons and the very crowded skies over Great Britain.

British women serving in the *Women's Auxiliary Air Force* (WAAF) proved effective in tracking German planes in plotting rooms during the critical Battle of Britain. Working in small shacks near radar towers that were targeted by German bombers, WAAF members were in constant danger.

AXIS COUNTRIES

In Nazi Germany, the role of women was more conservative. Women were encouraged to stay at home and raise large families. However, the demands of war forced the Nazis to allow women to serve in a number of capacities. The majority served in administrative roles or as nurses. Others served in the signals and air defense services.

Finland greatly depended on women to support its war effort, giving many important duties to the *Lotta Svärd* paramilitary organization for women. Created in 1918, the Lotta Svärds boasted more than 230,000 members during the war out of a population of less than 4 million. The Lottas worked to meet day-to-day needs of the military including constructing defenses, working in air raid posts and hospitals, and serving as typists and translators.

RUSSIA

Russian women, perhaps more than in any other country, consistently faced mortal peril in supporting the war effort. Though often treated poorly, women served alongside men in rifle regiments and as medics on the frontline. Men marching to the frontline were often greeted by peasant women offering a drink of milk or a bite of food and wishing them safety.

As in America, many Russian women took the place of men in factories. Soviet factories were crude and much more dangerous than American factories. It was not uncommon for young mothers to breastfeed infants while working long hours under difficult conditions in the factories.

At Stalingrad, women workers from the *Barricades* factory staffed artillery positions, slowing the German advance before they were overrun and killed. Hundreds of others fought in antiaircraft and signal units or served as medics in the besieged city. Russian women proved to be expert snipers.

Women of the 46th Guard's Night Bomber Regiment flew 24,000 sorties in wood and canvas *Parlikarpov PO-2* biplanes. Flying in low over enemy positions at night, the brave women dropped a few small bombs or hand grenades. The German troops lost much-needed sleep because of the "night witches" as they were forced to run to trenches or man antiaircraft guns.

In occupied countries, women commonly served in partisan groups that sought to disrupt and frustrate Axis efforts. Perhaps most famous were the women of the French resistance movement. The contribution of women working behind the scenes to ensure an Allied victory over Axis tyranny cannot be overstated.

The National World War II Museum

An American Army nurse finds time to smile while working at a field hospital.

REVIEW QUESTIONS

1. *Which type of occupation did American women undertake during the war?*
   a. Labored in mines.
   b. Tested machine guns.
   c. Worked in large factories.
   d. All of the above.

2. *What proved to be a big challenge to many women during the war?*
   a. Working long hours in jobs related to war production.
   b. Improvising because many items were rationed.
   c. Taking care of a household alone.
   d. All of the above.

3. _____ _____ *was the first woman photographer to fly on a combat mission and later wrote a book about Nazi death camps.*

4. *Women serving in the Army Nurse Corps were more likely to face _____ than women serving in other military organizations.*

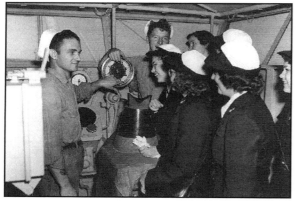

A group of WAVES (Women Accepted for Voluntary Service) personnel tour the escort carrier Mission Bay.

5. *Navy medics were trained by* _____ .
   a. special war medical schools
   b. Navy nurses
   c. doctors
   d. All of the above

6. *Both Douglas MacArthur and Dwight Eisenhower were impressed with the contribution of the Women's* _____ _____ *to the war effort.*

7. *Women serving in the U.S. Navy were known as* _____ .

8. *American women belonging to the* _____ *flew every kind of combat plane during the war.*

9. *British women serving in the Women's Auxiliary Air Force (WAAF) helped repulse the Germans in the Battle of* _____ .

10. *Finnish women supported the war effort against the Soviet Union by serving in the* _____ _____ *paramilitary organization.*

11. *Which country used women in combat roles on a regular basis?*
    a. Soviet Union
    b. Great Britain
    c. Germany
    d. Japan

12. *Russian women of the 46th Guard's Night Bomber Regiment who flew night bombing missions were named* _____ *by the German troops they continually bedeviled.*
    a. night guardians
    b. frau-devils
    c. night witches
    d. Russian renegades

Chapter 1
Neville Chamberlain

1. The Treaty of Versailles
2. 49
3. Weimar Republic
4. Fascist
5. The Munich Pact
6. Poland
7. Blitzkrieg
8. c
9. Germany and the Soviet Union
10. a
11. a

Chapter 2
Carl Mannerheim

1. d
2. Russia
3. Reds
4. The Mannerheim Line
5. a
6. They were excellent skiers.
7. the Molotov Cocktail
8. c
9. German
10. a
11. He opened negotiations with the Soviet Union
12. b

Chapter 3
Heinz Guderian

1. a
2. tank
3. c
4. Achtung! Panzer
5. b
6. Sweden
7. Denmark
8. d
9. Rotterdam
10. a
11. the Ardennes
12. Italy
13. He forced them to sign it in the same railway car that Germany had signed in at the end of the First World War.
14. Charles de Gaulle
15. Vichy France

Chapter 4
Karl Dönitz

1. U-boat
2. b
3. Athenia
4. c
5. Montevideo
6. Hood
7. A torpedo damaged her steering, causing her to go in circles.
8. a
9. Wolfpacks
10. Atlantic
11. d
12. b
13. Victory

Chapter 5
Winston Churchill

1. Boer
2. d
3. House of Commons
4. Gallipoli
5. a
6. Neville Chamberlain
7. Admiralty
8. d
9. Dunkirk
10. c
11. b
12. Dieppe
13. Italy
14. Potsdam

Chapter 6
Hermann Göring

1. Hermann Göring
2. d
3. Storm troopers
4. Luftwaffe
5. b
6. Fallschirmjägers
7. British
8. a
9. Hugh Dowding
10. bombers, fighters
11. c
12. b

Chapter 7
Erwin Rommel

1. the Desert Fox
2. c
3. Compass
4. b
5. Desert Fox
6. Tobruk
7. Rats of Tobruk
8. Crusader
9. a
10. Battle of El Alamein
11. d
12. Adolph Hitler

Chapter 8
Andrew Cunningham

1. Gibraltar, Suez
2. They were afraid the French fleet would join the Axis.
3. b
4. Regia Marina
5. a
6. c
7. d
8. Francisco Franco
9. a
10. Cape Matapan
11. Mercury
12. Malta
13. d

Chapter 9
Benito Mussolini

1. b
2. d
3. Fascist
4. 1922
5. Duce
6. France
7. a
8. Afrika Korps
9. c
10. Pietro Badoglio
11. b
12. c

Chapter 10
Erich von Manstein

1. Germany's
2. a
3. c
4. c
5. d
6. a
7. Minsk
8. Moscow
9. c
10. Sevastopol
11. Stalingrad
12. d
13. c

Chapter 11
George Marshall

1. d
2. General John Pershing
3. a
4. b
5. Ernest King
6. Torch
7. c
8. b
9. b
10. Five star
11. a

Chapter 12
Georgii Zhukov

1. b
2. Japanese
3. Smolensk
4. Vladimir Lenin
5. c
6. b
7. d
8. Blau (Blue)
9. Stalingrad
10. c
11. Kursk
12. Berlin

Chapter 13
George Patton

1. b
2. Pentathalon
3. c
4. tank
5. d
6. Kasserine
7. Africa
8. Husky
9. d
10. Patton
11. slapping
12. Battle fatigue
13. d
14. a
15. b

Chapter 14
Albert Kesselring

1. d
2. b
3. b
4. a
5. Sicily
6. Italy
7. c
8. Mark Clark
9. b
10. Mules
11. Monte Cassino
12. Anzio
13. c
14. c, though a and b can also be accepted.

Chapter 15
Dwight Eisenhower

1. b
2. a
3. George Marshall
4. c
5. d
6. c (*or* b: *Operation Sledgehammer* was a 1942 proposed invasion of Northern France)
7. a
8. Atlantic Wall
9. a
10. flanks
11. Pegasus
12. c
13. b
14. Sword, Juno, Gold, Utah and Omaha
15. Omaha (*or* Bloody Omaha)
16. Magic Carpet
17. President

Chapter 16
Bernard Montgomery

1. c
2. common (*or* everyday, enlisted)
3. b
4. El Alamein
5. d
6. a
7. airborne
8. c
9. 48

10. Arnhem
11. a
12. Nine
13. d
14. North Atlantic Treaty Organization

Chapter 17
James Doolittle

1. b
2. night
3. c
4. a
5. China
6. b
7. b
8. Hamburg
9. b
10. Ploesti
11. a
12. c
13. jet plane

Chapter 18
Omar Bradley

1. George Patton
2. d
3. Cobra
4. Paris, France
5. a
6. Antwerp, Belgium
7. d
8. c
9. b
10. d
11. Malmedy
12. c
13. The Great Blow
14. Remagen
15. b

Chapter 19
Josef Stalin

1. d
2. d
3. c
4. a
5. b
6. c
7. d
8. factories
9. Commissars
10. a
11. Japan
12. d

Chapter 20
Raoul Wallenberg

1. d
2. d
3. Holocaust
4. Nuremberg
5. c
6. a
7. Death squads
8. c
9. Gas
10. c
11. d (though primarily "a")
12. Final Solution
13. a
14. b

Chapter 21
Chiang Kai-shek

1. a
2. Mao
3. Marco Polo
4. b
5. China-Burma-India
6. d
7. b
8. c
9. d
10. The Hump (*or* the Himalayas)
11. Chindits
12. b
13. a
14. b

Chapter 22
Isoroku Yamamoto

1. a
2. b
3. opposed
4. b (d is also acceptable)
5. d
6. Midget
7. c
8. Mitsuo Fuchida
9. a
10. Arizona
11. d
12. Philippines
13. b
14. d

Chapter 23
Franklin Roosevelt

1. Theodore Roosevelt
2. d
3. polio
4. b
5. neutrality
6. isolationists
7. a
8. c
9. c
10. b
11. d

Chapter 24
Hideki Tojo

1. c
2. China
3. a
4. Singapore
5. b
6. oil
7. d
8. Sunda Strait
9. b
10. d
11. a
12. c
13. c

CHAPTER 25
FRANK FLETCHER

1. a
2. MAGIC
3. b
4. Port Moresy, New Guinea (Australia is also acceptable)
5. c
6. Aleutian
7. d
8. a
9. turning
10. Savo
11. b

CHAPTER 26
CHESTER NIMITZ

1. a
2. Pacific
3. Midway
4. Guadalcanal
5. c
6. d
7. Guadalcanal
8. Marianas
9. b
10. b
11. Japan
12. b
13. secret service

CHAPTER 27
WILLIAM HALSEY

1. d
2. White
3. d
4. b
5. Doolittle
6. b
7. a
8. Victory
9. four
10. d
11. a
12. destroyers (or destroyer escorts)
13. d
14. b
15. a

CHAPTER 28
MERRITT EDSON

1. a
2. airfield
3. b
4. b
5. a
6. d
7. Bloody Ridge
8. Betio
9. d
10. c
11. c
12. Okinawa
13. a
14. d
15. b

CHAPTER 29
DOUGLAS MACARTHUR

1. general
2. c
3. Corregidor
4. b
5. death
6. d
7. a
8. b
9. c
10. b
11. Japan
12. Harry Truman

CHAPTER 30
HARRY TRUMAN

1. a
2. b
3. Einstein
4. d
5. Leslie Groves
6. J. Robert Oppenheimer
7. b
8. d
9. Indianapolis
10. a
11. b
12. doctrine
13. d

CHAPTER 31
AUDIE MURPHY

1. decorated
2. c
3. a
4. c
5. d
6. d
7. movie (or Hollywood)
8. stress
9. b

CHAPTER 32
FAMOUS WOMEN

1. d
2. d
3. Margaret Bourke-White
4. combat
5. b
6. Women's Army Corps (WAC)
7. Women Accepted for Voluntary Service (WAVES)
8. Women Airforce Service Pilots (WASP)
9. Britain
10. Lotta Svärd
11. a
12. c

BIBLIOGRAPHY

GENERAL HISTORY

Badsey, Stephen, ed. *The Hutchison Atlas of World War II Battle Plans: Before and After.* Fitzroy Dearborn Publishers, 2000.

Cawthorne, Nigel. *Military Commanders: The 100 Greatest Throughout History.* Enchanted Lion Books, 2004.

Gilbert, Martin. *The Second World War: A Complete History.* Henry Holt and Company, LLC, 1989.

Goralski, Robert. *World War II Almanac 1931-1945.* Perigree Printing, 1982.

Keegan, John. *The Second World War.* Viking Penguin Group, 1989.

Kemp, Anthony. *Men-at-Arms: Allied Commanders of World War II.* Osprey Publishing, 1982.

O'Neill, William L. *World War II: A Student Companion.* Oxford University Press, 1999.

Parker, Robert. *The Second World War: a Short History, Student Companions to American History.* Oxford University Press, 1989.

Polowetzky, Nate, ed. *World War II: A 50th Anniversary History by the Writers and Photographers of the Associated Press.* Henry Holt & Co., 1989.

Salmaggi, Cesare and Pallavisini, Alfredo. *2194 Days of War: An Illustrated Chronology of the Second World War.* Gallery Books, 1977.

Sturgeon, Alison, Senior Editor. *World War II: The Definitive Visual History.* Dorling Kindersley, 2009.

Taylor, Mike. *Leaders of World War II.* Abdo Publishing Co., 1998.

Wagner, Margaret, David M. Kennedy, Linda Barrett Osborne, & Susan Reyburn. *The Library of Congress World War II Companion.* Simon & Schuster, 2007.

Weir, William. *50 Military Leaders Who Changed the World.* The Career Press, 2007.

Wight, Michael, ed. *The Reader's Digest Illustrated History of World War II.* Reader's Digest, 1939.

BIOGRAPHIES, MEMOIRS & DIARIES

Archer, Jules. *Man of Steel: Joseph Stalin.* Pocket Books, inc., 1965.

Browne, Courtney. *Tojo: The Last Banzai.* Holt, Rinehart and Winston, 1967.

Carter, Violet Bonham. *Winston Churchill: An Intimate Portrait.* Konecky & Konecky, 1965.

D'este, Carlo. *Patton: A Genius for War.* Harper Collins Publishers, 1995.

Devaney, John. *Franklin Delano Roosevelt: President.* Walker and Company, 1987.

Doolittle, James and Carroll V. Glines. *I Could Never Be So Lucky Again: An Autobiography.* Random House, 2009.

Feis, Herbert. *Churchill Roosevelt Stalin: The War They Waged and the Peace They Sought.* Princeton University Press, 1957.

Guderian, Heinz. *Panzer Leader.* Da Capo Press, 1996.

Ingram, Scott. *History's Villans: Joseph Stalin.* Blackbirch Press, 2002.

Jenkins, Roy. *Churchill: A Biography.* Faraux, Straus & Girouw, 2001.

Kobylyanskiy, Isaac; Stuart Bitton, ed. *From Stalingrad to Pilau: A Red Army Artillery Officer Remembers the Great Patriotic War.* University Press of Kansas, 2008.

Lash, Joseph P. *Eleanor and Franklin: The story of their relationship, based on Eleanor Roosevelt's private papers.* Smithmark, 1971.

"Life Visits Audie Murphy," *Life Magazine*, July 16, 1945. pp. 94-97.

Lundstrom, John B. *Black Shoe Carrier Admiral: Frank Jack Fletcher at Coral Sea, Midway and Guadalcanal.* Naval Institute Press, 2006.

Manchester, William. *American Caesar: Douglas MacArthur 1880-1964.* Little, Brown and Company, 1978.

McCullough, David. *Truman.* Simon & Schuster, 1992.

Meachem, John. *Franklin and Winston. An Intimate Portrait of an Epic Friendship.* Random House, 2003.

Meadowcroft, Enid Lamont. *The Story of Winston Churchill.* Grosset & Dunlap, 1957.

Montefiore, Sebag. *Young Stalin.* Alfred A. Knopf, 2007.

Mosely, Leonard. *Hirohito: Emperor of Japan.* Prentice-Hall Inc., 1966.

Mosley, Leonard. *Marshall: Hero for Our Times.* Hearts Books, 1982.

Muench, James F. *Five Stars: Missouri's Most Famous Generals.* University of Missouri Press, 2006.

Murphy, Audie. *To Hell and Back.* Henry Holt and Company, 2002). Originally published 1949.

Patton, George Smith. *War as I Knew it.* Houghton Mifflin Co., 1947.

Perret, Geoffrey. *Eisenhower.* Adams Media, 1999.

Perry, Mark. *Partners in Command.* The Penguin Press, 2007.

Potter, E. B. *Bull Halsey.* Naval Institute Press, 1985.

Potter, E. B. *Nimitz.* Naval Institute Press, 1976.

Potter, John Dean. *Yamamoto: The Man Who Menaced America.* The Viking Press, 1965.

Self, Robert. *Neville Chamberlain: A Biography.* Ashgate Publishing Company, 2006.

Simpson, Harold B. *Audie Murphy: American Soldier.* The Hill Jr. College Press, 1975.

Simpson, Michael. *A Life of Admiral of the Fleet Andrew Cunningham.* Frank Cass Publishers, 2004.

Spahr, William J. *Zhukov: the Rise & Fall of a Great Captain.* Presidio Press, 1993.

Thomas, Lowell and Jablonkski, *Edward. Doolittle: A Biography.* Doubleday & Company, 1976.

Whiting, Charles. *American Hero: The Life and Death of Audie Murphy.* Eskdale Publishing, 2000.

PREWAR

Elson, Robert T. *Prelude to War (World War II Time-Life Books).* Time-Life Books, 1982.

Keegan, John. *The First World War.* Vintage Books, 1998.

WESTERN EUROPE

Brook, Henry. *True Stories of D-Day.* Scholastic Inc., 2006.

Crookenden, Napier. *Battle of the Bulge 1944.* Charles Scribner's Sons, 1980.

Goolrick, William K. & Ogden Tanner. *The Battle of the Bulge (World War II Time-Life Books).* Time-Life Books, 1982.

Hastings, Max. *D-Day and the Battle for Normandy.* Random House, 1985.

Hook, Alex. *Illustrated History of The Third Reich.* TAJ Books 2004.

Hynson, Colin. *Days That Changed the World: D-Day.* World Almanac Library, 2004.

Jackson, Julian. France: *The Dark Years 1940-1944.* Oxford University Press, 2001.

Kemp, Anthony. *Men-at-Arms: German Commanders of World War II.* Osprey Publishing, 1982.

Kersaudy, François. *Norway 1940.* St. Martin's Press, 1987.

Lewis, Adrian R. *Omaha Beach: A Flawed Victory.* The University of North Carolina Press, 2001.

Mann, Chris & Jörgensen, Christer. *Hitler's Arctic War: The German Campaigns in Norway, Finland and the USSR 1940-1945.* Thomas Dunne Books, 2003.

Messenger, Charles; Keegan, John, ed. *The Second World War in Europe (Smithsonian History of Warfare).* Smithsonian Books, 2004.

Moss, Norman. *Nineteen Weeks: America, Britain and the Fateful Summer of 1940.* Houghton Mifflin Company, 1940.

Ryan, Cornelius. *A Bridge Too Far.* Simon and Schuster, 1974.

Wernick, Robert. *Blitzkrieg (World War II Time-Life Books).* Time-Life Books, 1982.

Young, Brigadier Peter. *D-Day.* Bison Books Corp., 1981.

EASTERN EUROPE

Bethel, Nicholas. *Russia Besieged* (World War II Time-Life Books). Time-Life Books, 1982.

Blassinggame, Wyatt. *Joseph Stalin and Communist Russia.* Garrard Publishing Company, 1951.

Elting, John R. *Battles for Scandinavia (World War II Time-Life Books).* Time-Life Books, 1982.

Freeman, Gregory. *The Forgotten 500.* NAL Caliber (Penguin Group), 2007.

Gottfried, Ted. *The Great Fatherland War.* Twenty-First Century Books, 2003.

Kowalski, Ludwik. *Hell on Earth: Brutality and Violence Under the Stalinist Regime.* Wasteland Press, 2008.

Lauterbach, Richard E. *"Zhukov: Stalin's Best general, Defender of Stalingrad and Moscow, Commands the Great Russian Drive to Berlin,"* Life Magazine, February 12, 1945. pp. 94-106.

Salisbury, Harrison E. *The 900 Days: The Siege of Leningrad.* De Capo Press, 1985.

Seaton, Albert. *The Russo-German War 1941-45.* Praeger Publishers, 1971.

Shaw, John. *Red Army Resurgent (World War II Time-Life Books).* Time-Life Books, 1982.

Vernadsky, George. *A History of Russia.* Yale University Press, 1969.

Ziemke, Earl F. *The Soviet Juggernaut (World War II Time-Life Books).* Time-Life Books, 1982.

PACIFIC THEATER

Ballard, Robert D. and Archbold, Rick. *Return to Midway.* National Geographic/Madison Press, 1999.

Busch, Noel F. *"Admiral Chester Nimitz: He Commands History's Greatest Fleet and a Watery Theater of 65,000,000 Square Miles."* Life Magazine July 10, 1944. pp. 81-92.

Dunnahoo, Terry. *Pearl Harbor: America Enters the War.* Franklin Watts, 1991.

Dunnigan, James F. and Nofi, Albert A. *Victory at Sea: World War II in the Pacific.* William Morrow and Co., Inc., 1995.

Flanagan, E. M. *Corregidor: The Rock Force Assault.* Presidio, 1995.

Glines, Carroll V. T*he Doolittle Raid: America's daring first strike against Japan.* Orion Books, 1988.

Griess, Thomas E., ed. *The Second World War: Asia and the Pacific (The West Point Military History Series).* Square One Publishers, 2002.

Marrin, Albert. *Victory in the Pacific.* Atheneum, 1983.

Mayer, S.L., ed. *The Rise and Fall of Imperial Japan.* The Military Press, 1984.

Merillat, Herbert Christian. *Guadalcanal Remembered.* Dodd, Mead & Company, 1982.

Nardo, Don. *World War II: the War in the Pacific.* Lucent Books, 1991.

Simons, Gerald, ed. *Japan at War (World War II Time-Life Books).* Time-Life Books, 1982.

Steinberg, Rafael, ed. *Return to the Philippines (World War II Time-Life Books).* Time-Life Books, 1982.

Stone, Scott C.S. *Pearl Harbor: The Way It Was — December 7, 1941.* Island Heritage, 1988.

Tanaka, Shelley. *Attack on Pearl Harbor: The True Story of the Day America Entered World War II.* Hyperion/Madison Press, 2001.

Wheeler, Keith. *The Road to Tokyo (World War II Time-Life Books).* Time-Life Books, 1982.

Wheeler, Keith. *War Under the Pacific (World War II Time-Life Books).* Time-Life Books, 1982.

Wheeler, Richard. *Iwo.* Lippinscott & Crowell, 1980.

Willmot, H. P. *Pearl Harbor.* Bison Books Corp., 1981.

Willmott, H. P.; Keegan, John, ed. *The Second World War in the Far East (Smithsonian History of Warfare).* Smithsonian Books, 2004.

Wukovits, John. *Pacific Alamo: The Battle for Wake Island.* New American Library, 2003.

Zich, Arthur, Ed. *The Rising Sun (World War II Time-Life Books).* Time-Life Books, 1982.

CHINA, BURMA, INDIA THEATER

Allen Louis. *Burma: The Longest War 1941-45.* Phoenix Press, 2002.

Moser, Don. *China-Burma-India (World War II Time-Life Books).* Time-Life Books, 1982.

NORTH AFRICA AND MEDITERRANEAN THEATER

Adams, Henry, ed. *Italy at War (World War II Time-Life Books)*. Time-Life Books, 1982.

Collier, Richard. *The War in the Desert (World War II Time-Life Books)*. Time-Life Books, 1982.

Ford, Ken. *El Alemein 1942: The Turning of the Tide*. Osprey Publishing, 2005.

Latimer, John. *Alamein*. John Murray Publishers, 2002.

Macksey, Kenneth. *Rommel: Battles and Campaigns*. De Capo Press, 1997.

Mitcham, Jr., Samuel W. Stackpole. *Military History Series – Rommels' Desert War: The Life and Death of the Afrika Korps*, Stackpole Books, 2007.

Porch, Douglas. *The Mediterranean Theater in World War II: The Path to Victory*. Farrar, Straus & Giroux, 2004.

Whipple, A.B.C. *The Mediterranean (World War II Time-Life Books)*. Time-Life Books, 1982.

Williamson, Gordon. *Afrika Korps 1941-43*. Osprey Publishing, 1991.

AIR WAR

Bailey, Ronald H. *The Air War in Europe (World War II Time-Life Books)*. Time-Life Books, 1982.

Bergstrom, Christer and Mikhailov, Andrey. *Black Cross Red Star: The Air War over the Eastern Front*. Pacifica Military History, 2000.

Bowman, Martin W. *Great American Air Battles of World War II*. Airlife Publishing, Ltd.

Fisher, David E. *A Summer Bright and Terrible: Winston Churchill, Lord Dowding, Radar, and the Impossible Triumph of the Battle of Britain*. Shoemaker Hoard, division of Avalaon Publishin Group, Inc., 2005.

Jablonski, Edward. *Flying Fortress: The Illustrated Biography of the B-17s and the Men Who Flew Them*. Doubleday & Company, Inc., 1965.

Mosley, Leonard. *The Battle of Britain (World War II Time-Life Books)*. Time-Life Books, 1982.

Woolf, Alex. *The World Wars: the Battle of Britain*. Steck-Vaughn Company, 2004.

NAVAL WARFARE

Arnold, James & Stinson, Starr. *U.S. Commanders of World War II (2): Navy and USMC, Volume 2*. Osprey Publishing, 2002.

Crawford, Steve. *Battleships & Carriers*. Barnes & Nobles Books, 1999.

Elpick, Peter. Liberty: *The Ships that Won the War.* Naval Institute Press, 2001.

Friedman, Kenneth I. *Afternoon of the Rising Sun: The Battle of Leyte Gulf*. Presidio Press Inc., 2001.

Gannon, Robert. *Hellions of the Deep*. The Pennsylvania State University Press, 1996.

Hoehling, A.A. *The Fighting Liberty Ships: A Memoir*. The Kent State University Press, 1990.

Hornfisher, James D. *The Last Stand of the Tin Can Soldiers: The Extraordinary World War II Story of the U.S. Navy's Finest Hour*. Bantam Books, 2004.

Hornfisher, James D. *Ship of Ghosts: the Story of the U.S.S. Houstin, FDR's Legendary Lost Cruiser, and the Epis Saga of her survivors*. Bantam Books, 2006.

Konstan, Angus, and Leo Marriott and George Grant. *Warships: From the Galley to the Present Day*. Gramercy Books, 2001.

Pitt, Barrie. *The Battle of the Atlantic (World War II Time-Life Books)*. Time-Life Books, 1982.

HOLOCAUST

Beir, Robert L. with Brian Josepher. *Roosevelt and the Holocaust: A Rooseveltian Examines the Policies and Remembers the Times*. Barricade Books, 2006.

Meltzer, Milton. *Rescue: The Story of How Gentiles Saved Jews in the Holocaust*. Harper & Row, 1988.

Talbott, Hudson. *Forging Freedom: A True Story of Heroism during the Holocaust*. G. P. Putnam's Sons, 2000.

Nicholson, Michael and David Winner. *Raoul Wallenberg: the Swedish diplomat who saved 100,000 Jews from the Nazi Holocaust before mysteriously disappearing*. Church Pub Inc., 1989.

OTHER

Barr, Gary. *World War II Home Front*. Heinemann Library, 2004.

Binney, Marcus. *The Women Who Lived for Danger: The Agents of the Special Operations Executive*. William Morrow, 2002.

Cohen, Daniel. *The Manhattan Project*. The Millbrook Press, 1999.

Levy, Patricia. *The World Wars: The Home Front in World War II*. Raintree, 2004.

Natkiel, Richard. *Atlas of Battles: Strategy and Tactics Civil War to Present*. Bison Books Corp., 1984.

Orso, Allen: Publisher. *Uncle John's Gigantic Bathroom Reader*. Portable Press, 2006.

Rolef, Tamara, ed. *The Atom Bomb: Turning Points in History*. Greenhaven Press, Inc., 2000.

Weatherford, Doris. *American Women and World War II: History of Women in America*. Facts on File, 1990.

GLOSSARY

Afrika Korps — A German military formation that gained a formidable reputation under the leadership of General Erwin Rommel. The German name was the *Deutsches Afrika Korps* (DAK).

appeasement — The political policy followed by European leaders in the 1930's that allowed Adolph Hitler to take over Austria and other countries in exchange for a promise of peace.

armistice — An agreement between combatants to stop fighting for a time, typically the first step in the establishment of a lasting peace.

atoll — A ring-shaped chain of islands created by coral.

auxiliary - A group or organization providing direct support to a country's military but is not actually part of the military.

AWOL — Acronym for "Absent without official leave."

Beachhead — A defended position at the edge of an ocean or river from which forces are gathered for an attack.

Blitzkrieg — A German word for "lightning war." A term used to describe the intense, mobile military campaigns employed by the German Wehrmacht in the early stages of the war.

bogie wheels — The small wheels that hold tank treads in place and propel the vehicle forward.

Bolsheviks — Led by Vladimir Lenin, members of the Russian Social Democratic Party who overthrew the czarist Russian government in a violent revolution in 1917 and installed a communistic government.

capitalism — A system in which an economy is based on private ownership rather than government control.

CinCPac — Abbreviation for Commander in Chief Pacific.

Cold War — *An extended standoff between the* United States and Russia that began after the Second World War and lasted until 1990. It was characterized by a nuclear arms race, propaganda, diplomacy and efforts to undermine each nation's interests.

commissar — An official of the Communist Party. Commissars were used by Josef Stalin during the Second World War to ensure the loyalty of military leaders.

Commonwealth — Great Britain was an empire, comprised of possessions around the world. These possessions were given varying levels of independence, but all contributed to the war effort. The Commonwealth included Canada, Australia, New Zealand, India and South Africa. The terms *Commonwealth* and *British* are used interchangeably in this book.

Communism — A social political theory first proposed by Karl Marx in which all property is owned by the government and apportioned to individuals based on skill and need.

corps — A military formation typically made up of two or more divisions.

defeatism — A view that defeat is inevitable.

delousing — American engineering term for finding and neutralizing land mines.

division — A unit of a military organization. The size of a division varied greatly by country and phase of the war.
- Panzer divisions had an average 328 tanks in 1941 but were down to 73 by 1943.
- U.S. Army divisions were made up of 8100 combat soldiers and 6000 in support roles. Airborne divisions had fewer than 9000 men.
- In 1944, British divisions were made up of 18,000 men.
- A Russian Rifle division was made up of 14,000 men.
- Italian divisions, normally 14,000 strong, were reduced to an average of 3200 each in North Africa in 1942.
- Chinese divisions varied between 6000 and 12,000 troops.

Enigma code machine — A German code machine. Believed unbreakable by the Germans, the Allies captured and broke the Enigma code, providing much useful information during the course of the war.

enlisted — Members of the military who are not officers.

envelopment — To wrap around or enclose. Envelopment is a proven military tactic in which an enemy is surrounded and cut off.

escarpment — A steep slope that separates two areas of land with different heights.

estuary — The place where the mouth of a large river meets the ocean. Estuaries are affected by tidal motions.

Fallschirmjäger — German airborne troops commanded by General Kurt Student. The term comes from words meaning "parachute" and "elite."

Fascist Party — The first Fascist Party was formed by Benito Mussolini of Italy in 1919. Fascism espouses a strong authoritarian form of political and social-minded government. It typically supports the superiority of one ethnic or national group over all others.

funnies — A series of modified Churchill and Sherman tanks developed by Major General Percy Hobart. Funnies were fitted with specialized gear to destroy land mines, "swim" to shore and clear hedgerows, among other tasks.

furrier — A merchant who deals with furs.

green troops — Soldiers who have not experienced actual combat.

guerilla tactics — Hit-and-run tactics used by smaller forces to harass and disrupt larger, better armed forces.

Heer — The name of Nazi Germany's army.

Holocaust — A Greek word meaning "sacrifice by fire." The term is used to specifically describe the mass murder of 6 million European Jews during the war. The term has also been used to broadly describe all people who were targeted for death by Nazi tyranny.

Holomodor — Literally "killing by hunger." This term describes the 1933 famine in the Ukraine created by draconian Communist policy under the leadership of Josef Stalin. The famine resulted in the estimated deaths of more than 3 million Ukranians.

indoctrination — Teaching an individual or group to accept a specific view or belief without questioning.

insurgent — Civilians of conquered territories who work to undermine the authority of the occupying army.

isolationists — Americans who believed that the United States should not get involved in the affairs of other countries, especially European.

Kamikaze — Japanese suicide pilots. Kamikaze meant "Divine wind." A wave of Kamikazes was known as *Kikusui* (floating chrysanthemums).

Kriegsmarine — The name given to the German navy during the Second World War.

Lend-Lease — A program in which weapons and materials were provided to American allies including Russia and Great Britain.

Low Countries — The Low Countries are Belgium, the Netherlands and Luxembourg.

Luftwaffe — A generic term for "air force." It was the name given to the German air force during the Second World War.

Medal of Honor — The highest award given by the U.S. government to members of the military who go above and beyond the call of duty while in action against an enemy force.

memoirs — The writings of an individual reflecting back on actions and feelings during historical events.

magazine — A storage place for ammunition.

Malakand — A tribal area in Asia that is today part of Pakistan.

Molotov cocktails — Bottles filled with rags and flammable liquid. The rag would be lit and the bottle hurled at a tank or other formidable target. The name originated during the Winter War in which Finnish soldiers named the crude weapon after Soviet Prime Minister Vyacheslav Molotov.

mulberry — A large artificial harbor used after the D-Day Normandy landings to facilitate the arrival of troops, weapons and materials.

NATO — The North Atlantic Treaty Organization was a coalition of Western European countries and the United States formed early during the Cold War to impede the expansion of Communism by assuring one another of mutual defense if attacked.

Nazi Party — German Workers Party, later to become the National Socialist German Workers Party.

NKVD — The People's Commissariat for Internal Affairs was a police organization that Josef Stalin used to control the Russian people by enforcing Soviet policy. The NKVD both publicly and secretly carried out executions and ran labor camps.

open city — A city that a government announces they will not defend in the hope that the approaching enemy will not attack or destroy, but merely occupy. The idea is to protect civilians, infrastructure and landmarks.

ordnance — An umbrella term encompassing guns, artillery, ammunition and the equipment necessary to use them.

Panzergruppe — A German sub-army formation containing more than one division but not enough to be considered an army.

partisan — A member of an armed group that actively fights against an occupying power.

Phoney War — The six-month period of time between the conquest of Poland and the invasion of France. Other names for the Phoney War included the *Twilight War* by Winston Churchill, *der Sitzkrieg* in German ("the sitting war": a play on the word Blitzkrieg), the *Bore War* (a play on the Boer War), the Polish *dziwna wojna* ("strange war"), and the French *drôle de guerre* ("bizarre war").

pillbox — A concrete fortification equipped with slits through which to fire weapons. Many are a cylindrical box shape similar to medical pill boxes.

POW — Acronym for "prisoner of war."

pretense — An attempt to make something appear true that is not.

pretext — A reason given to justify an action.

propaganda — Information of a dubious or misleading character intended to support a specific view, political cause or belief.

reparations — Monetary payments made by Germany to the Allies after the First World War.

sappers — Military engineers trained in placing or detecting mines.

scuttle — To intentionally sink a ship. Usually done as a precaution to prevent the ship from falling into enemy hands.

sennibari — A Japanese belt sewn together by 1000 women who each sewed one stitch. It was also known as the "Thousand stitch belt."

sniper — An expert marksman (or woman) who targets individual enemies from a concealed location and typically at a long distance.

socialism — A political and economic philosophy in which government takes an active role in developing and regulating economic and social life but does not control it completely, as in a communistic setting.

sortie — A flight made by an aircraft with a military mission.

Tokyo Express — A slang name given by U.S. troops to Japanese ships attempting to reinforce the island of Guadalcanal in the Solomon Islands.

Treaty of Versailles — The 1919 treaty officially marking the end of the First World War. The treaty forced Germany to accept responsibility for the war and to make substantial war reparations.

ultimatum — A final demand in which it is made clear that the alternative is to face severe consequences.

unrestricted warfare — War waged without consideration for damage to the civilian population. During the Second World War, both Germany and the United States waged unrestricted submarine warfare, targeting civilian cargo ships in addition to military vessels.

Western Allies — A political and geographic grouping among the Allied Powers of the Second World War. It generally includes the United Kingdom, the British Commonwealth countries (Canada, Australia, New Zealand, etc.), the United States, France and various other European and Latin American countries, but excludes China, the Soviet Union and Yugoslavia due to different economic, geographic and political circumstances.

Wehrmacht — The armed forces of Nazi Germany, including the *Heer* (army), *Luftwaffe* (air force) and *Kriegsmarine* (navy). The term literally means "defensive might."

INDEX

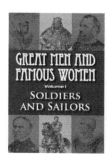
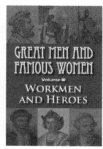

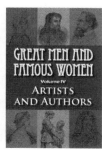

Made in the USA
Charleston, SC
04 August 2014